Public and Private

The public and private distinction is essential to our moral and political vocabularies as it continues to structure our social and legal practices. *Public and Private* provides an original and multidisciplinary perspective on this distinction which has been at the centre of intense and controversial debates in recent years. The focus of the debates has been on the delineation of acceptable boundaries between the public and private in the economic, social and cultural spheres of modern societies.

What is the nature and scope of citizenship? What are the implications of new reproductive technologies? And what is the fate of state sovereignty in the context of a globalised world economy? At first glance these questions may appear unrelated and yet they all raise underlying and serious concerns regarding the scope and proper boundaries between the public and the private.

Public and Private is a wide-ranging assessment of the changing nature and scope of this demarcation. It will both stimulate the current debate with its original approach and provide a valuable resource for all those interested in the role the public and private play in structuring our societies.

Maurizio Passerin d'Entrèves and **Ursula Vogel** are both Senior Lecturers in Political Theory at the University of Manchester.

Public and Private

Legal, political and philosophical perspectives

**Edited by
Maurizio Passerin d'Entrèves and
Ursula Vogel**

London and New York

First published 2000 by Routledge
11 New Fetter Lane, London EC4P 4EE

Simultaneously published in the USA and Canada
by Routledge
29 West 35th Street, New York, NY 10001

Routledge is an imprint of the Taylor & Francis Group

© 2000 selection and editorial matter Maurizio Passerin d'Entrèves and
Ursula Vogel; individual chapters © the contributors

Typeset in Times New Roman by BC Typesetting, Bristol
Printed and bound in Great Britain by Clays Ltd, St Ives plc

British Library Cataloguing in Publication Data
A catalogue record for this book is available from the British Library

Library of Congress Cataloging in Publication Data
Public and private: legal, political, and philosophical perspectives/
[edited by] Maurizio D'Entrèves and Ursula Vogel.
    p.   cm.
    Includes bibliographical references and index.
    1. Privacy, Right of.   2. Public interest.   3. Citizenship.
    I. Passerin d'Entrèves, Maurizio, 1953–   II. Vogel, Ursula, 1938–
JC596.P833 2000
323.44′8–dc21   00–028413

ISBN 0–415–16683–7 (hbk)
ISBN 0–415–16684–5 (pbk)

Contents

Contributors

Dario Castiglione is Senior Lecturer in Political Theory at the University of Exeter. He is the author of numerous essays on the history of early modern political thought and is co-editor of *Democracy and Constitutional Culture in the Union of Europe* (1995) and *Constitutionalism in Transformation: European and Theoretical Perspectives* (1996).

Jean L. Cohen is Professor of Political Science at Columbia University. She has published extensively in the fields of contemporary social and political theory and is the author of *Class and Civil Society: The Limits of Marxian Critical Theory* (1982) and co-author of *Civil Society and Political Theory* (1992).

Maurizio Passerin d'Entrèves is Senior Lecturer in Political Theory at the University of Manchester. He has published several articles in the fields of contemporary social and political theory and is the author of *Modernity, Justice and Community* (1990), *The Political Philosophy of Hannah Arendt* (1994) and co-editor of *Habermas and the Unfinished Project of Modernity* (1996).

Shane O'Neill is Reader in Politics at The Queen's University of Belfast. He has published a number of articles in the fields of political and social theory and is the author of *Impartiality in Context: Grounding Justice in a Pluralist World* (1997), co-author of *Contemporary Social and Political Theory: An Introduction* (1998) and co-editor of *Reconstituting Social Criticism* (1999).

Nigel Simmonds is Reader in Jurisprudence at Corpus Christi College, Cambridge University. He has published many articles in the field of legal philosophy and is the author of *The Decline of Juridical Reason* (1984), *Central Issues in Jurisprudence* (1986) and co-author of *A Debate over Rights: Philosophical Enquiries* (1998).

Hillel Steiner is Professor of Political Philosophy at the University of Manchester. He has written several essays in legal and political philosophy and is the author of *An Essay on Rights* (1994) and co-author of *A Debate over Rights: Philosophical Enquiries* (1998).

Christine Sypnowich is Associate Professor of Philosophy at Queen's University, Kingston, Ontario. She has published extensively in the fields of legal and political philosophy and is the author of *The Concept of Socialist Law* (1990).

Ursula Vogel is Senior Lecturer in Political Theory at the University of Manchester. She has published many articles on eighteenth- and nineteenth-century political thought and on contemporary feminism and is co-editor of *The Frontiers of Citizenship* (1991).

Introductory

1 Public and private

A complex relation

Maurizio Passerin d'Entrèves and Ursula Vogel

The categories of public and private have played, and continue to play, a central role in structuring human activities and delineating the main boundaries of social life. They have been the subject of extensive analysis and debate, at times of heated contestation, by philosophers, legal scholars, political theorists, feminist thinkers, anthropologists, cultural historians and economists operating in the public choice tradition. The categories themselves are highly complex and ambiguous, covering different features of social life depending on the framework adopted, while the distinction between public and private can by no means be conceived as a simple opposition or dichotomy, but must be viewed as multifaceted and protean, comprising a family of distinctions that are constantly shifting under the twin pressures of social change and political contestation.

The complex and ambiguous nature of the categories of public and private has been highlighted by several recent studies. Jeff Weintraub, for instance, has identified four broad frameworks in which different notions of public and private play an important role: (1) the liberal-economistic model, which sees the public/private distinction primarily in terms of the distinction between the state and the economy; (2) the civic republican tradition, which sees the public realm in terms of political community and citizenship, analytically distinct from both the market and the state; (3) the approach of cultural and social historians, which sees the public realm as a sphere of fluid sociability, distinct from both the structures of social organisation and the private domains of intimacy and domesticity; and (4) those trends in feminist scholarship that conceive of the distinction between private and public in terms of the distinction between the family and the larger economic and political order.[1]

As can readily be seen, each theoretical framework generates different understandings of public and private, as well as generating in some instances (frameworks (2) and (3)) a trichotomy in place of a dichotomy. We might then be led to conclude that public and private are 'complex-structured concepts', to use the helpful formulation of Stanley Benn and Gerald Gaus.[2] They are complex-structured concepts in two senses. First, the many senses of 'public' and 'private' are systematically related: embedded in a culture and its language are certain presuppositions that account for the continuity of the various meanings of public and private. However, the relations obtaining between the various meanings are not simply logical, but more often than not ideological, that is, traceable to a specific socio-theoretical framework that emphasises one aspect of the semantic relation at the expense of another. In this respect the very concepts of public and private are constantly open to contestation, notwithstanding some underlying continuity of meaning. Second, the distinction between public and private is inherently complex. Such a distinction could hardly be simple, given the broad range of activities and practices over which it ranges. Moreover, those activities and practices have a number of different features according to which they may be classified as either public or private. The public/private distinction, then, exhibits the same complex structure that is characteristic of the concepts themselves.

The lesson to be learned from these recent studies is that of avoiding simplified or reductive understandings of the public/private distinction in favour of a complex appreciation of the multifaceted meanings embodied in the distinction and of the shifting boundaries between public and private domains. For, as Weintraub has argued, the public/private distinction is 'inherently problematic', 'often treacherous', 'frequently confusing' and 'potentially misleading', but remains 'a powerful instrument of social analysis and moral reflection if approached with due caution and conceptual self-awareness'.[3]

The chapters in this volume aim to provide a rich and nuanced understanding of the complex theoretical, legal and political issues arising out of a study of the relations between the public and the private. They range from a conceptual analysis of the public/private demarcation (Steiner), to critical assessments of influential formulations of public and private by leading contemporary thinkers (Castiglione, O'Neill, Passerin d'Entrèves), to legal analyses of the concepts of privacy and civility (Cohen, Sypnowich), to a jurisprudential study of public and private law (Simmonds), to a historical reconstruction of public and private in marriage law (Vogel). They are all informed by an awareness of the variability and ambiguity of the public/private distinction, and by the recognition that no single disciplinary perspective would suffice to exhaust its multiple meanings and its shifting boundaries. Taken together, they offer a fresh and multi-disciplinary perspective on a distinction that remains essential to our moral and political vocabularies and, in virtue of its power to structure our social and political practices, unavoidably open to critical reformulation and ongoing contestation.

The book has two parts. Part 1, 'Philosophical and political perspectives', begins with Hillel Steiner's analytical reconstruction of the public/private demarcation. He argues that our standard conception of the relation between public and private domains is one that takes them as essentially asymmetrical. He characterises this conception as the 'asymmetry thesis': public and private domains are (a) entirely non-identical, and (b) the contents of the former are instrumentally derived from the contents of the latter. According to the asymmetry thesis, the sphere of public authority lacks any element of foundational independence from the sphere of private authority: its demands are entirely subservient to the demands originating in the private domain, whether these are conceived in terms of Lockean natural rights, Rousseauian moral liberty or Benthamite maximised utility. Steiner points out that, however common the asymmetry thesis might appear to contemporary scholars, it has been implicitly denied by legal and political theories in at least two ways. It has been denied by theories which hold that all the contents of the public domain are identical with at least some private ones (denial of (a)); and it is denied by theories which reject the reduction of the contents of the public domain to those of the private (denial of (b)).

As regards the former, a clear example of political theories upholding the identity of public and private domains is to be found in post-Reformation doctrines of the 'divine right of kings': here the public domain is a mere extension of the private domain of the monarch, and public law a mere appendix to private (the king's) law. Such a subsumption of the public domain by the private continues to operate even when sovereignty is held not by a monarch but by a larger set of persons, say, the 'people' or the citizen body.

If subsumption has been one way of denying the asymmetry thesis, another is the rejection of the reducibility of the public domain to the private (denial of (b)). To assess the non-reducibility argument Steiner provides, first, a clarification of the notion of public goods and, second, draws a distinction between Will and Interest theories of rights. If we adopt a simple characterisation of public goods, the claimed non-reducibility of the public domain to the private cannot be vindicated: public rights can in fact be shown to be instrumentally derived from private rights, regardless of whether we embrace the Will or the Interest theory of rights. But if we adopt a more complex characterisation of public goods, one that focuses, say, on long-term environmental protection, the argument turns out to be quite different. In such a case the rights pertaining to the public domain cannot be reduced to the private rights of each individual, not because they are endowed with foundational independence, but because such public rights do not secure goods that can be characterised as public goods. So the argument for the non-reducibility of public rights to private rights wins by default, since there are no public goods, strictly speaking, that can be shown to be reducible, or be instrumentally related, to the private rights of individuals. This conclusion is reached in all four cases examined by Steiner, namely, whether we adopt a Will or an Interest theory of rights for current or future generations. In none of the four cases can long-term environmental protection be described as a public good. Steiner's overall argument, then, demonstrates that the asymmetry thesis fails on two counts. It fails when public rights are shown to be identical with private ones (denial of (a)); and it fails when public rights secure goods which cannot be regarded as public goods (denial of (b)). Our standard conception of the asymmetric relation between the public and the private is thus shown to be deeply flawed, on both historical and conceptual grounds.

In 'Public Reason, Private Citizenship', Dario Castiglione offers a critical account of two key concepts in contemporary political theory, namely, John Rawls's idea of public reason and Bruce Ackerman's notion of private citizenship. He aims to show the mutual entailment of these two concepts, as well as the tensions they exhibit when they are fleshed out into ideals capable of providing a normative foundation to the institutions of constitutional democracy. Castiglione first examines Rawls's idea of public reason, which is defined as the reason of free and equal citizens in a well-ordered constitutional regime. Such a reason is public in three distinct senses: it is exercised by free citizens; it concerns exclusively the public good; and its nature and content are public, that is, justifiable according to public standards and open to public scrutiny. Public reason offers a common language through which citizens can address questions pertaining to the fundamental institutions and arrangements of their political society. Public reason represents the key idea on which Rawls establishes a 'freestanding' conception of political justice based on an overlapping consensus.

Castiglione's aim is not to probe the philosophical soundness of Rawls's idea of public reason, but to raise the twin questions of *when* citizens should engage in public reasoning and of *how to motivate* them to do so. According to Rawls, citizens and public officials must speak the language of public reason whenever they debate about constitutional essentials and matters of basic justice pertaining to the basic structure of society. The motivation to engage in public reasoning lies, for Rawls, in the duty of civility that binds the citizenry of a well-ordered society. But there is a certain parsimony in Rawls's account that Castiglione finds rather puzzling. Why should citizens only respect the limits of public reason on certain fundamental matters and not be guided by them in all matters political? Are constitutional essentials and questions of basic justice easier to judge within the parameters of public reason? Does the duty of civility apply only intermittently at times of elections? Why should it not guide all political dealings between citizens? Rawls himself, in the essay 'The Idea of Public Reason Revisited', has acknowledged the many ways in which the comprehensive views inhabiting the background culture of civil society may form and enrich public political culture itself. But with this admission, Rawls starts to blur the boundaries between public reason, as a normative idea, and the (plural) reasons used in public, in ways that may undermine his conception of an overlapping consensus. Moreover, the question of motivation remains unresolved, since Rawls does not provide a convincing argument linking the obligation of citizens to engage in public reasoning with their natural motivations (he only provides a 'philosophical' moral psychology, not an empirically grounded one).

An answer to the motivational question may be found in Ackerman's idea of dualist democracy, an idea that Rawls himself seems to have embraced in his most recent essay on public reason. Dualist democracy refers to a constitutional regime where the higher law, originating in the constituent power of the people, is protected from ordinary law-making through a variety of institutional mechanisms and anti-majoritarian procedures. According to Ackerman, dualist democracy is the best constitutional regime for societies whose experience of political participation takes the form of what he calls 'private citizenship'. Citizens of modern democratic societies do not, for Ackerman, behave in a purely self-interested way (as 'perfect privatists') nor in a purely other-regarding way (as 'public citizens'). Rather, they bring their personal concerns and preferences into the public domain, but are capable of being public-minded and impartial at those key moments in the political cycle when 'normal' politics is transformed into 'constitutional' politics.

Ackerman's model of private citizenship, and its associated idea of dualist democracy, offer an interesting solution to a number of overlapping difficulties that beset modern politics: how to reconcile private and public interests; how to give expression to both instrumental and expressive concerns; how to accommodate aggregative and deliberative views of democratic decision-making. But, as Castiglione argues, it fails to specify the conditions conducive to the flourishing of the virtues of private citizenship. Moreover, when it is employed to address the motivational problem intrinsic to Rawls's idea of public reason, it offers a solution that resembles far more a *modus vivendi* conception of political legitimacy than Rawls's strongly normative conception based on an overlapping consensus. But, as Castiglione observes, there may be some gain in acknowledging the mixed nature of citizens' motivations, and the wide latitude of discursive criteria employed in public justification, if we want to provide a realistic account of politics in modern constitutional democracies.

In 'Private Irony and the Public Hope of Richard Rorty's Liberalism', Shane O'Neill provides a critical assessment of Rorty's radical separation of public and private as articulated in his version of postmodern or postfoundational liberalism. For Rorty, liberal institutions and the values of liberal society require no philosophical justification of the kind that appeals to Enlightenment notions of reason or nature; their justification, rather, rests on a creative redescription of the practices they foster, of the possibilities they open up for individual self-fashioning and for collective solidarity. Liberal societies allow for a separation between a private sphere of self-creation in which we are free to pursue our conception of the good life, and a public sphere in which we try to find principles of civic coexistence based on toleration and the reduction of cruelty and suffering. The best defence of liberal institutions lies in the hope that they will inspire the allegiance of a progressively larger number of people, and not in the attempt to provide some kind of philosophical justification.

The clear demarcation of private irony and public hope is central to Rorty's attempt to show the superiority of his new vocabulary over the old rationalist vocabulary of the Enlightenment. In three tightly argued sections, O'Neill argues that Rorty fails in this attempt. First, regarding the (public) project of justifying principles of political morality, he shows that there are strong reasons for doubting the attractiveness of Rorty's redescription of liberalism. Second, regarding the (private) project of self-creation, he argues that there are serious inconsistencies in Rorty's conception of the self. Third, with respect to the relation between public hope and private irony, he shows that Rorty does not make a convincing case for maintaining the radical opposition between the two domains.

Rorty's redescription of liberalism rests on the claim that loyalty to our own liberal tradition(s) is the only political morality that we require. Morality is simply the area of overlap of beliefs and convictions shared by the members of a particular historical community. We develop our sense of morality by reinterpreting the story of our community, and the vocabulary that we employ for this purpose is thoroughly contingent. Rorty's post-foundational liberalism has no need for notions such as reason or human nature that could serve as trans-historical criteria by which the morality of a community could be judged. Rather, it offers us only an internal perspective that yields circular justifications for our political allegiances and allows for the creative redescription of our practices and institutions. Having abandoned the language of Enlightenment rationalism in favour of the language of ethnocentric pragmatism, Rorty ends up redescribing liberalism as a political morality of *convention* rather than one of *conviction*. Such a redescription fails, however, to capture one crucial aspect of liberal political morality, namely, the practice of normative justification by means of rational argument. The practice of normative justification rests on an important distinction that Rorty wishes to abandon, that between moral arguments that are held to be valid because supported by good reasons and moral arguments that are held to be valid because widely accepted in a particular community. If liberal values and principles are held as a matter of rational conviction, and not simply as a matter of social convention, they will seek a grounding in arguments that can be shown to be valid, rather than in arguments that happen to be widely acceptable. The importance of this distinction between validity and acceptability is that it supports a commitment to rational dialogue as the best institutional procedure of conflict-resolution and provides the normative tools to identify and criticise the exercise of illegitimate power. By abandoning this distinction it becomes unclear how Rorty could distinguish a process of rational deliberation from a ruthless quest for political power. Thus, Rorty's redescription of our public morality offers little support to his plea for substituting a morality of convention for the morality of rational conviction that lies at the heart of modern liberalism.

In addition to advocating the contingency of our moral vocabulary and the conventional nature of our practices of normative justification, Rorty enjoins us to accept the purely contingent character of the self. There is no human nature, no paradigmatic form of human flourishing, no completeness towards which we ought to strive in our lives. Each of us is simply a 'tissue of contingencies', a particular web of beliefs and desires that is constantly rewoven throughout each human life. This view of the contingent self seems to be in tension with the liberal value of personal autonomy, which Rorty interprets in terms of self-creation. It seems doubtful that Rorty can both espouse the view of the self as a 'tissue of contingencies' and at the same time give an adequate account of personal autonomy as self-creation. Rorty's image of the self is that of a network that is constantly reweaving itself in an adaptive fashion vis-à-vis its external environment, with no conscious agent standing behind the weaving. This rather passive image of the self sits uncomfortably with Rorty's celebration of the capacity we have to create and invent ourselves. There must be some activity involved in self-creation, some self-consciousness doing the weaving. We must conceive of ourselves as active spinners of our web of beliefs and desires in order to subscribe to Rorty's view of ourselves as self-creative beings. A more satisfactory alternative to Rorty's contradictory account of the self is to be found in the hermeneutic conception that accepts both the contingency and historicity of our being while retaining the notion of an agent actively involved in the weaving of beliefs and desires.

Rorty's depiction of the liberal ironist is that of a subject whose activities of self-making and creative redescription are firmly located in the private sphere. The liberal ironist is someone who has radical and continuing doubts about the final vocabulary she currently employs and who accepts that the choice of vocabularies is simply a question of 'playing the new off against the old'. But from a political perspective we might ask whether Rorty's ironists are not so troubled by their doubts that they will lack the motivation to act one way rather than another. There seems to be no reason why the ironist would be morally committed to the defence of liberal practices and institutions. Indeed, her awareness of the contingency of all vocabularies would undermine her belief that liberalism can be morally justified. She lacks that reason for hope that comes from the conviction that there are valid arguments which support a political defence of liberalism. More ominously, Rorty's glorification of the 'strong poet' has strong elitist tones and may be compatible with the rule of a political elite manipulating the people with inventive redescriptions of their political values and traditions. A post-philosophical aestheticised culture, as advocated by Rorty, would not generate a sense of loyalty and communal solidarity, but lead to social fragmentation and a weakening of civic bonds. Aware of these dangers, Rorty restricts the activities of the ironist to the private sphere, where he can playfully entertain his radical doubts without the danger of humiliating others. In the public sphere, by contrast, the liberal ironist will restrain himself so as not to cause humiliation or suffering. But can public and private domains be separated so rigidly? How can Rorty ignore the deep and complex interconnections between the two domains? Rorty seems rather naïve in his belief that we can draw a line around a range of activities and be confident that within that domain our activities of redescription will have no public consequences. Rorty's strict separation of private irony from public solidarity has an additional worrying implication, namely, that of privatising radical theory and assuming that we already have a community of citizens bound together in solidarity. In so doing, Rorty wishes away the many conflicts between competing vocabularies in the political realm and assumes that we can replace political struggle with technocratic social engineering. Rorty's political vision seems to envisage a depoliticised society with a shrunken public sphere: such a minimalist conception of politics bears little affinity with the democratic tradition of radical reform to which he claims his allegiance. In the end, it would appear that Rorty can only combine private philosophical radicalism with public political conservatism.

In the final chapter of Part 1, entitled 'Public and Private in Hannah Arendt's Conception of Citizenship', Maurizio Passerin d'Entrèves provides a reconstruction of Arendt's conception of citizenship and a critical evaluation of her distinction between the public and the private. The reconstruction is articulated around three major themes: the public sphere political agency, and collective identity, and political culture.

In the first section, d'Entrèves examines the connection between Arendt's conception of citizenship and the notion of the public sphere. For Arendt the public sphere comprises two distinct but interrelated dimensions. The first is the *space of appearance*, a space of political freedom and equality which comes into being whenever citizens act in concert through the medium of speech and persuasion. The second is the *common world*, a shared world of human artifacts, institutions and settings that separates us from nature and that provides a relatively permanent and durable context for our activities. Both dimensions are essential to the practice of citizenship, the former providing the spaces where it can flourish, the latter providing the stable background from which public spaces of action and deliberation can arise.

D'Entrèves then goes on to examine three features of the political sphere that are closely connected to Arendt's conception of citizenship. These are, first, its artificial or constructed quality, second, its spatial quality and, third, the distinction between public and private interests. As regards the first feature, Arendt always stressed the artificiality of public life and of political activities in general, the fact that they are humanly constructed rather than natural or given. She regarded this artificiality as something to be celebrated rather than deplored. Politics for her was not the result of some natural predisposition, or the realisation of the inherent traits of human nature. Rather, it was a cultural achievement of the first order, enabling individuals to transcend the necessities of life and to fashion a world within which free political action and discourse could flourish. The second feature stressed by Arendt has to do with the spatial quality of public life, with the fact that political activities are located in a public space where citizens are able to meet one another, exchange their opinions and debate their differences, and search for some collective solution to their problems. Politics, for Arendt, is a matter of people sharing a common world and a common space of appearance so that public concerns can emerge and be articulated from different perspectives. In her view, it is not enough to have a collection of private individuals voting separately and anonymously according to their private opinions. Rather, these individuals must be able to see and talk to one another in public, so that their differences as well as their commonalities can emerge and become the subject of democratic debate. This public or world-centred conception of politics lies also at the basis of the third feature stressed by Arendt, the distinction between public and private interests. According to Arendt, political activity is not a means to an end, but an end in itself; one does not engage in political action to promote one's individual welfare, but to realise the principles intrinsic to political life, such as freedom, equality, justice and solidarity. Our public interest as citizens is quite distinct from our private interest as individuals. The public interest has little to do with our private interests, since it concerns the world that lies beyond the self, a world that finds embodiment in activities and institutions with their own intrinsic purposes. The public interest concerns the interests of a public world which we share as citizens and which we can pursue and enjoy by going beyond our private self-interest.

In the second section d'Entrèves argues that Arendt's participatory conception of citizenship provides the best framework for addressing both the question of the constitution of collective identities and that concerning the conditions for the exercise of effective political agency. With respect to the first question, he argues that political action and discourse are essential to the constitution of collective identities, since they enable the construction of a collective 'we'. This process of identity-construction is a process in which actors articulate and defend competing conceptions of cultural and political identity and competing conceptions of political legitimacy. Arendt's participatory conception of citizenship is particularly relevant in this context, since it articulates the conditions for establishing forms of collective identity that can be acknowledged, tested and transformed in a discursive and democratic fashion. With respect to the second question, he argues that the connection between political action, understood as the active engagement of citizens in the public realm and the exercise of effective political agency, is one of the central contributions of Arendt's participatory conception of citizenship. For Arendt, the active engagement of citizens in the determination of the affairs of their community provides them not only with the experience of public freedom and public happiness, but also with a sense of political agency and efficacy, the sense, in Jefferson's words, of being 'participators in government'. In her view, only the sharing of power that comes from civic engagement and common deliberation can provide each citizen with a·sense of effective political agency.

In the last section d'Entrèves explores the connection between Arendt's participatory conception of citizenship and the constitution of an active and democratic political culture. He shows that for Arendt the possibility of reactivating the political capacity for impartial and responsible judgement depends upon the creation of public spaces for collective deliberation in which citizens can test and enlarge their opinions. Instead of remaining the expression of arbitrary preferences, these opinions can be shaped and transformed through a process of democratic debate and enlightenment. The same holds true for the formation of valid judgements: as the most political of our cognitive faculties, judgement can be exercised and tested only in a context of public deliberation and debate, a context where everyone is encouraged to enlarge his or her perspective and to acknowledge the standpoint of others. The cultivation of an 'enlarged mentality' requires, therefore, the creation of institutions and practices where the voice and perspective of everyone can be articulated, tested and transformed. As Arendt argued, a public culture of democratic participation which guarantees to everyone the right to action and opinion remains essential to the flourishing of our capacity for judgement and to the formation of valid opinions.

The four chapters that constitute Part 2 of this book, 'Legal perspectives', situate the public/private distinction in the domain of the law, encompassing legal philosophy and the history of jurisprudence as well as legal and administrative policies and the case studies of relevant court judgments. Although the chapters approach their subject from different epistemological and political perspectives, they can nonetheless be seen to address a common set of problems which are given in the specific character of legal norms and their relationship with authoritative judgment, prescriptive rules and coercive enforcement. All four contributions take issue with the liberal paradigm of the public/private demarcation, at least in its simplified, ideological expression which posits a fundamental distinction between a protected sphere of individual freedom and responsibility, on the one hand, and a domain of collective responsibility, citizenship and state interest, on the other. Moreover, to the extent that they focus on the political construction and historical variability of the divide, the chapters affirm the potential usefulness of a reconstructed distinction for the guarantee and the development of personal autonomy. Both Christine Sypnowich and Jean Cohen explore the conditions under which a constitutional right to privacy could be severed from its historical association with the injustice of economic inequality and the oppression of religious and sexual minorities. Nigel Simmonds emphasises the necessity of adopting a dual perspective, rather than a rigidly monolithic view, upon individual and collective responsibility which would leave the moral relevance of the distinction between private and public law intact. Ursula Vogel's historical analysis of European marriage discourses highlights the coercive effects of the public interest in the private domain of gender relations and considers the benefits that could be derived from present tendencies towards a genuine privatisation of marriage.

In 'The Civility of Law: between Public and Private' Christine Sypnowich takes Virginia Woolf's quest for 'a room of one's own' to emphasise the fundamental importance of privacy to the culture of modernity. She argues that the meanings and values that we associate with privacy can be ascertained from three perspectives. The first points to the private as a protected space with clear boundaries which secure individuals against the intrusions of others and against the invasive claims of the public power. The second set of meanings pertains to the private as an active constituent of freedom, i.e. as a necessary condition and incentive of personal self-development. The third perspective on privacy refers to its institutional embodiment in the rule of law and its task to set limits to the discretion of legislators, judges and administrators.

The first part of the chapter offers a response to those developments in contemporary political theory which pose a radical challenge to the notion of a public/private divide. Egalitarians and socialists, on the one hand, and feminists and defenders of minority rights, on the other, have made a powerful case to discredit the idea of privacy by pointing to its alignment with social injustice, patriarchal oppression and ethnic and religious domination. Sypnowich concedes that in all these cases we can, indeed, observe undeniable historical links between the defence of privacy and the features of a defective society which seems incapable of responding to our needs for equality, community and solidarity. However, these historical connections should not be taken to exhaust our conceptual resources which allow for a reformulation of the idea of privacy in ways that would remedy those grievances. Thus, the demand for privacy is not incompatible with the aim of imposing serious restrictions upon the extent of private ownership and of reducing the ambit of the private for the sake of social justice. To make the case for redistribution is, on the other hand, not to deny an egalitarian society's need for privacy under the protection of the rule of law. The quest for community still has to include a guarantee of the individuals' claims to a personal domain immune from intrusion and will have to rely upon the procedures and regularities of the rule of law to sustain a fair legal sytem.

Similarly, feminist critics of the public/private distinction as well as the advocates of minority rights have rightly emphasised that the values historically associated with the private sphere have served to conceal the structures of power and unjust domination. The author suggests that in this respect, too, we should not aim at a wholesale repudiation of the private, be it in favour of an 'ethic of care' or of the recognition of multiple group identities.

Rather, we should seek to disconnect the idea of privacy from its oppressive historical meanings and to reconfigure it in a new framework. What is needed is a reconceptualisation of the public/private distinction that will neither render individuals vulnerable to the forced public disclosure of private concerns nor serve as a shield for mere indifference to the needs and interests of our fellow-citizens.

The second part of the chapter examines the conditions of such reconceptualisations by reference to the idea of 'civility'. Sypnowich suggests that we interpret this concept as expressing a form of concern for others that is appropriate to the more distanced and impersonal relations of the public sphere. Civility, then, should not be mistaken for the constraints of politeness, etiquette and decorum upon public debate, but should be seen as a virtue of the institutions of a democratic society. When embedded in the institutional framework of the rule of law, civility – the treatment of other citizens as worthy of respect – will foster the conditions of trust that are both necessary and conducive to open debate. Civility in this sense would safeguard the boundaries of a personal domain while also opening up the space for an open and frank debate on the conditions of substantive justice which would allow us to address the injustice hidden and protected by traditional claims to privacy.

In 'Is Privacy a Legal Duty? Reconsidering Private Right and Public Virtue in the Domain of Intimacy' Jean Cohen emphasises the need for reconceptualising the boundaries of public and private in ways that can take account of the epochal changes which during the last quarter of the twentieth century have transformed the domain of intimate relationships. With particular reference to the continuing denial of full privacy rights to gays and lesbians she attempts to develop a conception of the particular goods that we expect privacy rights to grant and protect. Two conditions bear upon the task of such reconceptualisation: first, we have to move away from the myth that identifies the private with a natural, or prepolitical sphere and thus with concerns which are not open to political contestation. Second, we have to disconnect the understanding of privacy rights from the traditional liberal paradigm of mere toleration and forbearance which is incapable of guaranteeing equality to the members of a stigmatised minority. Third, the usefulness of privacy rights to the concerns of these groups can only be established if we avoid confusing the right to privacy with a duty of privacy. It was the latter, Cohen suggests, and not the former, that informed the new military policy of the Clinton administration in the early 1990s. That policy made the acceptance of gays and lesbians in the military conditional upon the rule of not revealing their orientation in speech and conduct. Given that no such duty of privacy pertained to the conduct of heterosexuals, the new policy preserved and reinforced the stigma attached to homosexuality.

How was this case of blatant discrimination legally possible? Cohen refers to the decision of the Supreme Court in the Hardwick case (1986) which upheld the constitutionality of the criminal prosecution of two homosexual men under the sodomy statutes of Georgia. She argues that although the statutes themselves are formulated in a gender-neutral way, they are in fact no longer applied to heterosexual acts, especially when these are sheltered by the privacy of marriage. In denying that the protection of constitutional privacy rights was at issue in the case of 'homosexual sodomy', the majority of the court constructed gays as criminal subjects under the law. That is, the court associated gay identity with a set of criminalisable sexual acts and, at the same time, took these acts to constitute all members of this group as a potentially criminal population.

Cohen claims that in both cases the evidence of a constructed and enforced identity points to the potential benefits of privacy rights. When properly re-constructed, constitutional privacy rights would protect the decisional autonomy of individuals with regard to a wide and diverse range of intimate relations against intolerant majorities. Understood in terms of a reflexive paradigm of the law and of constitutional rights, they would foster the personal autonomy that they protect. In this form, privacy rights would also entail endorsement constraints, i.e. the right of expressing sexual desires without having an unwanted collective identity forced upon one. The case for privacy under conditions of communicative liberty does not imply the with-drawal of the law from the private domain. Rather, it enjoins us to look for an appropriate form of the juridification of intimate relationships, which would protect individuals against the disintegrative effects of over-legislation and, equally, against the harmful effects of non-intervention.

Nigel Simmonds's chapter on 'Justice, Causation and Private Law' sets out from a critical comment upon the habitual unwillingness of practising law-yers and legal theorists to consider the relevance of the distinction between public and private law. While the first group is reluctant to engage in the futile task of exploring the philosophical foundations of this demarcation, the representatives of legal science (be it in the form of legal positivism or of economic theories of the law) will consider the classification as serving no useful function for a rigorously scientific and unitary construction of legal rules and principles. The reverse inclination, Simmonds argues, charac-terises the attempt to rehabilitate the distinctiveness and, indeed, complete autonomy of the private law by contrasting its immanent rationality and independence from political considerations with the politically chosen principles of distributive justice that pertain to the realm of the public law.

Simmonds argues for an approach that neither reifies nor collapses the distinction. What is required is a duality of perspective that enables us to differentiate between the principles of procedural civil justice and the attri-butes of social justice without losing sight of their interdependence. The dual perspective is exemplified in the biblical parable of the labourers in the vineyard who are hired by its owner at different times throughout the day and who are yet all paid the same wages irrespective of the time and effort they have invested in the work. If we consider the scenario in terms of the private law, i.e. as a series of discrete market transactions and separate contractual arrangements, the outcome is just. If, however, we look at the vineyard as a collective arrangement for the fair distribution of benefits and burdens, the undifferentiated remuneration will appear unjust.

Simmonds shows that this distinction between individual and collective responsibility can serve as a useful device for explaining the division of legal systems into the two domains of private and public law. However, such explanations should not be understood as a claim to establish an essential and thus invariable boundary between separate concerns. Nor can we expect to derive the demarcation of the two spheres from a coherent set of philosophical principles. We have to accept that the distinction is an artifice which draws upon historical contingency and the resilience of certain legal traditions as well as on deeply rooted moral intuitions. From a moral perspective, the distinction gives expression to two distinct and potentially conflicting concerns. It refers to our willingness and capacity to exercise collective responsibility over the profile of our community. But it also embodies the need to preserve the individual's accountability for her actions. The common-sense causal principles by which the private law attributes events to particular individuals as authors of their actions are necessary to sustain our sense of self in relation to other selves and to foster our mutual recognition as autonomous agents.

Considered from their historical origins, the characteristic institutions and ideas of the private law – i.e. the attribution of responsibility to individual agents – are owed to social and political conditions which preceded the evolution of the state and its capacity to penetrate all spheres of social life. In one sense, then, the assumptions that constitute the principles of the private law belong to the past and can be expected to be further eroded or transformed in the future. In another and more important sense, the relative backwardness of these assumptions and their resistance to change continues to provide modern law with a valuable resource in that the notion of individual responsibility preserves a necessary condition of autonomous agency.

In the last chapter of the book – 'Private Contract and Public Institution: the Peculiar Case of Marriage' – Ursula Vogel traces the construction and reconfiguration of public and private by reference to the discursive history of marriage. Present controversies and apprehensions about the uncertain future of 'the institution of marriage' serve as a starting point to explore the ambivalent status of a contractual relationship which is still widely understood as essentially different from and incommensurable with the normative principles that define contracts in modern private law. Historically, marriage has been a latecomer to the contractualisation of legal relationships and to the guarantee of individual agency and formal equality which underpin our understanding of the distinctive features and systematic coherence of private law. However, the author argues that the peculiar backwardness of the marriage law and its extra-territorial place in the legal system should not be attributed to historical contingency. At least in the domain of legal discourse the double perspective on marriage as both a contract and an institution has served the systemic function of reconciling notions of individual agency with the demands of public order.

The chapter examines the construction of marriage at the intersection of private and public law in three exemplary historical contexts. The first refers to the medieval canon law and its attempt to derive a coherent system of legal rules from the normative properties of contract and consent, on the hand, and from the demands of a pre-ordained sacramental order on the other. With this dual perspective the canon law set the terms that all subsequent debates about marriage were to follow. It established a private space for the personal commitment of the spouses while at the same time binding them into an order that was not at the disposal of their will. The second context details the radical epistemological shift towards an understanding of marriage as a purely civil contract which occurred in the natural law doctrines of the seventeenth and eighteenth centuries. In severing the nexus with the truths of divine revelation, the secular contractual paradigm placed marriage under the exclusive jurisdictional power of the state and opened the door to the legitimisation of divorce. On the other hand, however, the contract remained embedded in, and constrained by, an overall structure of distinctly public purposes which subjected individual freedom to the coercive imperatives of sexual discipline, orderly procreation and marital *Herrschaft*. Vogel argues that the dynamic inherent in the process of contractualisation left those public-order imperatives unsecured and open to contestation. The 'divorce revolution' of the late eighteenth century – the introduction of divorce by mutual consent in the civil legislation of the French Revolution and in the codifications of enlightened absolutism – appeared to many contemporary observers to shift the purposes of marriage from the public into the private domain.

It was against this background that the institutional reaction of the early nineteenth century – the third relevant context – cast the contractual marriage as an effective cause of revolutionary disorder. The 'institution of marriage' embodied the claim that the essence of marriage did not belong to the world of contracts and individual rights. It belonged to a higher order in which privacy, understood as the protected sphere of sentimental love, intimacy and gender hierarchy, appeared directly related to the non-contractual essence of the state. The chapter uses the recriminalisation of adultery and illegitimacy as public offences as evidence to show that the privacy discourse served to obscure and sustain a coercive discourse in which the meaning of public interest and public order focused in particular upon the deviance of women.

Like the other contributions to Part 2, the chapter argues that the liberal paradigm and its notion of the private as an essentially non-political, non-coercive sphere is of little help in reconstructing the legacies of the public/

private divide in legal discourse. But the critique of liberalism moves along a different route. The chapter shows that the liberal paradigm can give us no access to the peculiar history of marriage because it cannot account for the regulative and coercive presence of the public power in this domain of the private law. Moreover, the majority of nineteenth-century liberals shared in the general consensus which supported the institution of marriage as a safeguard against the corrosive tendencies of modern individualism. But this defence bought into the resources of the institutional discourse at the cost of abandoning liberal principles. In reviewing the massive changes in Western marriage law in the last half of the twentieth century, the conclusion suggests that the present form of marriage enables us to envisage its further transformation into a partnership of equals whose autonomy in a private space is protected by the law.

Notes

1 J. Weintrab, 'The Theory and Politics of the Public/Private Distinction', in J. Weintraub and K. Kumar (eds), *Public and Private in Thought and Practice* (Chicago: University of Chicago Press, 1997), pp. 1–42, at p. 7.
2 S. Benn and G. Gaus, 'The Public and the Private: Concepts and Action', in S. Benn and G. Gaus (eds), *Public and Private in Social Life* (London: Croom Helm, 1983), pp. 3–27, at pp. 5–7.
3 J. Weintraub, 'The Theory and Politics of the Public/Private Distinction', op. cit., p. 38.

Part 1

Philosophical and political perspectives

2 The 'public–private' demarcation

Hillel Steiner

Both common parlance and contemporary political philosophy would lead one to believe that the relation between the public and private domains is essentially *asymmetrical*. That is, our standard conception of these domains is one which, whatever their actual contents may be in any society, attributes the following two characteristics to the contents of the former: that they are entirely (a) non-identical with, and (b) instrumentally derived from, contents of the latter.

On this view, which I'll call the *Asymmetry Thesis*, the sphere of public authority lacks any element of foundational independence from the sphere of private authority, and makes no autonomously generated demands upon the conduct of members of society. Rather, the former presupposes the latter and, accordingly, any theory about what its demands *should be* is necessarily constrained by whatever set of principles determines the demands of private domains. Whether the demands of those private domains are construed as being ones for Lockean natural rights, Rousseauian moral liberty or Benthamite maximised utility, the public domain is conceived as a set of instruments for their fulfilment.

But strongly inclined as we are to subscribe to the Asymmetry Thesis, some hesitation is warranted. For it is by no means true that legal and political theories – and the more popular views they sometimes reflect – have invariably sustained it. In fact, the thesis has been implicitly denied in at least two different ways. It is denied by theories which maintain that all the contents of the public domain are identical with at least some private ones: that is, by theories which deny (a). And it is denied by theories which reject the full analytical reducibility of the public domain to an instrumental aggregation of private ones: that is, by theories which deny (b). Despite their significant mutual differences, what both of these types of theory share is the view that at least some of the contents of the public domain are not construable as instrumental derivations from those of the private domain. The public domain does not stand in a simple agent–principal relation to the private.

In order to explore these denials of the Asymmetry Thesis something needs first to be said about the concept of a 'domain'. Domains are normative entities. They can usefully be conceived as rule-assigned portions of action-space. That is, they are collections of rights whose owners hold Hohfeldian claims which each correlatively entail enforceable duties in others.[1] We can think of every particular owed duty as constituting a mini- or sub-domain for the person to whom it's owed. And we can thus construe that person's entire domain as composed of the entire set of duties owed by others to him or her, minus the duties he or she owes to others. Those sets of duties are, typically, mixtures of both negative (forbearance) and positive (performance) ones. In being owed those duties by others, a domain's owner is thereby endowed with an entitlement implying that certain changes or continuities, in how that portion of the world is, should be brought about by those others.

Now, as was suggested above, one way of denying the Asymmetry Thesis is to affirm the partial or complete identity of the public and private domains: to reject characteristic (a). For clearly, if items to be found in the former are identical with ones located in the latter, the two domains are imperfectly distinguishable and, to that extent, are not asymmetrically related to one another. It might appear, however, that the indisputable existence of separate bodies of public and private law – each with its own inventory of enforceable duties and correlatively entailed rights – is the decisive piece of evidence counting *against* such indistinguishability. But as Paton has tellingly observed,

> this distinction has not always been clearly marked. Until the State itself has developed, public law is a mere embryo. Even in the days of feudalism there is much confusion; for no clear line can be drawn between the public and private capacities of the king. Jurisdiction, office and even kingship are looked upon as property – indeed public law might almost be regarded as 'a mere appendix' to the law of real property so far as the feudal ideal is realized.[2]

That is, the rights of feudal kings counted as elements of the private domain. Are there sufficient reasons to suppose that the subsequent development of the state and, with it, the post-embryonic emergence of an extensive body of public law, has essentially altered this *subsumption* of the public domain by the private?

Perhaps the theories most comprehensively committed to such subsumption are those various doctrines of absolute monarchy – most notably, the 'divine right of kings' – that emerged in the post-Reformation period. Their guiding thought is that, although monarchs may be ultimately accountable to God for the manner in which they have exercised their rights, those rights are all-encompassing and extend to the regulation of every aspect of subjects' conduct. Accordingly, such entitlements as subjects may possess are ones held entirely on the sufferance of the monarch and are not ones which may be claimed against him/her. These entitlements form, in effect, the normative framework for a division of labour among subjects and, as such, vest them with only that liberty (in their dealings with one another) as is deemed necessary to execute the monarch's wishes. Subjects stand, in that respect, in an agent–principal relation to their monarch. My duty not to trespass on my neighbour's field is one owed to the monarch and not to my neighbour. In general, the territorial jurisdiction of any legal system simply *is* a single private domain – the monarch's – and, accordingly, the respective contents of the public and private domains are mutually identical.

It would, I think, be a serious mistake to imagine that such theories are ones of merely antiquarian interest. For we do not have to be anarchists to find it, at best, unclear how or why such subsumption ceases to be true in circumstances where sovereignty is held not by a monarch but rather by some larger set of persons. Nor is it clear, therefore, what precisely is implied by a current view like 'the personal is political'. Is it thereby intended that *all* norms regulating personal conduct properly fall within the public domain – a view with which those post-Reformation monarchists would certainly have concurred? Try as we might to harness them together, the questions of who controls the public domain and of how far it extends remain mutually distinct and independently answerable. So even where the proffered answer to the first of these is (implausibly) 'Everyone, jointly', that no more implies the replacement of private by public control than does an increase in the number of shareholders in a bank.

If subsumption has been one basis for denying the Asymmetry Thesis, another is the rejection of the public domain's complete instrumental reducibility: the rejection of characteristic (b). But here a clarifying qualification must immediately be registered. For few theories embracing that rejection suggest that *every* element of the public domain resists such reducibility: many evidently do not. On the other hand, it seems clear that the class of non-reducible items is often treated as more inclusive than closer scrutiny warrants.

What I have in mind is the sort of inference, about the contents of the public domain, that is sometimes drawn from the existence of *public goods*. A private good is a commodity or service whose consumption by one person either reduces or altogether excludes its consumption by anyone else: apples and medical treatment are standard examples. A public good, in contrast, possesses the characteristics of being (partly or wholly) non-rival in consumption and non-excludable: its consumption by one person does not reduce its availability to others and its producer is unable to exclude those others from consuming it. Hence, on standard economic theory, it will not be supplied by voluntary activity, including the network of voluntary contracts constitutive of private markets. And there is therefore a presumption that, despite being universally desired, it can be supplied only by imposed restrictions and/or funded only by compulsory taxation: environmental protection, military defence and street-lighting are common examples. Accordingly, so it is argued, the *rights* to such restrictions and/or revenue are authentically elements of the public domain, and cannot be located in the private domain.

While this line of reasoning is unassailable, it does not furnish sufficient grounds to reject (b). For it fails to show that those restriction and revenue rights, though exclusively located in the public domain, are not instrumentally derived from private rights. Clearly, they are. And this is true regardless of whether we embrace the Will Theory of rights or the rival Interest Theory. On the Will Theory, right-holders are themselves empowered to waive any of their protected liberties and claims, including claims to funds which they own, and to vest these in others. That, indeed, is how goods of any kind are purchased. So if vesting some such claims in governments can be shown to be the only *means* of securing certain goods desired by all private right-holders, then those public rights are construable as the results of exercises of those private rights and as standing in an unmistakably instrumental relation to them. And the argument from the Interest Theory reaches the same conclusion, albeit more directly. For although on this theory private right-holders are not necessarily empowered to waive their claims, the fact that each one's vital interests are better *served* by the transferral of some of those claims to the government is again sufficient to signify that those public rights are instrumentally related to private ones. In both cases, not only are the duties correlating to those public rights borne by private individuals, but so too are the rights which they subserve. The duties correlating to those public rights are instruments for the fulfilment of duties correlating to everyone's private rights.

But the case is quite otherwise when we focus our attention on certain other public rights. For although these are often associated with the provision of public goods, the case for doing so is, at best, considerably more complex than those we've just examined. Consider two alternative sets of government measures for environmental protection: EP_1 and EP_2. Suppose that these sets both protect exactly the same aspects of the environment but that, whereas EP_1 can be expected to do so for only a century, EP_2 will probably do so for at least a millennium: the life-spans of these two sets differ greatly.[3] Accordingly, it is plausible to assume that EP_2 will cost considerably more than EP_1. Let's call that difference between their respective costs D. It follows that, if what is to be supplied is EP_2 rather than merely EP_1, there must be a public right to D and private right-holders must bear the correlative duties to pay D. The question we need to address is whether that public right to D can similarly be construed as instrumentally related to each individual's private rights.

In addressing it, we find that there are two variables which are saliently in play: the nature of rights and the membership of the class of right-holders. The first of these has to do with whether we deploy the Will Theory or the Interest Theory of rights. And the second is concerned with whether the class of private right-holders is confined to *current persons* or also includes *future persons*. The phrase 'future persons' refers to persons whose lives share no element of contemporaneity – no temporal overlap – with those of current persons. Call the class of private right-holders that is confined to current persons the 'exclusive class' and its unconfined counterpart the 'inclusive class'. Accordingly, there are *prima facie* four possible ways of interpreting EP_2 as a public good and the public right to D as being instrumentally related to each individual's private rights:

1 It subserves the Will Theory rights of the exclusive class.
2 It subserves the Will Theory rights of the inclusive class.
3 It subserves the Interest Theory rights of the exclusive class.
4 It subserves the Interest Theory rights of the inclusive class.

Let's now consider each of these possible interpretations in turn.

Evidently 1 is the most easily assessed. For 1 to be true, it would need to be the case that *all* current persons would prefer to bear the cost of providing that form of environmental protection, to persons even a thousand years hence, than to deploy their respective shares of D in any other available way. They would all need to be more concerned for that environmental well-being of those temporally remote persons than for whatever other aspects of one another's well-being are purchasable with D. Whether all current persons' preference schedules do indeed reflect this ordering is, of course, an empirical rather than a philosophical question. So its apparent improbability cannot be taken as decisive.

In the case of 2, however, we have a genuine non-starter since the Will Theory itself is inconsistent with an inclusive class of right-holders. For an important feature of that theory is that it is logically incapable of attributing rights to future persons. As was previously noted, to have a Will Theory right is to be empowered to waive and alternatively demand and enforce compliance with its correlative duty. Having a right to such compliance certainly doesn't imply that the right-holder is actually able to exercise such powers, say, by personally wielding the requisite force: she can confer them on others (such as the state) and thereby authorise them to do so. But it does imply that there's nothing logically absurd or inconceivable about her exercising them, or about her authorising others to do so. And in this regard, it's perhaps worth emphasising that such powers can be conferred – their exercise by others can be authorised – only by the right-holder herself. For White's waiver or enforcement of Red's duty to do A to count as an exercise of the powers entailed by Blue's right that Red do A, it must be the case that Blue has conferred those powers upon White. If White's possession of those powers did *not* presuppose Blue's authorisation, there would be no reason why anybody else might not equally claim to be possessed of those powers and hence authorised to decide whether to enforce or waive Red's compliance with his duty to do A. In short, to be possessed of the power to uphold a Will Theory right is either to be, or to be authorised by, that right's holder.

It follows fairly readily from these considerations that whatever moral duties current persons have to future persons are not correlative ones. Future persons are able neither to waive nor to demand nor to enforce current persons' compliance with those duties. And this inability isn't merely a physical incapacity, an empirical impossibility.[4] A future person is necessarily incapable of either waiving or demanding a current person's compliance or preventing a current person's non-compliance or penalising him for it, because *ex hypothesi* two such persons lack any element of contemporaneity. And this necessary lack of contemporaneity also implies the logical impossibility of future persons authorising some current persons to exercise those powers. Hence such demands and enforcement cannot be regarded as an exercise of powers attached to future persons' rights. They have no Will Theory rights against current persons nor, therefore, any rights that current persons protect the environment for them.[5] So although members of the exclusive class – those existing within the life-span of EP_1 – can each owe one another correlative duties of environmental protection, the same cannot be said of members of the inclusive class. The public right to D cannot be described as being instrumentally related to each of its members' private rights since many of them simply have no rights. EP_2 is not a public good on this interpretation.

What about 3? Since we are here dealing with the Interest Theory, the issue of whether persons can correlatively owe duties to one another turns, not on whether they can be described as empowered with respect to one another's duties, but rather on whether those duties can be regarded as subserving one another's vital interests. Can the securing of EP_2, and the consequent duty to pay their respective shares of D, be understood as subserving the vital interests of the members of the exclusive class? We know, or are assuming, that the environmental protection afforded by EP_1 does indeed subserve those interests: EP_1 is, unproblematically, a public good and the public right to payment of its cost is therefore properly construed as being instrumentally related to each current person's private rights.

One condition necessary for EP_2 to be similarly construed appears to be that future persons' vital interests count as *components* of all current persons' vital interests. Let's call this the *component condition*. Now, nothing said so far precludes satisfaction of this condition: no analysis has been offered of what is undoubtedly the manifold of diverse items composing any person's vital interests, beyond supposing that some aspects of environmental protection are among them. Nor shall I embark on such an analysis here, since formidable conceptual obstacles confront the component condition itself.

These are chiefly associated with the very function of rights in our normative discourse. Rights are generally presumed to entail *distributive* demands on our conduct and ones that enjoy a *peremptory* status. They are peremptory inasmuch as the duties correlative to rights are taken to be such that, in any conflict with non-correlative sorts of duty, they prevail. And they are distributive in the sense that no consideration is to be given to the comparative importance of the conflicting duties nor, therefore, to the aggregately greater good that might be achievable by favouring performance of the non-correlative duty over the correlative duty with which it conflicts. But what if some correlative duties conflict with other correlative duties themselves?[6] Since such inter-right conflicts are evidently *not* resolvable by reference to the peremptory status of rights, they can be resolved only by reference to some aggregative calculus of the comparative importance of the rights in conflict. And it seems reasonable to suppose that, even if the component condition is satisfied – even if all current persons have a vital interest in, and hence some Interest Theory right to, the protection of future persons' vital interests – these will conflict with their other such rights.

So the question that needs to be asked is whether the vital interests of future persons in EP_2, as elements in every current person's vital interests, are *more important* than those current persons' interests in what could alternatively be purchased by their respective shares of D. For if they are not, then, again, the public right to D cannot be described as being instrumentally related to the private rights of each of the exclusive class's members. Accordingly, EP_2 would not be a public good. As in 1 above, the answer to the foregoing question obviously requires empirical information. So the most that can be said is that it would be surprising if the requisite superior importance of EP_2 were to prove true of the vital interests of *every* current person.

Which brings us to 4. Here what we want to know is whether combining the Interest Theory with the inclusive class of right-holders yields EP_2 as a public good. Leaving aside the problem of rights-conflicts just discussed, it seems undeniable that, if EP_1 is a public good for the exclusive class, then EP_2 must be a public good for the inclusive class – especially when considered from the perspective of the Interest Theory.[7] Since both EP_1 and EP_2 protect the environment in the same way, how could it be otherwise?

One way of seeing how it could, indeed, be otherwise is to take note of a preconception that seems to pervade many arguments for the longer-term protection of the environment. We might call this preconception the *Space-ships Perspective*. According to this view, the number of future persons and the number of generational cohorts into which they are marshalled are *preordained*. These persons occupy, so to speak, some gigantic convoy of space-ships which are 'already out there'. And as they await their respective turns to dock at Planet Earth, there is profound anxiety about whether its environment will prove to be a victim of current persons' self-indulgent prodigality or a beneficiary of their self-denying frugality.

The *Space-ships Perspective* is, I hope it goes without saying, profoundly erroneous. Its error lies in a failure to appreciate that there are two variables in play here – population size, as well as environmental quality – and not just one. Just how many future persons there will be, and how they will be distributed over successive generations, is incrementally and successively determined by the members of each generation's predecessor. Whether there will *be* a next generation, and how numerous its membership will be, are questions which are answered by aggregated estimates of the individual procreative choices of those preceding persons. And those answers are themselves needed if we are to form some idea of how much environmental protection is required, and for how long, to serve the vital interests of inclusive class right-holders. Put more directly, the vital interests of members of the inclusive class do not require as extensive a measure of environmental protection as is afforded by EP_2 if there are, say, only seven future generations in that class and/or their memberships are considerably less numerous than those of current generations.

So what factors *do* determine procreative choices? Here, to be sure, is a minefield best avoided. But one generalisation seems safe enough: *ceteris paribus*, persons will have fewer children as their living costs increase. The duty to pay D constitutes one such increase for current persons. Accordingly, in two otherwise identical societies, we might expect more procreation in the one which implements only EP_1 than in the one which implements EP_2. By extrapolation, and assuming the same subsequent rate of *per capita* procreation in both societies, we arrive at the conclusion that, at any given future date within the next century, the population of the prodigal former would be greater than that of the frugal latter. Thereafter, we might expect the rate of procreation in the former to drop precipitously. Just how much it would drop would vary with the magnitude of the environmental degradation faced and the cost of living increase that current persons incur in protecting themselves from it.

Can we say, on this basis, that the prodigal society – in contrast to the frugal society – violates the private Interest Theory rights of its inclusive class? It's hard to see how. What EP_2 does is to squeeze current persons' living standards more in order to create more environmental space for more, but also less sparsely populated, generations than does EP_1. But the latter does not disserve any *individual*'s vital interests. Persons who *would have existed*, but for the higher living costs confronting their predecessors, cannot be described as ones whose vital interests are disserved by the causes of those costs. The frugal society is one whose future persons outnumber its current ones. But since the reverse is true for the prodigal society, all that can be concluded is that the frugal society itself will probably enjoy an enhanced *longevity* which the prodigal society will lack. And since enhanced social longevity is not construable as a component of individuals' vital interests, we seem warranted in concluding that – under interpretation 4 – EP_2 is not a public good and that the public right to D cannot therefore be described as a means to one.

The Asymmetry Thesis, then, fails in the face of two kinds of counter-example. It fails when public rights are simply identical with private ones. And it fails when public rights secure goods which cannot be regarded as public goods. Whether, in the latter case, it is fruitful to regard those public rights as associated with some conception of irreducible *group* rights, is a question which would doubtless repay further study.

Notes

1 Disagreement persists over some aspects of how rights and, hence, their correlative duties should be conceived. According to the *Will Theory*, these duties are ones the fulfilment of which owners themselves (or persons whom they authorise) are empowered both to waive and, alternatively, to demand and enforce at their discretion – whereas the *Interest Theory* regards neither owners nor those whom they might authorise as *necessarily* the persons who are possessed of these duty-controlling powers. Although I defend the Will Theory – and criticise the Interest Theory – in *An Essay on Rights* (Oxford: Blackwell, 1994), ch. 3, and more extensively in *A Debate Over Rights: Philosophical Enquiries*, Matthew Kramer, Nigel Simmonds and Hillel Steiner (Oxford: Oxford University Press, 1998), the argument of the present essay is neutral with respect to these rival theories. I should perhaps add that the centuries-long debate about the nature of rights has failed to reveal any distinct third theory that even approaches the level of formal generality attained by the Will and Interest Theories.

2 G. W. Paton, *A Text-book of Jurisprudence* (Oxford: Oxford University Press, 1972), p. 328.

3 We can imagine that the two sets of measures respectively require, say, the use of toxic waste containers of differing minimum durability, or the employment of products or processes with differing rates of ozone-layer depletion.

4 As it *is* in the case of right-holders who are ill, asleep or geographically remote from persons who owe them duties.

5 Cf. *An Essay on Rights*, pp. 259–61.

6 Elsewhere I have argued that the Interest Theory is particularly likely to foster such inter-right conflicts; see *An Essay on Rights*, p. 92, and *A Debate Over Rights: Philosophical Enquiries*, pp. 290–3; cf. Jeremy Waldron, 'Rights in Conflict', *Ethics*, 92 (1981), 21–39.

7 Since it leaves less latitude than the Will Theory for individuals' preferences to produce variations in their rights.

3 Public reason, private citizenship[1]

Dario Castiglione

There is no Mandevillian ring to the title of this chapter. No attempt is here made to ground public justification and public reasoning on a self-interested conception of political membership. The defining concepts of 'public reason' and 'private citizenship' are instead borrowed from the recent work of John Rawls and Bruce Ackerman respectively, who conceive them as mutually sustaining, without any paradox being intended. The scope of this chapter is to explore the complexities of this relationship and to suggest that the virtuous circle between the ideals[2] of public reason and private citizenship cannot be assumed in the form explicitly suggested by Ackerman in *We the People*[3] and implied by Rawls in *Political Liberalism*.[4]

I Rawls's public reason

Rawls understands public reason as the reason of free and equal citizens in a political community. It is 'public' in three distinct but mutually reinforcing senses. It is characteristic of a free citizenry, forming the public body to whom it applies and from whom it originates; its exclusive scope is the public good; and its nature and content are public, that is, justifiable according to public standards and open to public scrutiny.[5] Public reason offers a common language and a minimum of shared values through which citizens can argue about and agree upon the fundamental institutions and arrangements of their political society, without having necessarily to resort to force or to appeal to forms of authority not justifiable to each other, at least in principle.[6]

Public reason is central in the overall structure of Rawls's own version of political liberalism. It represents the key idea on which he establishes a 'free-standing' conception of political justice based exclusively on an overlapping consensus.[7] Because of its importance in Rawls's and others' versions of *political* liberalism, and because it also represents an important idea in the justification of deliberative democracy, public reason has recently been at the centre of much discussion.[8] Probing questions have been asked on its specificity as a form of reason; on its grounds of justification; on its 'neutralist' appeal; on its moral compulsion; and on the institutions that either embody or represent it. These are important questions on which depend the philosophical standing and coherence of the very idea of public reason. But they need not concern us within the context of this chapter, for its scope is a more modest one. I wish instead to ask *when* citizens should engage in public reasoning and *how to motivate* them to do so (that is, *why* should they heed the demands of public reason).[9] Within the strict limits of these questions, I am happy to take for granted Rawls's own definition of public reason, without questioning its meaning and import. In the concluding section, however, I shall briefly discuss some of the implications that my analysis seems to entail for Rawls's formulation of the idea of public reason.

To remain with the conditions of the use of public reason, Rawls suggests that magistrates and public officials (or would-be public officials) must speak the language of public reason whenever they debate about constitutional essentials and about matters of fundamental liberty and justice involved in what Rawls takes to be the basic structure of society.[10] Citizens are restricted within the rhetorical[11] confines of public reasoning only when they act *as if* they were public officials.[12] Within the context of modern constitutional democracy this clearly means when they act so to affect directly (through referendums) or indirectly (through the selection of their representatives) the kinds of issue which fall under the province of public reason.

The general motivation that citizens and public officials at large have to speak (or, indeed, to *act*) within the limits of public reason lies in the duty of civility that binds the citizenry of a well-ordered society.[13] For magistrates and public officials this duty of civility is compounded by the responsibility they have in wielding political and ultimately coercive power.

As here outlined, Rawls's answers to our questions would therefore seem both clear and fairly uncontroversial. But there is a certain parsimony in Rawls's answers that makes them rather unsatisfactory. Why should citizens only respect the limits of public reason on certain fundamental matters and not be guided by them in all matters political? Are constitutional essentials and questions of basic justice easier to judge within the limits of public reason? Given their complexity, it may be more, and not less difficult, to reach an overlapping consensus on them. Does the duty of civility apply only intermittently at momentous elections? And why should it not guide all political dealings between citizens? Rawls himself suggests that there is a virtuous circle between the institutions of a well-ordered society and the citizens' ability to use and make appeal to public reason. If that is so, given that the motivational push discussed by Rawls is based on what he calls a 'philosophical' (not natural) moral psychology,[14] there seems to be no particular reason why we should economize on virtue. Moreover, in revisiting the idea of public reason Rawls has expounded on the social roots of democracy and on the many ways in which the comprehensive views inhabiting the 'background culture' of civil society may form and enrich 'public political culture'[15] itself. This, however, starts blurring the distinction between public reason, as a normative idea, and reasons used in public, in ways that, as we shall see below, may undermine Rawls's own conception of overlapping consensus.

If we wish to understand the particular force that Rawls attributes to his convictions on 'when' and 'why' to resort to public reason, we may perhaps have to start looking between the lines of his text in order to thicken out his own argument. There is nothing surprising, or illegitimate, in this. Much of ordinary moral philosophy seems to presuppose a motivation to do the right thing,[16] so that it is sometimes necessary to spell out the link between moral obligations and natural motivations[17] in order to establish the political feasibility of certain moral injunctions. In the case at hand, this may also be justified by the restriction of public reason to particular questions, so that a certain explanation of the motivational shift from one set of political questions to another may be required.

The suggestion of a motivational shift may indeed be the key to solving our problem. Although confusedly,[18] Rawls seems to embrace a conception of constitutional democracy as a 'dualist regime', where the higher law, subject to the constituent power of the people, is protected from the ordinary legislation of the constituted powers through a variety of institutions and anti-majoritarian procedures. Such a line of argument, as acknowledged by Rawls himself, owes a great deal to Ackerman's analysis of American constitutionalism in *We the People*.[19] Ackermnan's own defence of dualist democracy rests on the recognition that in modern societies the common experience of political participation takes the form of what he calls 'private citizenship'. Dualist democracy, and its two-track lawmaking system, is only an institutional means for giving expression to the political values of a community of private citizens.[20] Ackerman's understanding of such values and of how they translate in both normal and constitutional politics seems partly to address the kind of questions I have raised in connection with Rawls's public reason, for Ackerman's private citizens are indeed capable of public reason when they engage in matters of constitutional politics. It is to Ackerman's arguments, therefore, that we may want to turn in search of more fully developed answers to the motivational problems only implicitly addressed by Rawls. But before doing so, we should make clear a more general context for our discussion of public reason and private citizenship.

II The private voter's paradox

Ackerman's own conception of private citizenship indirectly addresses current preoccupations with solving the dispute between economic and deliberative views of democracy. The dispute is often couched in the well-known voter's paradox, showing that rational actors may find it difficult to take themselves to the polling booth on the basis of simple cost-benefit calculations, given the very small probability that their vote may make the difference.[21] Moreover, election results belong to that group of public goods (or bads) that in Olson's classical analysis are subject to free-riding problems.[22] Ackerman himself captures the voter's paradox in the image of the 'last election', which is said to come about if voters behaved according to such narrow and calculating standards. The 'perfect privatist' represents, according to Ackerman, the model of citizenship which would indeed give rise to the last election scenario. However, as he also notices, although there are plenty of people who, by following such a model, forgo the opportunity to express their political opinions and preferences, their number in democratic regimes has not yet reached that critical point when democracy may die not with a bang, but with a whimper. In fact, there is plenty of literature showing that the voter's paradox is such only for rational choice theory, for the motivational assumptions it attributes to voters are too narrowly defined.[23] Citizens who make use of the ballot do not act irrationally, even when they are aware of the fact that their individual vote can hardly matter. In voting, they are concerned with a host of other reasons, besides cost-benefit analysis. Such reasons comprise additional satisfactions attached to the act of voting, symbolic goods of various kinds and, most importantly, the expressive nature of voting itself as part of broader processes of self-identification in politics.[24] As suggested by Hirschman, for many citizens the act of voting should be considered not amongst the costs but amongst the benefits, and that is where the economic model of voting fails to capture reality.[25]

However, what the voter's paradox fails to do for the economic view of democracy and politics, the paradox of the 'private voter' may be more successful at achieving. This paradox does not question whether citizens may find any reason for going to the polling booth, since indeed very many of them still do, but the kind of reasons they bring to the polling booth itself. The dispute here involved is the more subtle one between a preference-based, or market view of voting and a judgement-based, or forum view of voting. We shall see in the next section how fundamental such a distinction is to Ackerman's own idea of private citizenship, but it should also be noticed that, according to Rawls, when citizens follow public reason, they should model themselves on the judgement-based view, which Rawls himself takes to be very similar to the Rousseauian conception of the general Will.[26]

But what is the private voter's paradox? Let me formulate it first with an anecdote. Recent British elections (May 1997) were not only a vindication that New Labour works, at least as an electoral machine, but also that opinion pollsters are not just cranks. In Britain, they were under scrutiny since the previous general election (1992), which turned out to be a disaster not only for Neil Kinnock's Labour Party, but also for opinion pollsters, for their predictions at the eve of election day went badly wrong. One of the reasons adduced for such a poor performance was that many voters had changed their mind at the very last minute. This might have been the case – though a very difficult one to prove – but such an explanation fails to account for a similarly noticeable discrepancy between exit polls and actual results (indeed the real picture only emerged slowly during the night as the results came in). Since normally exit polls are fairly reliable, at least as a guide to the main trends of an election result, their failure in the circumstances suggests that something else went wrong with opinion polls, regardless of the fickle nature of the electorate.[27]

One possible explanation – although one based on nothing more than anecdotal evidence – was that a number of conservative voters were at the time reluctant to declare their true voting intentions (or behaviour), because they felt that the only way they could justify their choice was by an appeal to narrow motives of self-interest. Questioned in the streets, they therefore tended to mask their likely voting intentions (or their actual vote) in ways that systematically underrepresented conservative support. In the secrecy of the ballot box, however, such niceties seemed to have counted for very little, with the unintended consequence that opinion pollsters got egg on their faces.[28] If one discounts the surprise element induced by this collective behaviour, there does not seem to be anything particularly odd about it. A number of electors, who had definite ideas about their preferences, felt uneasy to express them, even in front of a perfect stranger asking questions for a general survey that preserved their anonymity. But, on reflection, there is something paradoxical about all this, for these electors opted to be high-minded in their *private* capacity of passers-by and narrow-minded in their *public* role of citizens. Here lies the private voter's paradox.

This paradox, I submit, is not just a curiosity, since it crucially concerns the nature of the relationship between citizens and their own image of citizenship. What the paradox suggests is that one cannot automatically assume that dispositions normally (and normatively) associated with a particular realm will always apply in practice, while there is often scope for the mixing of motivations and for their transference from one realm to another. At first, and as the example I related may indicate, this gives new hope to a preference-based interpretation of democratic choice by restoring self-interest to its central place as the main motivational push. But my contention is that this is only one of the possibilities and that the paradox must be read both ways, giving food for thought to the supporters of both preference- and judgement-based views.

To see this we must be clear about the precise nature of the paradox, since, as some may be quick to point out – and as was argued for the classical voter's paradox – the paradox may only be in the eye of the beholder. Indeed, the paradox itself rests on the assumption that voting is a 'public act', in which citizens perform a public role. In democratic societies voting is often regarded as the paradigmatic form of public action, to which we have a right as citizens. If this were not the case, as for instance Jon Elster maintains against Alan Ryan,[29] there would be nothing paradoxical in citizens expressing their voting preferences by a simple appeal to their own self-interest, as indeed a strictly economic view of the preference-based interpretation of democratic choice contends. There is, however, some ground for saying that voting *is* a form of public act. The question turns on how one conceives the nature of the right to vote. There is evidence that many citizens see voting not just as a right but also as a public duty.[30] However, since there are plenty of others who do not share the same view, this may prove very little. Institutional practices of imposing sanctions on citizens who do not vote vary from one democratic regime to another, and, on the whole, there is no great enthusiasm for compulsory voting. But a simple thought experiment may convince us that there is indeed something 'public' in the right to vote.

In democracies, people are generally free to cast their vote as they please. But there are certain motives that are clearly considered unacceptable. For instance, the buying and selling of votes is generally excluded and widely condemned. One can see the moral and prudential reasons that underpin such a prohibition in cases in which candidates make use of public money in the transaction; or when the buying of votes is only a prelude to using public office for entirely personal gain. Such considerations are however excluded in cases in which candidates use their own personal money, and when there is no particular reason to believe that they aspire to more than the normal trappings of power. The prohibition is perfectly understandable if one considers voting – as the forum view of democratic choice does – not just as a right but as a duty or a public act. In modern post-feudal societies people cannot dispose of public offices as if they were their patrimonial rights. But a conception of the right to vote as a purely personal right may have some difficulty in mounting the same argument against the use of bribes. Indeed, as the market view maintains, there is nothing particularly wrong in casting one's vote by following self-interested calculations. Such a motivation is considered both legitimate and respectable by political scientists who refer to it as standard. But if 'political exchange' of this kind is admitted, it seems curious that the option of selling one's vote should be foreclosed to the rational voter. John Stuart Mill was making the same point when criticizing the view that there is a 'right' to vote, since this may seem to carry with it the impression that people can dispose of it as they do with other property rights.[31] Indeed, it would be entirely in the rational voter's interest to accept a bribe in exchange for his or her vote, since this represents a more certain net gain than, say, voting into office a party promising tax cuts. The gain is more certain, because in the bribe-taking scenario the voter is not the first performer in the exchange. The gain is greater, because a change in direct taxation would affect the population at large, so increasing one's comparative purchasing power less than in the bribe-taking case, which presumably would not apply with equal universality.

So, what are the moral or practical grounds on which a market view of democracy would exclude the buying and selling of votes, when one discounts current legal provisions against it?[32] From a practical point of view, one could argue that by allowing people to buy and sell votes the wrong people may get elected and that this would then result in a licence to use public money and public patronage to buy yet more votes next time around, so that even a purely self-interested rational voter may want to exclude such a possibility. Notice that this argument is exclusively concerned with the buyer's motivations and not the seller's. However, the same consideration ushers in the more principled objection that the buying and selling of votes may prevent electoral democracy from working as a market mechanism in the selection of a governing class that reflects the real preferences of the electorate.[33] In fact, such an objection implicitly shifts the focus from the individual voter's preferences to the aggregating mechanism. By doing so, it presupposes a collective (public) interest above that of the single individual. Indeed, it is akin to the more intuitive and non-reflective objection against bribe-taking, that this is not, in a way, in the spirit of the electoral game.[34] Moreover, and this is the crucial argument that distinguishes economic from political markets, there seems to be some deep-rooted prejudice that excludes political opinions and preferences from exchange transactions, in the same way that a person's bodily attributes are.[35] More to the point, and as already suggested, this exclusion is very similar in nature to the one that applies to public offices and public duties, like military or jury service.[36]

It should now be evident that even from a preference-based perspective there is something 'public' – in the sense of inherently collective and linked to rules that are bound to the interests of the collectivity as a whole – in the act of voting. I do not want here to suggest that this, in itself, makes the market view of democracy incoherent or unfeasible, as for instance, in another context and with different arguments, Brennan and Pettit have maintained.[37] I only wish to stress how, from the market view perspective, there is indeed a private voter's paradox. But this is not less so from the perspective of the forum view of democratic politics. Supporters of such a position are right in stressing that voting is a public act and that in strict coherence voters should express their judgement about the public good rather than their raw preferences, but the fact is that in free democratic elections there is no way of filtering voters' motivations and reasons, so that the very existence and diffusion of 'private voters' in modern democracies (or indeed in any democracy) is a paradox for them too.

III Ackerman's private citizens

As suggested at the beginning of the previous section, Ackerman's idea of private citizenship can be seen as a possible solution to the above paradox. In this sense, it can also be taken as an attempt to outline the conditions for Rawls's public reason and for Rousseauian deliberation in modern societies. This section explores Ackerman's idea. The next one focuses on its limits.

Ackerman's private citizen is not the 'private voter' of our paradox, however. Ackerman suggests that there are three models of citizens' involvement in matters political. The first, which has already been mentioned, is the 'perfect privatist', who more accurately reflects the private voter's attitudes and dispositions as described above. A society of perfect privatists would often be on the brink of the last election scenario; but assuming that even in such a society elections would carry on, citizens would be at pains to justify to themselves the particular nature of political markets and political rights as separate from general economic transactions. In short, they would be unable to solve the private voter's paradox.

Ackerman's second model is that of the 'public citizen'. From the perspective of the forum view of democracy, this is a more encouraging model. Public citizens take their political duties extremely seriously. They are very much concerned about the public good to which they devote much time and energy. In a classical republican fashion, or at least according to an idealized version of it, they firmly harness their private interests to their public virtue. A modern society based on this model is both unthinkable, given the extreme demands that it would make on the material and moral resources of its citizens, and also threatening, given the obvious danger of turning such heightened ideals into coercive measures. The private voter's paradox would not be solved by a society of public citizens, because such a society could simply not live with it.

There is, however, some comfort in thinking that a great number of citizens in modern societies fall into neither camp. They act, instead, either of the two roles depending on personal and other circumstances. This is why Ackerman calls them 'private citizens', so as to emphasize the combined nature of their virtues, dispositions and motivations. Ackerman also suggests that 'private citizens' are capable of shifting involvements between private and public concerns, a fact that he emphasizes graphically by using the device of stressing one or the other of his compound expressions (*private* citizen vs. private *citizen*). But the simple consideration that there is a group of people who alternate between the two simple models of citizens' behaviour seems scant reason for comfort. This would only amount to the fact that, *at any given time*, the citizenry of a polity comprises people from each of the two main models. So, is there anything particular about private citizenship, such as can be construed as a distinct third model? Ackerman outlines two possible answers to this question: one more sceptical, while the other is more sanguine about private citizens' virtues. Together, these answers form the basis for his model of 'dualist democracy' within which public reason can play an important part. Let us examine them in turn.

The more sceptical answer starts from the observation already mentioned that neither of the simple models of citizens' behaviour offers a reasonable solution to the stability problems of a modern polity and to the mixed preoccupations of its citizens. Private citizens are, in a sense, a classical second-best solution. Ackerman assumes that in times of normal politics, the great majority of citizens approximate the perfect privatist model, since they are generally preoccupied with their own private affairs and look at politics as an extension of such exclusive interests. This is no ideal situation, but has advantages over the reverse case of a stable majority of public citizens, for the latter could only be sustained by force. However, this limited supply of civic involvement poses a number of problems to democratic politics. First, there is the scarce amount of information and knowledge that citizens, who are mostly preoccupied with their own business, bring to the process of decision-making in complex societies. Second, there is the vicious double circle created by a citizenry of privately-minded people, in so far as this both fosters a culture of collective apathy, discouraging public involvement, and reinforces a selfish perspective across the whole spectrum of public and private affairs.

Since the option of forcefully increasing the supply of civic involvement is excluded, we can only try to maximize its use. According to Ackerman, this is done by two political strategies[38] that partly depend on the fact that, although private citizens behave most of the time as perfect privatists, they are also capable of more public-minded attitudes and dispositions. The first strategy involves the maximization of the limited supply of civicness in normal politics by the use of representation. The demand on civic involvement is reduced in terms of both time and effort through the device of voting in people to whom the onerous task of decision-making on behalf of the collectivity is delegated. But elections have also the function of increasing the value of citizens' limited involvement by giving to this act a particular strategic importance in the decision-making process. Furthermore, and against a simple economic view of democratic choice, the universality of voting rights confers a symbolic aspect to electoral moments, so that citizens recognize themselves within a political community, while recognizing each other as equal partners in it.

Representation, however, does not solve the cognitive problems associated with limited civic involvement. The scarce time and thinking that citizens may devote to matters political produce what Ackerman calls a 'soft vote'. It is as though private individuals were taking important decisions (like changing jobs, buying a house, starting a family) only on impulse and with very little thinking. This would suggest a failure on their part to appreciate the importance either of the decisions themselves or of their consequences in terms of welfare and quality of life. The second political strategy aimed at maximizing scarce civic involvement comes in here by drawing on the neo-republican insight that, although the main purpose of the machinery of government in modern societies is that of economizing on virtue, a certain amount of it is still necessary. Admittedly, this is the natural starting point of Ackerman's discussion of dualist democracy, where phases of 'normal politics' are intermittently punctuated by what he calls 'constitutional politics'. This is meant to express the 'voice' of the people more directly. There is no suggestion here that constitutional politics must take the form of direct democracy, rather that it is a kind of politics done by the people (or a significant majority of them) in a more deliberative tone, when the simple aggregation of and trading-off between individual preferences gives way to debate on the basis of publicly justifiable reasons. Constitutional politics takes place in critical circumstances only, when a large majority of the people is aware of the great importance of the issues at stake and is sufficiently mobilized. Its fundamental aim is to express the considered 'voice' of the people and not just the will of all.[39] Ackerman's implicit suggestion is that there are enough citizens in the polity who recognize the importance of certain public decisions and are prepared to give them time and due consideration. This is, so to speak, the *natural* stuff of constitutional politics.

There are, of course, *artificial* constraints – the institutional framework and various filtering preference mechanisms – within which constitutional politics needs to be channelled. Ackerman discusses at length the kind of constraints that may give scope and meaning to a more immediate and forceful representation of people's 'voice';[40] but all this presupposes the willingness on the part of a large section of the citizenry to shift both their involvement and their style of involvement: from a politics of bargains, trade-offs and simple aggregation of individual preferences, to one where people tend to discuss with each other, so as to arrive at a consensual (or at least, fairly consensual) agreement over the general principles regulating the polity. According to Ackerman, the art of institutional design consists in devising a set of institutions and mechanisms that maximize civic involvement *both* in normal and in constitutional politics while balancing one against the other.

At the core of this two-pronged second-best strategy lies, however, the assumption that private citizenship is something more than the simple sum of the other models of citizenship. This requires a more positive justification for it – one which has already begun to emerge from the neo-republican and deliberative gloss that Ackerman gives to constitutional politics. Indeed, he offers a more straightforward defence of private citizenship by painting a more fulsome portrait of its virtues and underlying ethical values, particularly if pitted against those characterizing the alternative models. In comparison to public citizenship, which Ackerman describes in more classical republican terms, private citizenship fits in better with some important values of modern society. First, it allows for the centrality that the work ethic has acquired in the modern world by recognizing the intrinsic value of labour and by seeing political action as the result of the roles we perform in private life. Second, it acknowledges one of the important lessons of the post-classical world, that there is spirituality outside politics and the pursuit of the common good. Finally, it emphasizes the importance of the modern conception of freedom that sees in the plurality and diversity of life choices a positive good. These contrasts are perhaps overdrawn, since the classical republican alternative is identified with a narrow Aristotelian conception of public life, but Ackerman's general point stands: there is something good in a view of citizenship not entirely cut off from the resources of private interests and pursuits.

Against the libertarian and narrow individualist concerns underlying the perfect privatist model, Ackerman argues for the moral superiority of private citizenship on the basis of three other important differences. First, private citizens recognize the importance of taking into account long-term considerations in decision-making. Perfect privatists' natural tendency to focus on first-order preferences,[41] thus narrowing the range of rational calculation in time and space, is something that often rebounds against their own interests. Second, Ackerman believes that behind the veil of ignorance one would choose the duty of civility against a purely selfish view of life in a community. Third, and along a similar line of argumentation, Ackerman suggests that private citizens distinguish themselves from perfect privatists in that they accept that we owe recognition to others as members of the same community. In sum, whereas Ackerman's comparison with public citizenship places private citizens on the firm ground of private virtues, that with perfect privatists suggests that to some degree private citizens also possess virtues such as far-sightedness, fairness and sympathy.

IV The limits of private citizenship

Having followed Ackerman in his analysis of the virtues of private citizenship, we are now in a position to assess whether it addresses the preoccupations outlined in Sections II and III. Indeed, private citizenship (and the kind of dualist democracy that Ackerman derives from it) offers a considered solution to the private voter's paradox. It does so by two combined moves. First, there is the recognition that private and selfish interests, also of a strict economic nature, are fundamental to the well-being of a modern polity. Their expression in public actions is therefore fully legitimate. This is not new, of course, but its meaning is qualified by the second move. Ackerman assumes that in politics private interests and unreflective preferences must be harnessed to an institutional structure that both mirrors and gives normative substance to the instrumental as well as the expressive aspects of citizens' participation in public life. In Ackerman's scheme, the solution to the paradox is mechanically achieved by a clear institutional separation between moments in which the citizenry expresses its will by simple aggregation of raw preferences (the will of all), and moments in which the 'voice' of the people is articulated in a more deliberative form (a kind of General Will).[42] But, in fact, Ackerman's recognition of the double-faced nature of modern citizenship is more fundamental to the solution of the paradox than the mere mechanics of dualist democracy.

Private citizenship also goes some way towards clarifying the motivational and institutional conditions of public reason, thus bridging the gap between its normative demands as an idea and its feasibility as an ideal. On the motivational side, the ideal of private citizenship only assumes that enough people should follow a 'realistic' pattern of motivation. As to 'when' public reason is required, Ackerman avoids giving excessive weight to individual subjective perceptions, while relying instead on the inter-subjective filtering of opinions and expectations done through a complex set of institutions.

Thus Ackerman's answers, with which I find myself in general sympathy. But the sanguine optimism underlying his conception of private citizenship is, I believe, overstated. A more considered discussion of private citizens' shifting involvements will show, as I shall argue in this section, that the conceptual fabric of Ackerman's dualist democracy may need revision; and that, as will be briefly suggested in the conclusion, Ackerman's model of private citizenship makes Rawls's own idea of public reason feasible, but incoherent.

To examine first the inner logic of Ackerman's own discussion of private citizenship, let us consider Albert Hirschman's classic discussion of shifting patterns of private and public involvement.[43] He observes that, to be convincing, cycle theories need to rely on endogenous mechanisms. If upswings and downswings are the exclusive result of external and contingent events, there is little of general value that can be learnt from their cyclical recurrence, unless those exceptional circumstances can in some way be shown to derive from factors endogenously connected to the very nature of the cycle. As he suggests, 'in the case of changes in collective behaviour along the public–private dimension, outside events can generally be credited with much of the responsibility'.[44] He mentions foreign threats, oppression and reform processes (in a Tocquevillian sense) as examples of factors that *pull* towards public involvement; while focusing on the one hand on periods of heightened repression and on the other on times of great economic opportunities, or conversely of deep economic crisis, as instrumental towards private retreat. Without denying the importance of such and much discussed pull factors, Hirschman wishes to turn the attention to the *push* factors of the public–private cycle, those that convince people, after 'dwell[ing] for some time in either . . . sphere' to 'evaluate the ensuing experiences'.[45]

Accordingly, Hirschman's book is a study in 'disappointment', which he takes to be the main endogenous factor in public and private shifting involvements.[46] For he considers mistake-making to be an intrinsic characteristic of human beings leading them inevitably to some form or other of disappointment. Indeed, sustained and protracted involvement in either public or private pursuits is often based on over-exaggerated expectations and/or mis-perceived benefits. In the course of time, the realization of such mistakes results in disenchantment with the idea of the good associated to that particular sphere and in the search for compensation in a different direction.

But, as Hirschman admits, to take disappointment as the main push factor in the public–private cycle may be saying either too much or too little. By considering disappointment as a general feature of the human condition one may be inclined to discount its relevance for the evaluation of people's satisfaction – thus inevitably ending up in disappointment. Moreover, even admitting that disappointment is relevant to the individual evaluation of public and private involvement, it is not yet obvious how this bears on general cycles of involvement across society. To take disappointment seriously, we must therefore assume that there are *variations* in intensity and across activities and that *aggregate* disappointment may change across time. We do not need to go into the details of Hirschman's analysis, besides noticing the main lines of his argument. In discussing shifts from private to public, he focuses on the variety of consumption experiences associated with different goods and services, and on how strong feelings of disappointment may arise from such experiences in periods of intensive change in the structure of production and/or consumption. Feelings of dissatisfaction are also compounded by the complex moral backlash that new wealth and new (positional and non-positional) goods seem to generate. When turning to shifts from public to private, Hirschman notes that they are generally the product of two symmetrical conditions which ordinary citizens experience in public life. On the one hand, and perhaps because of a certain failure of imagination, ordinary citizens seem unaware at first of the burdens of overcommitment that come with public involvement. There is a natural expansionist tendency in public activity that squeezes out other more private pursuits, so that unless one gets addicted to this lifestyle, its demands are progressively perceived as excessive and intolerable. On the other hand, disillusionment is caused by the strict limits imposed upon ordinary citizens' involvement in public affairs – what one may call the burdens of underinvolvement. Voting is the classical example of such a limit, by offering a '*minimum* share in public decision-making' it also 'sets something of a maximum or *ceiling*'.[47] Frustration sets in when citizens, who often perceive the importance of public action's objectives in direct proportion to their own personal involvement, start feeling powerless. Hirschman sums up his discussion of disappointment with public action by making the seemingly contradictory observation that 'the trouble with political life is that it is either too absorbing or too tame'.[48]

Returning now to our discussion of Ackerman's thesis, one may ask whether endogenous factors are at play in shifts between normal and constitutional politics, and if so, what are the mechanisms through which the aggregation of cycles in the life of individuals become socially relevant. It would seem at first that the answer must be negative.[49] Ackerman explicitly suggests that constitutional politics is very often the product either of momentous transformations within the polity or of external crises.[50] At best, constitutional politics can be seen as originating, in Tocquevillian fashion, from the very expectations aroused by the beginning of a reform process, expectations that Ackerman wishes to be firmly kept under control by the institutions of dualist democracy. Such processes have indeed a dynamics of their own, but, as Hirschman notices, they can only be regarded as pull factors in the public–private cycle. If no endogenous factor can be mustered to explain the normal/constitutional cycles of politics, we are left with the alternatives that either Hirschman's categories do not apply to Ackerman's thesis, or that Ackerman's own conception of dualist democracy is not cyclical in an interesting sense.

But after some more considered reflection it would appear that by focusing our attention on Ackerman's shifts between normal and constitutional politics, we have been talking at cross-purposes. In *We the People* Ackerman, on the one hand, engages in a sustained analysis of the stable motivational components of *private* citizens and of how these are institutionally expressed and harnessed in normal politics; on the other, he outlines the different phases through which constitutional politics gives voice to private *citizens*. His main focus is on the institutional frameworks that regulate the expression of the double-sided nature of modern citizenship, not on private citizens' motivational shifts. In normal politics, private citizens' motivations are taken as fixed. Their shift towards constitutional politics, however this is triggered, reflects citizens' dissatisfaction *with* what normal politics can do, but not *because* normal politics promises more than it can deliver. In constitutional politics, things are rather different. Ackerman's description of it as a process – the emergence of a new constitutional consensus ('signalling phase'), its gaining in authority and concreteness ('proposal functi0n'), the testing of its support ('mobilized deliberation'), and its final constitutional sanctioning ('codification') – presupposes that throughout that very process an increasing number of private citizens are induced to look at political life and at their own involvement in it in a new way, with a more deliberative purpose and a broader view of their contribution to the common good. But this picture of the shifting motivations of private citizens throughout the phases of constitutional politics looks still too close to a Tocquevillian reform process, where people are pulled into action by external circumstances.

One may observe at this point that, even though there are no endogenous mechanisms regulating the cycles of dualist democracy, it is possible to assume that such mechanisms operate in private citizens' shifting involvements and that they are the very same as those discussed by Hirschman. I take this to be true, but with an important difference. What Hirschman's classic study describes is a genuine shift from private (consumer-oriented) pursuits to more public (citizen-oriented) activities. Indeed, Hirschman often refers to the 'consumer-citizen', and his discussion of the opposition between private and public life is underscored by the other important opposition between consumption and action. Such oppositions do not take centre stage in Ackerman's analysis, mainly because his private citizens do not shift between spheres. Instead it is their *views* of politics and of citizens' attitudes that shift.

All this said, it remains true that by shifting their views, private citizens are shifting between a consumer-oriented and a citizen-oriented view of political involvement. This often requires fundamental lifestyle changes as those described by Hirschman. However, if one assumes as much, Ackerman's optimism about private citizenship looks unwarranted for the very reasons that Hirschman gives in the conclusions to his book. There he expounds on the moral of his story as he sees it. First, he suggests that the pattern of change he has described 'is not only inevitable, but outright useful and desirable'.[51] This is something on which Ackerman fully agrees, given his positive defence of private citizenship. But the second piece of moralizing offered by Hirschman cautions against too optimistic a view of the 'movement back and forth between the public and private life'. This is indeed 'wholesome for individuals as well as for society as a whole'; but its 'oscillations can obviously be overdone'.[52] The issue therefore at stake is not so much to guarantee expression for both styles of life and involvement at different times, but to make sure that concerns from both domains are present *at the same time* and, whenever appropriate, mixed. In other words, individuals and societies must learn from their shifting involvements to transfer attitudes and preoccupations from one sphere to the other, tempering the single-mindedness that particular spheres may ask of them.[53]

From such a perspective, Ackerman's view of private citizens and dualist democracy suffers from two main weaknesses. First, the line of demarcation between the two styles of politics is overdrawn. Although, as Ackerman himself occasionally admits, in practice it may be difficult to distinguish between normal and constitutional politics and between the different attitudes associated with them, the whole conception of dualist democracy relies on a sharp separation between the two forms of representation embodied in the two-track lawmaking system. This separation is also evident in the kind of split personality complex which private citizens seem to suffer, unless, as argued above, they are capable of learning from their own shifting experiences. The second weakness comes in here, for Ackerman relies entirely on the natural diffusion of private citizens and on their ability to shift between styles of political involvement effortlessly. As Hirschman remarks, modern societies are singularly unprepared to educate people to the values, and to nurture the habits, of a mixed citizenship. They themselves go through 'long periods of privatization during which they live through an impoverishing "atrophy of public meanings", followed by spasmodic outbursts of "publicness" that are hardly likely to be constructive'.[54] Moreover, advanced forms of industrialization and the bureaucratization of modern society have exacerbated the split between instrumental and expressive aspects of people's lives. This dichotomy superimposes itself on, and reinforces the separation between private and public spheres. On the face of it, the virtues of private citizenship cannot be taken for granted, but need careful cultivation, something that Ackerman's neutralist liberalism may find difficult to accommodate.

In conclusion, Ackerman's third way between perfect privatists and public citizens offers a direction for solving a number of overlapping difficulties that beset modern politics: how to reconcile private and public interests; how to give expression to both instrumental and expressive needs; how to accommodate aggregative and deliberative views of democratic decision-making. But it does not deliver its promises in full, for it fails to indicate the precise grounds on which the virtues of private citizens may flourish.[55]

V Conclusion: public reason for private citizens

To return to the theme from which this chapter started, can public reason, as Rawls defines it, play a role in the politics of modern society? In spite of the reservations discussed in Section IV, it was suggested (Section III) that Ackerman's theory of private citizenship gives some feasibility to Rawls's expectation that constitutional essentials will be decided by public reason. However, if one reviews the substantive arguments on private citizens' virtues canvassed in the last two sections, new questions emerge. At the beginning, we took Rawls's conception of public reason for granted, in the attempt to see whether the obligation to abide by it carried some natural motivation. Having done this, doubts seem now to emerge about the integrity of Rawls's own normative conception of it.

In brief, if one takes the ideal of private citizenship seriously, there are at least three main difficulties with Rawls's idea. When one considers the importance that Ackerman, for instance, gives to the institutional filtering of constitutional consensus, Rawls's strongly normative and substantive conception of public reason looks problematic. From such a perspective, public reason becomes instead the contingent product of institutional design, with some touch of social engineering, in given cultural conditions.

The second difficulty is that, if one gives proper weight to the suggestion that in matters political a mixture of interest-based and judgement-based considerations is inevitable, and to a certain degree desirable, it becomes far more controversial to establish how an argument may fit the criteria of public reason. This is something on which Rawls himself has given ground in his revisitations of public reason, when, for instance, he allows for a wider view of public reason,[56] so that arguments first formulated in terms of a comprehensive moral view can in due course[57] – or indeed must (this is what he calls the 'proviso') – be formulated or re-formulated according to the more strict criteria of public reason. Moreover, Rawls seems now to suggest that there is a rhetoric of public justification, comprising forms such as 'declaration', 'conjecture' and 'witnessing',[58] besides public reasoning. Although these other forms may not meet the duty of civility in full, they represent legitimate attempts to formulate a reasonable (or, at least, reasonably convincing) discourse addressed to others. The upshot of all this is that public reason's own logic of argumentation becomes difficult to identify with precision and is certainly more contested than Rawls would admit.

The third, and from Rawls's own perspective more troublesome, difficulty is that by allowing a certain contingency in the establishment of consensus on the basis of public reason (difficulty one) and a greater latitude of discursive criteria in public justification (difficulty two), Rawls's overlapping consensus starts looking more like a *modus vivendi*. There would be nothing particularly wrong in this, if it were not for the fact that Rawls has made a virtue of strongly distinguishing his position from the view that social union is mainly based on a *modus vivendi*.[59] This he identifies with unstable compromises and agreements reached out of a sense of *force majeure*.[60] He also sees in such a form of coexistence a certain insincerity and underlying hypocrisy that directly contradict the duty of civility. In this connection, it may be interesting to return briefly to some of the oppositions characterizing the image of third-way citizenship sketched in the previous sections. Jon Elster has for instance suggested that there is a third mode in which citizens relate to each other and try to reach agreements, besides bargaining, as in economic and political markets, and arguing, as in the forum. This he calls 'strategic arguing' and consists in the attempt to dress self-interested arguments in a form that may appear impartial.[61] However, to develop an argument that may *appear* impartial often means to appeal to values and arguments that, in a given situation, may indeed *be* impartial, or at least be perceived by most as being impartial.[62] More intriguingly, Elster suggests that, even from a selfish perspective, the normative and cognitive constraints of impartiality that come with arguing contribute to reach agreements that are to a large degree socially equitable. This is so, on the one hand, because privileged groups may refrain from using the full contractual force of their own position – this being ruled out by the strategy of impartiality they have opted for. On the other, because the pretension to impartiality may have rubbed off on the self-interested agent, so that the repeated appeal to impartial (or seemingly impartial) arguments has become a habit not just of the mind, but also of the heart. Elster calls this double process the 'civilizing effect of hypocrisy', and it could be argued that such a process contributes to the stability of a social union founded on a *modus vivendi*. Whether Rawls himself may find convincing an argument that enrols hypocrisy on the side of public reason is, however, a different matter.

On this note, I may perhaps draw this chapter to a close. I said at the beginning that there was no Mandevillian ring to the title of this chapter. On reflection, there is perhaps something Mandevillian in some of its arguments.

Notes

1 Thanks to Richard Bellamy, Robert Goodin, Iain Hampsher-Monk, Andrew Hindmoor, Cécile Laborde, Albert Weale and participants at seminars in Oxford, Sussex, Prague and Exeter for comments and advice, always helpful but regretfully not always heeded in the present chapter. The chapter, however, would not have been written if not for Maurizio Passerin d'Entrèves's gentle prodding and sympathetic patience. Support is also acknowledged from the ESRC (Research Grant R000222446) and the EUSSIRF programme at the European University Institute (Florence).

2 Notice that what I am doing in this chapter, is to take Rawls's and Ackerman's *ideas* (i.e., conceptual constructions) at their face value, and try to show that they fail to translate into the kinds of *ideals* that according to the same authors are capable of sustaining constitutional democracy. Rawls himself distinguishes between 'ideas' and 'ideals' in 'The Idea of Public Reason Revisited', *The University of Chicago Law Review*, 1997, 64, pp. 765–807, at pp. 768–9.

3 B. Ackerman, *We The People. Foundations*, Cambridge MA, The Belknap Press, 1991.

4 J. Rawls, *Political Liberalism*, New York, Columbia University Press, 1993.

5 Rawls, *Political Liberalism*, p. 213.

6 Rawls, *Political Liberalism*, p. 217.

7 Rawls, *Political Liberalism*, p. 10.

8 I mention here only a few recent texts where authors have engaged with one or another aspect of the public reason debate: G. F. Gaus, *Justificatory Liberalism*, New York and Oxford, Oxford University Press, 1996, chs 8–11; W. Galston, *Liberal Purposes*, Cambridge, Cambridge University Press, 1991, ch. 5; C. Larmore, *The Morals of Modernity*, Cambridge, Cambridge University Press, 1996, ch. 7; F. D'Agostino, *Free Public Reason: Making It Up As We Go*, Oxford, Oxford University Press, 1996; G. J. Postema, 'Public Practical Reason: An Archeology', in E.F. Paul, F.D. Miller and J. Paul (eds), *Contemporary Political and Social Philosophy*, Cambridge, Cambridge University Press, 1995; D. Ivison, 'The Secret History of Public Reason: Hobbes to Rawls', *History of Political Thought*, 1997, vol. XVIII, pp. 125–47; T. McCarthy, 'Enlightenment and the Idea of Public Reason', *European Journal of Philosophy*, 1995, vol. III, pp. 242–56; J. Bohman, 'Public Reason and Cultural Pluralism. Political Liberalism and the Problem of Moral Conflict', *Political Theory*, 1995, vol. XXIII, pp. 253–79; C. Audard, 'The Idea of "Free Public Reason"', *Ratio Juris*, 1995, vol. VIII, pp. 15–29; B.W. Brower, 'The Limits of Public Reason', *The Journal of Philosophy*, 1994, vol. XCI, pp. 5–26; C. Bertram, 'Review Article: Theories of Public Reason', *Imprints*, 1997, vol. II, pp. 72–85. Cf. also the recent exchange between Habermas and Rawls: J. Habermas, 'Reconciliation Through the Public Use of Reason: Remarks on John Rawls's Political Liberalism', *The Journal of Philosophy*, 1995, vol. XCII, pp. 109–31; and Rawls's reply in the same issue, pp. 132–80. David Gauthier has also discussed public reason, though his essay is not particularly concerned with the role that this has in political liberalism: 'Public Reason', in E.F. Paul, F.D. Miller and J. Paul (eds), *Contemporary Political and Social Philosophy*, Cambridge, Cambridge University Press, 1995. Both Joshua Cohen, 'Procedure and Substance in Deliberative Democracy', and particularly Seyla Benhabib, 'Toward a Deliberative Model of Democratic Legitimacy', discuss the idea of public reason in relation to deliberative democracy, in S. Benhabib (ed.), *Democracy and Difference. Contesting the Boundaries of the Political*, Princeton, Princeton University Press, 1996.

9 To avoid misunderstanding, I emphasize that 'why' is here meant to formulate a question of motivation, not obligation.

10 Rawls, *Political Liberalism*, pp. 214–16.

11 I use 'rhetorical' advisedly and not at all in a disparaging sense. By it, I mean the rules that govern public language when this reflects the idea of public reason. I briefly return to this topic in the conclusion.

12 Rawls, *Political Liberalism*, p. 215, but the distinction between officials and ordinary citizens is clarified in 'The Idea of Public Reason Revisited', pp. 767–9.

13 Rawls, *Political Liberalism*, pp. 217 and 236.

14 Rawls, *Political Liberalism*, pp. 86–8.

15 Rawls, 'The Idea of Public Reason Revisited', pp. 783–7, in particular p. 785, n. 52.
16 On this cf. R.E. Goodin, *Motivating Political Morality*, Cambridge MA and Oxford, Blackwell, 1992; in particular ch. 1 and p. 4, n. 3.
17 Of course, by doing this, we shall go beyond the limits of the philosophical moral psychology as Rawls conceives it (see text referred to above at n. 14). However, the boundary between 'ought' and 'is' questions is more slippery than many modern philosophers believe.
18 I say confusedly, because in trying to show how the Supreme Court's reason must conform to public reason, Rawls describes 'constitutional democracy' at large as a dualist regime (*Political Liberalism*, VI.6.1). In the following paragraph, however, he refers to a regime of 'parliamentary supremacy', such as the British, and a firmly entrenched constitution, such as in the German case, as alternative regimes that may also conform to the principles of public reason. Since, however, at various points Rawls speaks of the idea of public reason as 'belonging to a conception of a well ordered constitutional democratic society' ('The Idea of Public Reason Revisited', p. 765) it is unclear whether, in Rawls's view, 'dualism' is a necessary feature of constitutional democracy.
19 Ackerman's own position on dualist democracy is also subject to some confusion, since on the one hand he seems to advocate the virtues of 'dualism' on normative grounds, but on the other he indicates a preference for a more entrenched constitutional regime. For a closer criticism of Ackerman's inconsistencies, cf. Bellamy and Castiglione, 'Constitutionalism and Democracy', *British Journal of Political Science*, 1997, vol. 27, pp. 611–12 and notes to the text.
20 Ackerman, *We The People*, p. 300.
21 The classical account is in A. Downs, *An Economic Theory of Democracy*, New York, Harper and Row, 1957. An insightful discussion of the value and limits of the paradox is to be found in B. Barry, *Sociologists, Economists and Democracy*, Chicago and London, University of Chicago Press, 1978, pp. 13–23.
22 M. Olson, *The Logic of Collective Action. Public Goods and the Theory of Groups*, Cambridge MA, Harvard University Press, 1971.
23 The literature on the voter's paradox is vast. For recent discussions of it, cf. M. Laver, *Private Desires, Political Action. An invitation to the politics of rational choice*, London, Sage, 1997, pp. 91–8, who takes a critical, but generally sympathetic view of the 'economic' approach to voter turnout; and D.P. Green and I. Shapiro, *Pathologies of Rational Choice Theory*, New Haven and London, Yale University Press, 1994, ch. 4, who take a more negative view of the rational choice scholarship in political studies.
24 Of course, this is too quick as a critique of the paradox. For interesting insights that go some way towards resolving it (i.e. re-stating the issue without generating a new paradox), cf. G. Brennan and L. Lomasky, *Democracy and Decision. The Pure Theory of Electoral Preference*, Cambridge, Cambridge University Press, 1993, in particular ch. 3, on the role of intrinsic elements in preference revelation and on how expressive returns may diverge from instrumental calculations; and R.E. Goodin and K.W.S. Roberts, 'The Ethical Voter', *The American Political Science Review*, 1975, vol. LXIX, 3, pp. 926–8, where a distinction is made between egoistic and ethical preferences, which are not as affected as the former by the voter paradox. (Both texts have interesting repercussions for the paradox that I discuss in the remainder of this section, which is concerned on *how* people vote rather than on *why* they do it.) The critique as I have here briefly stated it, however, mainly follows A. Pizzorno, 'On the rationality of democratic choice', in P. Birnbaum and J. Leca (eds), *Individualism. Theories and Methods*,

Oxford, Clarendon Press, 1990. Notice that much discussion of the paradox has centred on the possibility of enlarging the 'economic' elements of cost-benefit analysis, so as to include symbolic goods, feelings of obligation and expressive elements. By doing so, some rational choice theorists have tried to fit the 'economic' model to the empirical findings. On the other hand, critics of the rational choice approach have maintained that this is a sleight of hand. Expounding on this idea, Pizzorno's analysis offers a considered discussion of where the 'economic' model fails. It is indeed true that symbolic goods cannot be 'added' to material goods (there are no simple ways of quantifying their marginal utility). Moreover, they pose the problem of intersubjective recognition, which equilibrium theories find it difficult to account for. Pizzorno suggests instead that theories of identification can provide 'rational' explanations for political activity, by accounting for the role that this has in both *transforming* needs and *constituting* identities. In the rest of the chapter, I use 'expressive' as a shorthand equivalent of these aspects of politics.

25 A.O. Hirschman, *Shifting Involvements*, Princeton, Princeton University Press, 1982, p. 86; cf. also G. Lavau, 'Is the Voter an Individualist?', in Birnbaum and Leca (eds), *Individualism*.

26 Rawls, *Political Liberalism*, pp. 219–20.

27 It is interesting to note that the prediction failure was mainly due to opinion polls at the time of the election. David Sanders's own forecasting model, based on voters' perceptions of the state of the economy and elaborated well in advance of the elections themselves (some 18 months beforehand), proved to be more accurate even of the exit polls. Cf. D. Sanders, 'Government Popularity and the Next General Election', *Political Quarterly*, 1991, vol. 62, pp. 235–61; and 'Forecasting Political Preferences in Election Outcomes in the UK: Experiences, Problems and Prospects for the Next General Election', *Essex Papers in Politics and Government*, no. 96, January 1994, *passim*, but in particular, footnote 9.

28 A similar kind of justification was advanced in Italy, where opinion pollsters' early projections of the result of the 1990s municipal elections consistently underestimated the neo-fascist vote.

29 J. Elster, 'The Market and the Forum: Three varieties of political theory', in J. Elster and A. Hylland (eds), *Foundation of Social Choice Theory*, Cambridge, Cambridge University Press, 1986, p. 127; cf. also A. Ryan, 'Two concepts of politics and democracy: James and John Stuart Mill', in M. Fleischer (ed.), *Machiavelli and the Nature of Political Thought*, New York, Atheneum, 1972.

30 Cf. Lavau, 'Is the Voter an Individualist?', p. 285.

31 Cf. John Stuart Mill, *Representative Government*, in *Utilitarianism, On Liberty and Considerations on Representative Government*, London, Dent, 1972, ch. X.

32 In a sense, this question asks supporters of a market view of democracy to pro-- vide a moral rationale for the legal exclusion of the buying and selling of votes; that is, a conception of the right to vote as a form of entitlement that one can use but not exchange.

33 This seems to me to reflect better Schumpeter's competitive view of democracy, cf. *Capitalism, Socialism and Democracy*, London, Unwin, 1987, ch. XXII.

34 Cf. I. Kopytoff, 'The cultural biography of things: commoditization as process', in A. Appadurai (ed.), *The Social Life of Things. Commodities in Cultural Perspective*, Cambridge, Cambridge University Press, 1986, p. 77.

35 An argument on the same line is offered by Hirschman in *Shifting Involvements*, p. 20, when he suggests that 'social arrangements often have the specific effect and probable purpose of making sure that [certain] activities are *not* compared

with income-producing and consumption activities', in other words, they 'prevent equalization at the margins'. J. Buchanan and G. Tullock, *The Calculus of Consent: Logical Foundations of Constitutional Democracy*, Ann Arbor, Michigan University Press, 1962, ch. 18, in particular at pp. 267–76 put forward an intriguing argument for the partial rejection of vote-trading, which seems to rest entirely on the calculation of the external costs that such a trade would impose on the voter. The crucial reason they give for this is that market imperfections would seem likely to arise, thus imposing external costs, which are better avoided by enforcing a legal prohibition. But they also conclude that the 'optimal' solution lies in the sanctioning of 'indirect' methods of vote-trading. Without wanting to enter into a discussion of the counter-intuitive way in which Buchanan and Tullock account for what is more economically explained by a clear distinction of the background conceptions that, *in modern democratic societies*, still underlie the operations of political and economic 'markets', it is worth noticing that their 'partial' rejection of vote-trading is tantamount to re-stating the paradox of the 'private voter', who publicly condemns the marketing of one's vote, but does it in conditions of relative secrecy. This is not very different from what, in talking about the 'role of interests', Brennan and Lomasky refer to as either *akrasia* (weakness of the will) or hypocrisy (*Democracy and Decision*, pp. 51–3). Both are character flaws indicating a dissonance between one's action and one's principles. There is no reason to treat such a dissonance in moralizing terms. As the rest of the chapter will show, it can also be taken as part of the condition of modern citizenship.

36 The point here made is that 'political markets' and acting a 'role' in a political market are distinctive arenas/activities that presuppose a sense of the 'public' (not necessarily intended in holistic terms). Similar kinds of arguments can be found in B. Barry, *Political Argument*, New York, Harvester Wheatsheaf, 2nd edn 1990, where he suggests that there are grounds for arguing that 'political action may elicit wider sympathies than the market' (p. 299) and that 'people make "better" choices when they make them as citizens than when they make them as private persons' (p. 74); and S.I. Benn, 'The Problematic Rationality of Political Participation', in P. Laslett and J. Fishkin (eds), *Philosophy, Politics and Society. Fifth Series*, Oxford, Blackwell, 1979, pp. 291–312, in particular pp. 299–304 on 'role rationality'.

37 G. Brennan and P. Pettit, 'Unveiling the vote', *British Journal of Political Science*, 1990, vol. 20, pp. 311–33. I take them to say that the *ideal* of preference-based voting is unfeasible; not that actual voters cannot follow their unreconstructed preferences in voting.

38 Both the strategies discussed in the next few paragraphs are meant to articulate the more sceptical (second-best) answer to the question of how to maximize a given supply of civicness; the more positive answer that will be examined below in the main text tends to emphasize instead the intrinsic qualities of civicness that come with the private citizen model.

39 For Rawls's position on this point see Rawls, *Political Liberalism*, pp. 219–20.

40 Cf. Ackerman, *We the People*, ch. 10, *passim*.

41 On the question of first- and second-order preferences there is a vast literature, but for a classic statement see A.K. Sen, 'Rational fools', in F. Hahn and M. Hollis (eds), *Philosophy and Economic Theory*, Oxford, Oxford University Press, 1979. For an attempt to argue that rational actors are no fools, cf. D. Gauthier, *Morals by Agreement*, Oxford, Clarendon Press, 1986.

42 Of course, such a distinction is not original to Ackerman. His distinction is very similar to the one between constituent and constituted power, which was central, for instance, to Sieyès's constitutional theory.

43 Hirschman, *Shifting Involvements*.
44 Hirschman, *Shifting Involvements*, p. 4.
45 Hirschman, *Shifting Involvements*, p. 5.
46 Hirschman, *Shifting Involvements*, ch. 1, *passim*.
47 Hirschman, *Shifting Involvements*, p. 104.
48 Hirschman, *Shifting Involvements*, p. 119.
49 I am grateful to Sandro Ferrara and other participants in the 1997 Philosophy Colloquium in Prague for challenging such a simple negative answer. The next couple of paragraphs are partly meant to deal with their objections, though I fear I may not have met them in full.
50 For a more general discussion of constitutional politics and its contexts outside the American experience, cf. B. Ackerman, *The Future of the Liberal Revolution*, New Haven and London, Yale University Press, 1992.
51 Hirschman, *Shifting Involvements*, p. 131.
52 Hirschman, *Shifting Involvements*, p. 132.
53 An intriguing example of the way in which public and private concerns may mix in ways that are not always clearly discernible is given by Hirschman himself in his other classic study on *Exit, Voice and Loyalty*, Cambridge MA, Harvard University Press, 1970, pp. 102–5, when he discusses the issue of private and public education.
54 Hirschman, *Shifting Involvements*, p. 132.
55 Other authors have tried to sketch a third-way citizenship. Jon Elster, for instance, propounds a middle way between forum and market politics, by suggesting that citizens should look at politics as 'public in nature, and instrumental in purpose', cf. 'The Market and the Forum', p. 128. Martin Hollis has similarly advanced a third way between 'consumers' (or maximisers) and 'Romans' (or morally bound citizens), by suggesting that there is a whole group of 'friendship' relationships (meant in the broad sense of 'small scale and fragmented') that metaphorically position citizens in 'midstream', where they can more easily see the imperative of 'the blending of personal aims and public good', cf. 'Friends, Romans and Consumers', in P. King (ed.), *Socialism and the Common Good. New Fabian Essays*, London, Frank Cass, 1996.
56 Cf. his introduction to the paperback edition of *Political Liberalism* also adapted as a Postscript to the reproduction of the chapter 'The Idea of Public Reason', in J. Bohman and W. Rehg (eds), *Deliberative Democracy. Essays on Reason and Politics*, Cambridge MA, MIT Press, 1997, p. 135.
57 Rawls, Postscript, p. 135 says as much; but, is there any time-frame that qualifies how to understand 'in due course', or should one interpret it as open-ended?
58 Rawls, 'Public Reason Revisited', pp. 786–7.
59 For more positive attitudes towards a *modus vivendi* type of social union, cf. Bellamy and Castiglione, 'Constitutionalism and Democracy'; D. Ivison, 'Modus Vivendi Citizenship', *RUSEL Working Paper*, No. 31; M. Philp, 'The Demands of Citizenship', *RUSEL Working Paper*, No. 32.
60 For a more positive understanding of compromise in politics, cf. R. Bellamy and M. Hollis, 'Consensus, Neutrality and Compromise', in Bellamy and Hollis (eds), *Pluralism and Liberal Neutrality*, London, Cass, 1998; and Erik O. Eriksen, 'Deliberative Democracy and the Politics of Pluralist Society', *Arena Working Paper*, no. 94, 1996.
61 J. Elster, 'Strategic Uses of Argument', in K. Arrow *et al.* (eds), *Barriers of Conflict Resolution*, New York, Norton, 1995. For a more critical discussion of the idea, cf. J. Johnson, 'Arguing for Deliberation: Some sceptical considerations', in J. Elster (ed.), *Deliberative Democracy*, Cambridge, Cambridge University Press,

1998; and E.O. Eriksen and J. Weigard, 'Conceptualizing Politics: Strategic or Communicative Action?', Mimeo.
62 Elster notices that the importance, or indeed the viability, of strategic arguing depends on the existence of a group of people who are genuinely impartial, or try to act as such. However small, such a group has an essential role, otherwise impartiality would never be taken seriously.

4 Private irony and the public hope of Richard Rorty's liberalism

Shane O'Neill

Richard Rorty combines a professional commitment to the deconstruction of all metaphysical foundations with a political commitment to the institutions and practices of liberal democracy. One significant feature of Rorty's foundationless liberalism is his highly original account of the separation of public and private domains. As a liberal, Rorty conceives of the private sphere as a domain in which each of us is free to pursue an individual plan of life. In this sphere of self-creation we may seek to realize our conception of a good life and to indulge our personal fantasies. In the public sphere however we must take the personal visions of others into account. There, as citizens, we must work out and justify to one another principles that could provide some basis for social harmony while also allowing for the toleration, and flourishing, of a wide diversity of personal visions.

Rorty is, it seems, rather straightforwardly liberal in this respect. Since he has, however, abandoned all possible philosophical justifications for his allegiance to liberalism he has had to conceive of the separation of public and private without the tools that have been available to liberals such as Kant or John Stuart Mill. He has faced the consequences of moving to this new terrain with courage, imagination and no little ambition. As we will see later on, Rorty thinks of the private sphere as the domain of self-creation in which we may well be inspired by the ironic redescriptions of our culture's 'strong poets'.[1] But in the public sphere we will be inspired by the liberal hope that Rorty assumes 'us' (liberal Westerners?) to share: that cruelty be minimized. It is this shared hope, and not philosophical reflection, that provides a supportive basis for liberal public institutions.[2] Rorty is offering us a redescription of, not a rational justification for, liberal institutions and the values of liberal society and culture. He is trying to change the subject, to substitute a vocabulary revolving around notions of metaphor and self-creation for the old vocabulary of Enlightenment rationalism which had been so important historically in establishing liberal democratic institutions that would respect the separation of public and private.[3]

In this chapter I hope to evaluate critically the separation of public and private as Rorty conceives of it in his redescription of liberalism. The clear demarcation of private irony and public hope is crucial to Rorty's attempt to show that the attractions of his new vocabulary outweigh those of the Enlightenment vocabulary which he is intent on discarding. I will be arguing in three stages that Rorty fails in this attempt. First, regarding the public project of justifying principles of political morality, there are compelling reasons for doubting the attractiveness of Rorty's redescription of liberalism. Furthermore, to deny that liberalism is a political morality that defends itself on the basis of rational conviction is to fail to grasp the normative core of the liberal tradition. Second, regarding the private project of self-creation, there are certain theoretical inconsistencies in the way in which Rorty conceives of the human self. Third, regarding the relation between public hope and private irony, Rorty does not make a convincing case for maintaining the radical disjuncture between these domains that his liberalism would seem to require. If Rorty's liberal democratic aspirations are not to be undermined by political naïveté then the relation between these domains will have to be reconceived in a way which eschews such an implausibly strict separation.

Liberalism of convention versus liberalism of conviction

In his introduction to *Consequences of Pragmatism* Rorty characterizes philosophy as a literary genre founded by Plato. The history of philosophy is the history of attempts to say something interesting about the essence of truth. From a pragmatist point of view this has been a story of repeated failures, so that we now must see 'the Platonic tradition as having outlived its usefulness'.[4] There is apparently no interesting philosophical work to be done since it would appear that there is nothing interesting to say about truth.

In a later paper, Rorty spells out the implications of this view for liberal political theory. Since we can no longer appeal to anything like a theory of true human nature, we need only justify our political beliefs and practices according to the traditions and the cultural beliefs of our own particular community, thought of as a historical product. 'For pragmatist social theory, the question of whether justifiability to the community with which we identify entails truth is simply irrelevant.'[5] But Rorty's liberalism of convention is not the only alternative to the metaphysics of truth that is entailed in the Platonic ideal which he rejects. Between these opposing views lies the possibility of defending liberalism on the basis of rational conviction. It seems to me that this third way represents not only the most accurate description of a committed liberal political morality but it is also the most attractive ideal on which the public hopes of liberalism might be pinned.

Rorty criticizes liberals who support democratic institutions and practices with philosophical arguments that rest on notions such as 'intrinsic human dignity' or 'the rights which are appropriate to the respect of persons as rationally autonomous beings'. Such views depend on a typically Kantian 'account of "rationality" and "morality" as transcultural and ahistorical'.[6]

While Rorty is concerned with the preservation of those same liberal institutions, he wants to convince us that loyalty to our own liberal traditions is the only morality we require. Morality is simply the area of overlap of beliefs and convictions shared by the members of a particular historical community. We develop our sense of morality by reinterpreting the story of our community, of how we came to develop the conventions and practices to which we now feel morally bound.

The vocabulary we use to develop our sense of morality is thoroughly contingent. We use it because it serves our purposes better than whatever vocabulary it may have replaced. It is for this reason that Rorty is so dismissive of any attempt to 'discover' philosophical foundations for political beliefs or to ground liberal commitments in a theory of human nature. We should, Rorty suggests, 'avoid thinking of philosophy as a "discipline" with "core problems", or with a social function'.[7] Philosophy wrongly assumes a natural order of justification which privileges logic and rational means of persuasion over literature, rhetoric and non-rational ways of attempting to change people's minds about what they find desirable. Once people are persuaded rather than forced, it is irrelevant how and why they come to choose one political option rather than another. All that matters for Rorty is that people find x (say liberalism) more desirable than y (say fascism). There is no point in trying to look under the surface for any deep reason as to why x is found to be more desirable.

Rorty is advocating a post-philosophical political culture, one 'that doesn't have any surrogate for God'.[8] Historically the Enlightenment was a philosophical culture which was the successor of religious culture. It substituted notions like reason and human nature for God. They were thought to act as reference points beyond history by which the morality of a community could be judged. Rorty's post-philosophical culture would, in contrast, be entirely 'de-divinized'. It would afford us only an internal perspective that could yield only circular justifications for our political allegiances and redescriptions of our institutions and practices.

Rorty speaks of this task of redescription as being 'more like refurnishing a house than like propping it up or placing barricades around it'.[9] A redescription provides a new vocabulary, a new way of talking about things. In a liberal society this can be presented as a challenge to the old Enlightenment vocabulary of truth and reason, an invitation for us to think of ourselves differently. We are invited to think of ourselves as products of historical contingency without any intrinsic human nature. The language of Enlightenment foundationalism is no longer a useful tool for us and it should be replaced with the language of ethnocentric pragmatism. Since the conventions and norms that constitute a political morality are created in a particular historical context, liberals should content themselves with circular justifications that redescribe the political institutions of Western democracies.[10] Rorty redescribes liberalism as a political morality of convention rather than one of conviction.

But this redescription fails to capture at least one crucial aspect of the liberal tradition of political morality. The attempt to provide a normative justification for the process of rational argument remains central to the concerns of contemporary liberals.[11] This project draws on an important distinction that Rorty would appear to abandon. The distinction I have in mind is that between moral arguments that are held to be valid and moral arguments that are held to be widely accepted in given circumstances. Liberals are typically concerned to show that the justification of their political morality does not depend, at least not entirely, on its being widely accepted throughout a democratic society. Rather it is justified as the most reasonable morality available to citizens of modern pluralist societies. Claims of justification do not rest on empirical evidence that can demonstrate the popularity of some moral view but rather on the defence of that view on the basis of good reasons. Acceptance need not entail validity and valid arguments are, we assume, not always found to be acceptable. If liberal views are held as a matter of rational conviction, and not simply as a convention, then they will seek a grounding not simply in arguments that could be widely acceptable but in arguments that can claim to be valid.

The importance of this distinction between validity and acceptability is that it underscores a commitment to rational dialogue and a vigilance against subtle elements of power that could distort the outcome of a political discourse. Jürgen Habermas accuses Rorty of committing an objectivistic fallacy by thinking that he can 'replace the normative conception of "valid arguments" with the descriptive concept of "arguments held to be true at this time"'.[12] A participant who is genuinely seeking a solution to some problem of pluralism could only understand the process of argument as the critical evaluation of validity claims. Rorty tries to step outside this context so as to adopt the perspective of an observer who redescribes what is going on in discourses of moral justification. On the inside however participants hold political beliefs as moral convictions not because they find them attractive but rather because they appear to be supported by the most convincing reasons. While the reasons given for holding the belief as a matter of conviction may constantly be challenged, the arguments that support it remain valid, at least until some better reason is given for believing otherwise. This practice of rational argument is not justified simply by the fact that it helps us to cope with practical problems but because it helps us to cope in a way that can itself be normatively justified. For those who participate in such a practice it does not just look better than any alternative ways of coping but it is understood to be the most reasonable practice available.[13]

There are important consequences for Rorty's abandoning this distinction between valid arguments and arguments that are widely accepted at a particular time. It is not clear how Rorty could distinguish between a process of rational deliberation and a ruthlessly instrumental quest for political victory. Liberal principles are grounded in rational conviction if they can be justified as the outcome of a process where all participants are genuinely committed to working towards a reasoned agreement. There is, from this perspective, an obvious justificatory deficit if the process had allowed political actors to explore any non-discursive avenues (money, promises of favour, protection from a threatened harm) that would lead them to persuade, cajole or manipulate others into accepting their arguments. Without a commitment to rational dialogue as a procedure of normative justification there is simply no adequate check on the use of power in our political ways of coping with disagreement.

It is also worth bearing in mind that a commitment to rational dialogue allows us to tolerate another person's holding a political view with which we disagree without committing us to agree with the view itself.[14] We tolerate such views but we need not stop short of arguing against them according to the norms of rational dialogue. Indeed we must do so. A commitment to rational argument involves both a respect for those who disagree with us and a determination to challenge arguments and views that cannot rationally be defended. By showing respect for each other in a political dispute, each participant can affirm a morality of rational conviction. Again it is not clear whether or not Rorty's view of political discourse need involve this respect for all participants. Since he refuses to privilege rational over non-rational forms of persuasion it would appear that any strategy, reasonable or otherwise, can be used in our encounter with those who disagree with us. There is no guarantee at all that these strategies will require the participants to respect each other. Nor is there any good reason to believe that participation in political discourse will foster such respect.

Furthermore, if Rorty wants to claim that we take as our morality whatever norms are acceptable in this particular historical context then he will have to agree that there are certain norms of rational argument which are in fact generally accepted in liberal societies today as the appropriate criteria for evaluating competing political arguments. If it is the political morality of liberalism that Rorty really wants to redescribe, then even according to his own historicist perspective, he must invoke the distinction between valid arguments and arguments that are widely accepted. Rorty's redescription of public hope does very little to support his call for substituting a morality of convention for the morality of rational conviction that is the very core of liberalism. So much, for now, for Rorty's liberal hopes. Before returning to them in criticizing the way he conceives of the relation between private and public, I will focus in the next section on his views on the self and on the ideal of self-creation in the private domain.

Self-creation and the value of autonomy

For Rorty, it is not enough for us to recognize the contingency of our vocabulary and language as nothing more than the way we choose to cope with the world. We must also think of ourselves as thoroughly contingent beings. There is no human nature, no paradigmatic human being, no completeness to which we strive in our lives. Each of us is simply a 'tissue of contingencies', a particular web of beliefs and desires that is constantly rewoven throughout each human life.[15] There is nothing going on inside or behind the attributes which distinguish each of us and tell the story of our individuality. There is no more to the self than the effects of personal historical experience.

This view of the contingent self seems to be in tension with another value which has been at the heart of liberal culture, the ideal of personal autonomy. Rorty seems to understand this value in terms of self-creation and it is captured, for him, by the notion of self-enlargement.[16] It seems very doubtful that Rorty can both espouse the view of the self as a 'tissue of contingencies' and at the same time give an adequate account of personal autonomy as self-creation. If self-creation is to be consistent with the public hopes of liberalism, it would be better supported by an alternative hermeneutic conception of self-interpretation.

Philosophical conceptions of the self have provided one focus to recent debates between liberal and communitarian political theorists.[17] Rorty adds an interesting twist to this debate about the self. He agrees with many communitarian criticisms of liberalism but he wants to take the critique in a very different direction.[18] He maintains that in continuing to argue in terms of philosophical justification, communitarian critics mistakenly take the vocabulary of Enlightenment rationalism for granted.[19] This metatheoretical point has not been an issue of great contention between the various key protagonists, although Rorty is right to point out that almost all contributors involved are still committed to giving philosophical justifications for their respective positions. What has divided them is the distance we must place between the identity of the self and its ends.

To what extent are our ends, goals and purposes in life chosen voluntarily? Can we think of ourselves as independent of our ends, standing back from them and deciding autonomously which collection of goals and aims we want to pursue? Such questions have led to much serious reflection and some very insightful work but they have also led to an unhelpful polarization which has tended to obscure the better arguments on both sides.[20] On the one hand, in emphasizing our freedom to pursue our ends voluntarily, liberals have often made it seem as if they were drawing on a model of the self as a presocial, atomistic, self-sufficient being. On the other hand, in stressing the fact that our identity is actually constituted by some communal ends, communitarians have often given the impression that they assume us to be incapable of reflecting critically on the values which governed our socialization.[21] Of course neither of these extreme positions is either tenable or illuminating.

We cannot understand ourselves without some constitutive ends. We do not choose many of the most significant of our relationships with others, relationships which determine to a large extent our identities. We are all marked by the fact that we are born to two particular natural parents, that each of us is born male or female, that we are socialized into a particular context with a certain social, historical, cultural, political and (non-)religious pattern of values. All of these factors are crucially formative in any evolving sense of personal identity. Every human being is thrown into life at a particular starting point from which each of us begins to reflect on personal values and individual ends. We are all biased and prejudiced by our experience of socialization.

This however is not to say that our identities are in some sense determined by that starting point or that we cannot get any critical distance from our constitutive ends. While it would certainly appear to be impossible for any of us to step entirely outside the process of socialization, we will all have new experiences of life which will distance us somewhat from the pattern of values into which we were originally thrown. This distance facilitates critical reflection on our constitutive ends. Indeed it may eventually, depending on the extent to which we seek this distance, allow for a radical change of values where an almost entirely new set of ends replaces the set that would typify the expectations of one's culture of origin. Identities often evolve through encounters with new spheres of influence that can empower a struggle against the expectations of significant others.

We may wonder what room there is in this sketch of the self for the notion of autonomy. Do we make any choice entirely independently of the influence of others? Are our choices in life to be thought of as rational or are they merely the product of a particular network of beliefs and desires which are the resultant force of our encounters with various spheres of influence? How are we to know that we have any control over our own destiny, that we are in any sense self-creative creatures? Liberals are typically committed to the view that we are, as human agents, capable of critical reflection and free choice based on reason. This view must be supported however with an appropriate normative conception of the person that can make sense of autonomy and self-creation. But it is not at all clear if Rorty's idea of the self as a 'tissue of contingencies' can give adequate support to the liberal view that we should value autonomy so highly.

In fact Rorty does not think that we need any normative conception of the self in order to give a philosophical grounding to liberal democratic institutions because no such grounding can, or should, be provided. However he does believe that while we do not need it some liberals like himself who have a 'taste for philosophy . . . will want a picture of the self'.[22] Rorty thinks that while the Kantian conception which presents the self as antecedent to the ends its chooses may provide us with some metaphysical comfort, it is, like all other metaphysical conceptions, simply a product of historical contingency. It cannot inform us as to the 'true' nature of the self because there is no true nature of anything.

On the one hand, therefore, he agrees with communitarian critics who argue that Kantian liberalism is grounded on an ahistorical and untenably individualistic conception of the self. On the other hand, however, he criticizes those who want to substitute an alternative 'true' metaphysical conception of the situated self for this 'false' atomistic conception. As we have already noted, Rorty considers all metaphysical conceptions to represent a variety of attempts to provide a substitute for God. We are urged to resist this hankering for metaphysical comfort so that we might 'de-divinize' the self. For those who are philosophically inclined it would be more beneficial to adopt a view of a purely contingent self. It is to Freud, Rorty suggests, that we owe our greatest debt in developing such a view.

We can think of Freud as the 'moralist who helped de-divinize the self by tracking conscience home to its origin in the contingencies of our upbringing'. He allows us to de-universalize our moral sense 'making it as idiosyncratic as the poet's inventions'.[23] Each life is a poem, a dramatic narrative. What was new about Freud's work was the detail he gave us in providing specific causal explanations of particular obsessions and neuroses. This helps us to blur the distinction between prudence and morality by making moral deliberation just as complex and multiform as prudential calculation had always been assumed to be.[24] We must turn away from the universal, the general theory of the self and look at the concrete, the particular idiosyncrasies of each human life which stand in need of some explanation.

Freud shatters any hope we may have harboured of discovering a paradigmatic human being. His work underlines for us the claim that no one way of life should be privileged over all others. Freud explains how lives come to be lived the way they are by reference to contingent life histories. Each life is a process of overcoming the contingencies of the past and the creation of a future as the individual wills it. Life is best thought of as the acting out of idiosyncratic fantasies. Occasionally one individual's private fantasies become popular in a given time with the result that that person is hailed as a genius. It is meaningless to think of the genius as somebody who expresses human nature more fully than the rest of us. Rather a genius is characterized by the fact that the metaphor of her life becomes literalized in our vocabulary. This is to be explained purely by reference to the contingencies of the particular historical situation. It is her good fortune (perhaps) that her private obsession happens to coincide with a public need.[25]

How does Rorty's Freudian view of the self make sense of autonomy? To what extent is the self active in the process of self-creation? According to Rorty, the individual is 'a network that is constantly reweaving itself . . . in the hit-or-miss way in which cells readjust themselves to meet the pressures of the environment'. The extent to which the self is a morally responsible being is explained by the fact that 'rational behaviour is just adaptive behaviour of a sort which roughly parallels the behaviour, in similar circumstances, of the other members of some relevant community'.[26] But this is a rather passive image of the self, one that sits rather uncomfortably with Rorty's celebration of the capacity we have to create and invent ourselves. It is not clear what is going on as each network of beliefs and desires is rewoven. Can everything that is going on be explained, as Rorty seems to suggest here, by some combination of psychoanalysis and neuro-physics?

A liberal commitment to the protection of private space for autonomous self-creation cannot be content with such a passive image of the self. There must be some activity involved in self-creation, some self-consciousness doing the weaving. As Martin Hollis has put it, 'the web of belief needs its active spinners'.[27] Rorty seems to suggest that the network remains passive in the reweaving process. His image draws on the anti-foundationalism of thinkers such as Heidegger ('man does not speak; rather, language speaks man') as well as Freud ('we are "lived" by unknown and uncontrollable forces').[28] Without an image of an active spinner, or a conception of self-consciousness, Rorty will need to provide an alternative explanation for our capacity to be self-creative.

The notion of an active self-consciousness therefore seems to be indispensable if we are adequately to explain to ourselves how we can make sense of our experience, our place in the world and our relationships with other persons. We are not merely passive objects responding to the pressures of our environment but are rather actively involved in making our own unique contribution to that environment.[29] Adapting to the environment can hardly be thought of as the limit of activity for a human self. In reweaving our web we are constantly engaged in active thought and interpretation. It is not clear what further argument might convince Rorty that if we are, as he believes us to be, self-creative creatures, then we must think of ourselves as active spinners of our web of beliefs and desires. Nonetheless it might help to look at an alternative conception of the self with which he might have some sympathy.

It is interesting to note that many of the anti-foundationalist thinkers Rorty admires, including Heidegger, have managed to combine a notion like Hollis's active spinner with a historicist philosophical hermeneutics.[30] These writers give an account of the self as unified and focused. The self is a web of self-interpretations which is set in a context of our particular historical existence. Our starting point is given to us and defines who we are as well as the possibilities for our self-development. It is our tradition and our heritage that we must draw on to formulate our goals and aims. Through critical dialogue with the past and with the alternatives of the present we can formulate a meaningful action-guiding perspective which directs our future choices as we play our own part in the development of our culture.

> On the one hand, we find ourselves thrown into a concrete historical context which lays out the range of possible interpretations we can take over in being agents in the world. On the other hand, action has a teleological structure – it is directed towards realizing goals in the future.[31]

This then is, for hermeneuticists, the essential structure of a human life. A self seeks an interpretive coherence that leads it to live in a particular way.

According to this perspective the individual has a sense for the better possibilities available in the alternative visions of life given to us through our historical traditions. Through critical reflection we can deliberate over and then choose our aims for the future and dedicate ourselves to their realization. We can do this best by focusing on the values which underlie our present context without getting too distracted by the immediate demands of the present. Only by such self-focusing can a self get an authentic sense of the coherence of its life and its deepest purposes. We are in this sense all called on to further the most worthy of the ends which are available to us at this historical juncture.

Rorty rejects this hermeneutics of the self as yet another failed attempt to discover the essential features of a human life. Rather than seeking coherence and unity, we should, from his perspective, simply revel in the playful, self-inventing experimentalism that our radical contingency leaves open to us. But it is still not clear that this would be possible unless we can also give an account of an active self-consciousness directing our choice of ends. A hermeneutic conception of the self offers an alternative perspective on self-creation that allows us to accept the historicity of our being without discarding the notion of an active spinner of our web of beliefs and desires. Rorty's liberal commitment to creating social conditions that best facilitate self-creation would be better supported by that conception than by the passive image of the self that he sometimes endorses.

Liberal irony and democratic politics

We have already examined certain important features of the conception of both the public and the private in Rorty's redescription of liberalism. I have suggested that there are many good reasons for scepticism with regard to the attractiveness of Rorty's redescription. Liberalism still looks better when described, not in Rorty's conventionalist terms, but as a political morality of public conviction that seeks to protect the privacy of self-creative beings who are actively engaged in a process of critical self-interpretation. In this section I want to focus more directly on the way Rorty conceives of the relation between public and private and on the implications of this conception for democratic politics. We can do this by assessing his character ideal, that of the liberal ironist.

Rorty wants to privatize irony, to make it part of our pursuit of personal perfection. He wants to suggest that the great ironist philosophers (Nietzsche, Heidegger, Derrida) have nothing to say to our politics of liberal hope. Nor can they promote the solidarity necessary for mutual accommodation and liberal tolerance. The traditional association of literature with private life and philosophy with public concerns should therefore be reversed. Rorty's liberal ironist fulfils three conditions:

(1) She has radical and continuing doubts about the final vocabulary she currently uses, because she has been impressed by other vocabularies, vocabularies taken as final by people or books she has encountered; (2) she realizes that argument phrased in her present vocabulary can neither underwrite nor dissolve these doubts; (3) insofar as she philosophizes about her situation, she does not think that her vocabulary is closer to reality than others', that it is in touch with a power not herself. Ironists who are inclined to philosophize see the choice of vocabularies as made neither within a neutral and universal metavocabulary nor by an attempt to fight one's way past appearances to the real, but simply by playing the new off against the old.[32]

It is by accepting her 'radical and continuing doubts' and allowing her idiosyncratic fantasies to redescribe the world that the ironist alone, and not the truth-seeking metaphysician, can make a genuinely progressive contribution to our culture. The metaphysician who tries to live up to a universal ideal fails to realize that it is only the concrete idiosyncratic contingencies of her own life which can set her free to create herself according to her will.

But from a political perspective we might wonder whether Rorty's ironists are not so troubled by their doubts that they will be lacking motivation to act one way rather than another. If everything is so thoroughly contingent then is something so complex as democratic politics not likely to move in ways that are simply out of our control?[33] Rorty might argue that far from abandoning moral and political commitments the ironist freely undertakes them as the best strategy for dealing with the radical contingency of our lives. But there is no reason why the ironist would undertake a moral commitment to the defence of specifically liberal practices and institutions. While she revels in redescription, an effective defence of those institutions requires concerted vigilant action by citizens and a strong sense of communal responsibility to further the values of liberal democratic culture.

It is difficult to see why an ironist who is so busy giving birth to herself would make that particular choice to fight for the preservation of liberal institutions should they come under attack. Her awareness of the contingency of life would surely make it appear that there is no reason to believe that liberalism is in fact morally justified. She does not have that reason for hope that comes from the conviction that there are valid arguments which support a political defence of liberalism.

In celebrating irony what Rorty seems to want is for us to take ourselves less seriously, to become more spontaneous, more inventive, more playful, more light-minded. This would be, he suggests, a vehicle for moral progress rather than a degeneration to narcissism. He wants to 'josh' us out of our needless seriousness about questions of true selves, rationality and the like, to treat philosophical controversy with the same light-mindedness with which we have successfully dealt with formerly divisive theological issues. This can serve our moral purposes.

Moral commitment, after all, does not require taking seriously all the matters that are, for moral reasons, taken seriously by one's fellow citizens. It may require just the opposite. It may require trying to josh them out of the habit of taking those topics so seriously.[34]

Irony then opens the way to greater freedom, tolerance and diversity by providing new possibilities that help us to escape the constraints of any moral strait-jacket.

It seems very doubtful however that the type of moral concern which is necessary for a strong sense of communal responsibility could survive in a society of ironists. While Rorty thinks that morality is a matter of whatever we take to be the accepted conventions of our culture, any moral consensus would be undermined persistently by the redescriptions of ironists. Rather than giving us reasons for changing our old morality for something new, these 'strong poets' merely seek to josh us out of taking things too seriously. But in our search for moral agreement in public we do not necessarily want to be inventive or spontaneous. What we want is to work out what is right through a process of rational argument. An excess of irony can destroy this practice, and with it our attempts to deal reasonably with the many complex and highly-charged moral issues that divide us. As Alasdair MacIntyre points out, with characteristic astuteness, what Rorty's vision exhibits 'is not moral argument freed from unwarranted philosophical pretensions, but the decay of moral reasoning'.[35] Rather than acting as a vehicle for moral progress unconstrained irony may well subvert the very basis of moral agreement itself.

Rorty has recognized that there are some difficulties involved in demonstrating that his character ideal is compatible with democratic politics. The glorification of the 'strong poet' in Rorty's post-philosophical aestheticized culture smacks of individualistic elitism. It may even be compatible with a political elite capable of manipulating the populace with fantastic visions, dressed in the language of utopian idealism but concealing the perverse cruelty driving their own 'will to power'. Freudian psychoanalysis could also show us how very few people actually succeed in breaking free from their past and reinventing themselves. Our projects can so easily be undermined by the contingencies of our existence. Many of us may be happy to look up to an elite who appear to have subjected contingency to their own will. Given this danger of elitism how could Rorty defend democracy?

Nancy Fraser has traced a tension in Rorty's work between a certain Romantic impulse and his commitment to liberal democracy.[36] At times Rorty seems to be quite optimistic about the prospects for a post-philosophical culture that could generate among the citizens a strong sense of loyalty to one another and so foster a community bound together in solidarity.[37] But I have already argued that there is no good reason to think that solidarity will be fostered by our embracing a post-philosophical culture. In a society as diverse and pluralist as that advocated by Rorty it is more likely that it would lead to further fragmentation and a weakening of bonds of solidarity. And why should this aestheticized culture give any priority to the values of liberty and equality which are central to liberal democracy? The continuing doubts and the spontaneous playfulness of the ironist can humiliate the vast majority of the people by scoffing at the beliefs they hold most dear.[38]

Rorty's hope is that irony will remain in the private domain. There the 'strong poet' can humiliate with inventive redescription to her heart's content. In the private domain it is her own business what she thinks and does. In the public sphere, however, there is a real possibility of humiliating others and so the liberal ironist will avoid cruelty and will restrain herself. But is it so easy to make this assumption, that the public and private can be separated so rigidly? If it is then are we not, as Fraser argues, going to have to turn our backs on the insights of all Marxists, feminists and leftists like Gramsci, Foucault and others who have shown that the economic, the domestic, the cultural, the educational and the medical are all political?[39] In ignoring these insights Rorty seems to think that we can maximize negative liberty and be confident that the public good will not be detrimentally affected. It is simply not possible to draw a line around a certain range of activities and to be sure that within that area our redescriptions will have no public consequences.

There are other reasons why Rorty cannot defend the separation of public and private in this way. By privatizing radical theory Rorty is assuming that we already have a community of citizens bound together by solidarity. He wishes away the many conflicts between competing vocabularies in the political realm and imagines a docile unity. This dichotomy naïvely splits theory from political practice. It fails to recognize the fact that, given the many divisive issues which abound in modern pluralist democracies, it is most unlikely that theory could remain confined to the private realm. It will be used by competing social groups as they argue with each other and engage in the type of political struggle which is inevitable in liberal democratic societies. Rorty's assumption that we can pull together to solve common problems without resort to theory assumes that we can replace political struggle with technocratic social engineering.[40] Any consensus that would emerge in those circumstances could hardly be thought of as the outcome of political discourse. It would rather be an engineered outcome that would presumably be in line with Rorty's vision of bourgeois liberalism.

In fact what Rorty envisages is a depoliticized society with a shrunken public space. He is advocating a minimalist conception of politics which can have little to do with the democratic tradition. It seems to ignore the fact that the freedom of a democratic society requires the vigilant participation of the people. Such a society is based on a notion of equality which as Sheldon Wolin has argued is wary of a sharply defined distinction between public and private and its inevitable accompaniment, the corruption of the public domain by private motives that are activated by the magnitudes of money, resources and legal authority connected with the daily actions of the few who typically are in charge of the modern state.[41]

Rorty's sterile political domain would inevitably favour those who are in a position to set the ground rules and so the views of the powerful would be privileged over those of other citizens. In the end it appears to be the case that Rorty combines private philosophical radicalism with public political conservatism.

We might also wonder what has happened to the ironist's 'radical and continuing doubts' when it comes to this strict separation of public and private or indeed when she considers the merits of liberal democracy as a political system. If liberalism is without foundations then why not engage in experimental inventive redescription of the public sphere? Is it not inconsistent of Rorty to celebrate private irony while protecting liberal democracy from the ironist political critiques of Foucault, Lyotard and Derrida?[42] These thinkers see their irony as intrinsically political so it is difficult to see how Rorty can draw on their insights and then claim that they are useful for anything but the political. Rorty celebrates the contingency of our descriptions but yet this very specific division between public and private reveals his desire to close off the political and to censure irony from redescribing what goes on inside the boundary. This irony would seem rather tame to the radical critiques of liberalism that could be found, for example, in the work of Foucault.

There are then many reasons to believe that Rorty's conception of the public and private, which is a crucial feature of his vision of a post-philosophical culture, is not at all suited to supporting liberal democratic politics. There is no convincing defence in his work of the radical disjuncture between these domains. If, as I have argued, this is an implausible disjuncture then it seems likely that the elitism of ironist culture will spill over from the private sphere and will subvert Rorty's liberal egalitarian aspirations. Despite Rorty's optimism there would not be a sufficient basis for the kind of solidarity that would be needed to sustain a vigilant democratic regime. Widespread ironism would be just as likely to feed a narcissistic culture where social fragmentation and political cynicism act as substitutes for social responsibility and political commitment. The liberal ironist is not an attractive ideal for citizenship.

Liberals would be best advised to reject Rorty's redescription of their political morality. In a pluralist society, public deliberation on the justification of moral principles of accommodation calls for a politics of rational conviction rather than an ethnocentrically pragmatic politics of convention. Some of these principles are intended to protect a private sphere of self-creation.

The self who creates is best thought of in a way that avoids the passive imagery that Rorty seems to embrace. A conception of an actively self-interpreting agent is a far more satisfactory alternative. Finally Rorty's liberal ironist is an inappropriate model for citizenship in a democratic society. There would appear to be no sound argument that Rorty could consistently use that might convince us that irony can, or should, be restricted to the private sphere. Rorty's defence of liberalism actually presents a serious danger to his own political hopes.

Notes

1 A 'strong poet' shapes our language by providing metaphoric redescriptions of some aspect of our actions, our beliefs or our lives. These redescriptions allow for radically new understandings of ourselves to emerge and they can eventually, after some form of Kuhnian paradigm shift, become part of a new vocabulary. In this sense 'strong poets' are for Rorty 'the vanguard of the species'. In our (Western) culture we can include in their number scientists such as Galileo and Newton as well as philosophers such as Hegel, Nietzsche, Heidegger and Derrida. Reading the history of science and the history of philosophy in a way that stresses the importance of metaphoric redescription can, Rorty suggests, lead us to accept the contingency of language itself. See *Contingency, Irony and Solidarity* (hereafter CIS), Cambridge, UK: Cambridge University Press, 1989, 3–22.

2 Rorty deals most directly with the public and private in 'Private Irony and Liberal Hope' in CIS, 73–95 and 'Trotsky and the Wild Orchids', *Common Knowledge* (Winter 1992), 140–53.

3 Rorty, CIS, 44. Some of Rorty's most important essays on liberalism are included in his *Objectivity, Relativism and Truth: Philosophical Papers Volume 1* (hereafter ORT), Cambridge, UK: Cambridge University Press, 1991.

4 Rorty, *Consequences of Pragmatism*, Minneapolis: University of Minnesota Press, 1982, xiv.

5 Rorty, 'The Priority of Democracy to Philosophy' in *The Virginia Statute for Religious Freedom: Its Evolution and Consequences in American History*, Merrill D. Peterson and Robert C. Vaughan (eds), Cambridge, UK: Cambridge University Press, 1988, 257–82, here at 259. See also ORT, 177.

6 Rorty, 'Postmodernist Bourgeois Liberalism' in *Hermeneutics and Praxis*, Robert Hollinger (ed.), Notre Dame: University of Notre Dame Press, 1985, 214–21, here at 216, also ORT, 198.

7 CIS, 83.

8 'A Post-Philosophical Politics: An Interview with Danny Postel', *Philosophy and Social Criticism*, 16 (1990), 199–204, here at 200.

9 CIS, 45.

10 CIS, 57, but see also 'On Ethnocentrism: A Reply to Clifford Geertz' in ORT, 203–10.

11 See especially John Rawls, *A Theory of Justice*, Oxford: Oxford University Press, 1972 and *Political Liberalism*, New York: Columbia University Press, 1993; Bruce Ackerman, *Social Justice and the Liberal State*, New Haven: Yale University Press, 1980 and Charles Larmore, *Patterns of Moral Complexity*, Cambridge, UK: Cambridge University Press, 1987.

12 'Questions and Counterquestions' in *Habermas and Modernity*, Richard J. Bernstein (ed.), Cambridge, UK: Polity Press, 1985, 192–216, here at 194.

13 This distinction is highlighted in Habermas's discourse ethics but see also Joshua
    Cohen, 'Deliberation and Democratic Legitimacy' in *The Good Polity: Norma-
    tive Analysis of the State*, Alan Hamlin and Philip Pettit (eds), Oxford: Blackwell,
    1989. The distinction is also crucial for Rawls's political liberalism despite
    Rorty's interpretation of his recent work (in 'The Priority of Democracy to
    Philosophy'). See Rawls, 'The Domain of the Political and Overlapping Consen-
    sus', *New York University Law Review*, 64 (1989), 233–55.
14 See Jean Hampton, 'Should Political Philosophy Be Done without Metaphysics?'
    Ethics, 99 (1989), 791–814.
15 CIS, 32.
16 See especially 'Freud and Moral Reflection' in *Pragmatism's Freud: The Moral
    Disposition of Psychoanalysis*, Joseph H. Smith and William Kerrigan (eds),
    Baltimore: The Johns Hopkins University Press, 1986, 1–27, also in Rorty's
    Essays on Heidegger and Others: Philosophical Papers Volume 2 (hereafter
    EHO), 143–63. We enlarge ourselves by enriching our lives constantly with
    vocabularies, possibilities and perspectives that are new, spontaneous and
    inventive.
17 The most notable contribution on this aspect of the debate is Michael Sandel's
    Liberalism and the Limits of Justice, Cambridge, UK: Cambridge University
    Press, 1982. The label 'communitarian' is somewhat problematic but its use
    here is intended to identify a set of concerns that are exemplified most clearly
    in Sandel's book. See also contributions of Charles Taylor, Alasdair MacIntyre
    and Michael Walzer in *Communitarianism and Individualism*, Shlomo Avineri
    and Avner de-Shalit (eds), Oxford: Oxford University Press, 1992.
18 For an overview of the key issues in the debate see Stephen Mulhall and Adam
    Swift *Liberals and Communitarians*, Oxford: Blackwell. 1992.
19 CIS, 46.
20 See the comments of Michael Walzer in 'The Communitarian Critique of
    Liberalism', *Political Theory*, 18 (1990), 6–23, here at 20–1.
21 Will Kymlicka, 'Liberalism and Communitarianism', *Canadian Journal of
    Philosophy*, 18 (1988), 181–204.
22 'The Priority of Democracy to Philosophy', 270.
23 CIS, 30. See also the more detailed account in 'Freud and Moral Reflection'.
24 CIS, 32.
25 CIS, 37.
26 ORT, 199.
27 Martin Hollis 'The Poetics of Personhood' in *Reading Rorty* (hereafter RR),
    Alan Malachowski (ed.), Oxford: Blackwell, 1990, 244–56, here at 247.
28 Both of these brief quotations are cited in Charles B. Guignon and David
    R. Hiley, 'Biting the Bullet: Rorty on Public and Private Morality' in RR,
    339–64, Heidegger at 345, Freud at 351.
29 Hollis in RR, 253.
30 See Guignon and Hiley in RR, 347–50.
31 Guignon and Hiley in RR, 347.
32 CIS, 73.
33 A variation on this question is put by Richard J. Bernstein, 'Rorty's Liberal
    Utopia', *Social Research*, 57, 1 (Spring, 1990), 31–72.
34 'The Priority of Democracy to Philosophy', 272.
35 'Moral Arguments and Social Contexts: A Response to Rorty' in *Hermeneutics
    and Praxis*, Robert Hollinger (ed.), Notre Dame: University of Notre Dame
    Press, 1985, 222–3.
36 'Solidarity or Singularity: Richard Rorty between Romanticism and Tech-
    nocracy' in RR, 303–21.

37 See for example 'Postmodernist Bourgeois Liberalism' and 'Solidarity or Objectivity?' in *Post-Analytic Philosophy*, John Rajchman and Cornel West (eds), New York: Columbia University Press, 1985, 3–19, also in ORT, 21–34.
38 CIS, 89.
39 Fraser in RR, 312–13.
40 Fraser in RR, 315.
41 'Democracy in the Discourse of Postmodernism', *Social Research*, 57, 1 (Spring 1990), 5–30, here at 25.
42 See for example Rorty's views on Foucault, CIS, 61–5 and 'Moral Identity and Private Autonomy: The Case of Foucault' in EHO, 193–8, on Lyotard, 'Habermas and Lyotard on Postmodernity' in EHO, 164–76 and 'Cosmopolitanism without Emancipation: A Response to Jean-François Lyotard' in ORT, 211–22, and on Derrida, CIS, ch. 6.

5 Public and private in Hannah Arendt's conception of citizenship

Maurizio Passerin d'Entrèves

In recent years there has been a renewal of interest in the question of citizenship and the related distinction between the public and the private. In Britain the Conservative Party launched in the early 1990s the so-called 'Citizens' Charter', while the current Labour administration has implemented policies, such as welfare to work, that rest upon the idea of responsible citizenship, linking the idea of rights to that of duties each individual owes to the community. In Italy the current governing coalition, led by the Democratic Party of the Left, has stressed the theme of citizenship rights and placed it at the centre of its political programmes. Citizenship has also been linked to the debate concerning the distinction between the public and the private. The feminist movement has been at the forefront of a struggle to redefine the boundaries between the public and the private, arguing that many issues previously regarded as falling under the domain of private choice or individual preference, such as pornography and surrogate motherhood, should become a topic of public debate and in specified cases of public legislation. The same attempt to transform into public issues questions that had been seen to belong to a private and non-political domain has characterized the activities of the gay and lesbian movements, of ethnic and cultural minorities, of orthodox religious groups, and of associations representing the physically handicapped and the mentally disabled. All these groups have attempted to gain some form of public recognition and support, including public legislation, so as to protect their distinctive way of life, their cultures and practices, their values and identities, or their individual and communal well-being. These movements could be seen as an attempt to redraw the boundaries of citizenship, in the sense of enlarging the scope of what is public by transforming what seemed to be purely private issues into matters of public concern.

My chapter will attempt to address these questions by looking at Hannah Arendt's conception of citizenship. Her conception of politics and of public life in general is in fact based on the idea of active citizenship, that is, on the value and importance of civic engagement and collective deliberation about all matters affecting the political community. The practice of citizenship is valued because it enables each citizen to exercise his or her powers of agency, to develop the capacities for judgement, and to attain by concerted action some measure of political efficacy. In what follows I will reconstruct Arendt's conception of citizenship around three major themes: (1) the *public sphere*; (2) *political agency* and *collective identity*; and (3) *political culture*. I hope in this way to show that Arendt's conception remains important for contemporary attempts to revive the practice of citizenship and to redraw the boundaries between the public and the private.

Citizenship and the public sphere

Throughout her writings Arendt attempted to articulate the question of citizenship around the constitution of public spaces of action and political deliberation. For Arendt the public sphere refers to that sphere of appearance where citizens interact through the medium of speech and persuasion, disclose their unique identities, and decide through collective deliberation about matters of common concern. This public sphere of appearance can be established only if we share a common world of humanly created artifacts, institutions and settings that separates us from nature and that provides a relatively permanent or durable context for our activities. The constitution of public spaces of action and political discourse depends, therefore, upon the existence of a common, shared world, and upon the creation of numerous spheres of appearance in which individuals can disclose their identities and establish relations of reciprocity and solidarity.

Arendt's conception of the public sphere, of the sphere within which the activity of citizenship can flourish, has therefore two meanings, since it refers both to the *space of appearance* and to the *world we hold in common*. According to the first meaning, the public realm is that space where everything that appears

> can be seen and heard by everybody and has the widest possible publicity. For us, appearance – something that is being seen and heard by others as well as by ourselves – constitutes reality. Compared with the reality which comes from being seen and heard, even the greatest forces of intimate life – the passions of the heart, the thoughts of the mind, the delights of the senses – lead an uncertain, shadowy kind of existence unless and until they are transformed, deprivatized and de-individualized, as it were, into a shape to fit them for public appearance ... The presence of others who see what we see and hear what we hear assures us of the reality of the world and of ourselves.[1]

Within this space of appearance, therefore, experiences can be shared, actions evaluated, and identities disclosed. Indeed, Arendt maintains that

> since our feeling for reality depends utterly upon appearance and therefore upon the existence of a public realm into which things can appear

out of the darkness of sheltered existence, even the twilight which illuminates our private and intimate lives is ultimately derived from the much harsher light of the public realm.[2]

In sum, the public realm as a space of appearance provides the light and the publicity which are necessary for the establishment of our public identities, for the recognition of a common reality, and for the assessment of the actions of others.

For Arendt the space of appearance is created every time individuals gather together politically, which is to say, 'wherever men are together in the manner of speech and action', and in this respect it 'predates and precedes all formal constitution of the public realm and the various forms of government'.[3] It is not restricted to a set of institutions or to a specific location; rather, it comes into existence whenever action is coordinated through speech and persuasion and is oriented towards the attainment of collective goals. However, since it is a creation of common action and collective deliberation, the space of appearance is highly fragile and exists only when actualized through the performance of deeds and the sharing of words. Its peculiarity, Arendt says, is that

> unlike the spaces which are the work of our hands, it does not survive the actuality of the movement which brought it into being, but disappears not only with the dispersal of men – as in the case of great catastrophes when the body politic of a people is destroyed – but with the disappearance or arrest of the activities themselves. Wherever people gather together, it is potentially there, but only potentially, not necessarily and not forever.[4]

The space of appearance must therefore be continually re-created by action; its existence is secured whenever actors gather together for the purpose of discussing and deliberating about matters of public concern, and it disappears the moment these activities cease. It is therefore always a *potential space* that finds its actualization in the actions and speeches of individuals who have come together to undertake some common project. It may arise suddenly, as in the case of revolutions, or it may develop slowly out of the efforts to change some specific piece of legislation or policy, e.g. saving a historic building or a natural landscape, extending the public provision of housing and health care, protecting groups from discrimination and oppression, fighting for nuclear disarmament, and so on. Historically, it has been re-created whenever public spaces of action and deliberation have been set up, from town hall meetings to workers' councils, from demonstrations and sit-ins to struggles for justice and equal rights.

The second meaning that Arendt assigns to the public realm, that which supports the space of appearance and provides action with its proper concerns, is the world, or more precisely, the world that we hold in common.

This is the world which 'is common to all of us and distinguished from our privately owned place in it'.[5] It is not identical with the earth or with nature; it is related, rather, 'to the human artifact, the fabrication of human hands, as well as to the affairs which go on among those who inhabit the man-made world together'.[6] Thus 'to live together in the world means essentially that a world of things is between those who have it in common, as a table is located between those who sit around it; the world, like every in-between, relates and separates men at the same time.'[7] In this respect the public realm, as the common world, 'gathers us together and yet prevents our falling over each other, so to speak. What makes mass society so difficult to bear is not the number of people involved . . . but the fact that the world between them has lost its power to gather them together, to relate and to separate them.'[8] By establishing a space between individuals, an in-between which connects and separates them at the same time, the world provides the physical context within which political action can arise. Moreover, by virtue of its permanence and durability, the world provides the temporal context within which individual lives can unfold and, by being turned into narratives, acquire a measure of immortality. As Arendt writes:

> The common world is what we enter when we are born and what we leave behind when we die. It transcends our life-span into past and future alike; it was there before we came and will outlast our brief sojourn in it. It is what we have in common not only with those who live with us, but also with those who were here before and with those who will come after us. But such a common world can survive the coming and going of the generations only to the extent that it appears in public.[9]

It is this capacity of human artifacts and institutions – i.e. the world we have in common – to endure through time and to become the common heritage of successive generations, that enables individuals to feel at home in the world and to transcend, however partially, the fleetingness of their existence. Indeed, without a measure of permanence and durability provided by the world, 'life would never be human'.[10] 'Permanence and durability [are what] human beings need precisely because they are mortals – the most unstable and futile beings we know of.'[11] For Arendt, therefore, the transitoriness of life can be overcome by constructing a lasting and stable world that allows for human remembrance and anticipation, that is, for both memory and a measure of trust in the future. As she expressed it:

> Life in its non-biological sense, the span of time each man has between birth and death, manifests itself in action and speech, both of which share with life its essential futility. The 'doing of great deeds and the speaking of great words' will leave no trace, no product that might endure after the moment of action and the spoken word has passed . . . [Thus] acting and speaking men need the help of *homo faber* in his

highest capacity, that is, the help of the artist, of poets and histori-
ographers, of monument-builders and writers, because without them
the only product of their activity, the story they enact and tell, would
not survive at all.[12]

Human mortality can thus be partly transcended by the durability of the
world and the public memory of individuals' deeds. By building and pre-
serving a world that can link one generation to the next and that makes possible forms of collective memory, we are able, in Arendt's words, 'to absorb
and make shine through the centuries whatever men may want to save from
the natural ruin of time'.[13]

The public realm: three features

I would like now to turn to an examination of three features of the public
realm and of the sphere of politics that are closely connected to Arendt's conception of citizenship. I will rely for this on an interesting essay by Margaret
Canovan entitled 'Politics as Culture: Hannah Arendt and the Public Realm',
in which she argues that Arendt's conception of the public realm is based on
an implicit analogy between politics and culture.[14] For the purpose of exploring Arendt's conception of citizenship, there are three features of the public-
political realm identified by Canovan that deserve out attention: first, the
artificial or constructed quality of politics and of public life in general;
second, its *spatial* quality; third, the distinction between *public* and *private*
interests.

The artificiality of public life

As regards the first feature, Arendt always stressed the artificiality of public
life and of political activities in general, the fact that they are man-made and
constructed, rather than natural or given. She regarded this artificiality as
something to be celebrated rather than deplored. Politics for her was not
the result of some natural predisposition, or the realization of the inherent
traits of human nature.[15] Rather, it was a cultural achievement of the first
order, enabling individuals to transcend the necessities of life and to fashion
a world within which free political action and discourse could flourish. It is
for this reason, we might note, that Arendt's political philosophy cannot
be easily located within the neo-Aristotelian tradition, notwithstanding
their common emphasis on the importance of the *vita activa*. Indeed, if we
take Michael Oakeshott's distinction between the tradition of political
thought based on Reason and Nature and that based on Will and Artifice
(characterizing respectively the ancient and the modern conception of
politics), it would appear that Arendt fits more easily into the latter, since
for her politics was always an artificial creation, a product of action and

speech, and not the result of some natural or innate trait shared by all human beings.[16]

The stress on the artificiality of politics has a number of important consequences. For example, Arendt emphasized that the principle of political equality among citizens is not the result of some natural condition that precedes the constitution of the political realm. Political equality for Arendt is not a natural human attribute, nor can it rest on a theory of natural rights; rather, it is an artificial attribute which individuals acquire upon entering the public realm and which is secured by democratic political institutions.[17] As she remarked in *The Origins of Totalitarianism*, those who had been deprived of civil and political rights by the Nazi regime were not able to defend themselves by an appeal to their natural rights; on the contrary, they discovered that, having been excluded from the body politic, they had no rights whatsoever.[18] Political equality and the recognition of one's rights (what Arendt called 'a right to have rights') can thus be secured only by membership in a democratic political community.[19]

A further consequence of Arendt's stress on the artificiality of political life is evident in her rejection of all neo-romantic appeals to the *Volk* and to ethnic identity as the basis for political community. She maintained that one's ethnic, religious, or racial identity was irrelevant to one's identity as a *citizen*, that it should never be made the basis of membership in a *political* community, and praised the American Constitution for having excluded in principle any connection between one's ethnic or religious identity and one's political status as a citizen.[20] Similarly, at the time of establishment of the state of Israel, she advocated a conception of citizenship based not on race or religion, but on the formal political rights of freedom and equality that would have extended to both Arabs and Jews.[21]

Finally, it is worth pointing out that Arendt's emphasis on the formal qualities of citizenship made her position rather distant from those advocates of participation during the 1960s who saw it in terms of recapturing a sense of intimacy, of community, of warmth, and of authenticity.[22] For Arendt political participation was important because it permitted the establishment of relations of civility and solidarity among citizens. In the essay 'On Humanity in Dark Times' she wrote that the search for intimacy is characteristic of those groups excluded from the public realm, as were the Jews during the Nazi period, but that such intimacy is bought at the price of worldlessness, which 'is always a form of barbarism'.[23] Since they represent 'psychological substitutes ... for the loss of the common, visible world',[24] the ties of intimacy and warmth can never become political; the only truly political ties are those of civic friendship and solidarity, since they 'make political demands and preserve reference to the world'.[25] In other words, for Arendt the danger of trying to recapture a sense of intimacy and warmth, of authenticity and communal feelings, is that one loses the public values of impartiality, civic friendship, and solidarity. As Canovan has put it:

[Arendt's] conception of the public realm is opposed not only to society but also to community: to *Gemeinschaft* as well as to *Gesellschaft*. While greatly valuing warmth, intimacy and naturalness in private life, she insisted on the importance of a formal, artificial public realm in which what mattered was people's actions rather than their sentiments; in which the natural ties of kinship and intimacy were set aside in favour of a deliberate, impartial solidarity with other citizens; in which there was enough space between people for them to stand back and judge one another coolly and objectively.[26]

The spatial quality of public life

The second feature stressed by Arendt has to do with the spatial quality of public life, with the fact that political activities are located in a public space where citizens are able to meet one another, to exchange their opinions and debate their differences, and to search for some collective solution to their problems. Politics, in this respect, is a matter of people sharing a common world and a common space of appearance in which public concerns can emerge and be articulated from different perspectives. For politics to occur it is not enough to have a collection of private individuals voting separately and anonymously according to their private opinions.[27] Rather, these individuals must be able to see and talk to one another in public, to meet in a public space so that their differences as well as their commonalities can emerge and become the subject of democratic debate.[28]

This notion of a common public space helps us to understand how political opinions can be formed which are neither reducible to private, idiosyncratic preferences, on the one hand, nor to a unanimous collective opinion, on the other. Arendt herself distrusted the term 'public opinion', since it suggested the mindless unanimity of mass society.[29] In her view representative opinions could arise only when citizens actually confronted one another in a public space, so that they could examine an issue from a number of different perspectives, modify their views, and enlarge their standpoint to incorporate that of others.[30] Political opinions, she claimed, can never be formed in private; rather, they are formed, tested, and enlarged only within a public context of argumentation and debate.

Opinions will rise wherever men communicate freely with one another and have the right to make their views public; but these views, in their endless variety, seem to stand also in need of purification and representation.[31]

Where an appropriate public space exists (the example chosen by Arendt is the US Senate, at least in its original conception, but we can extend her example to all those spaces of relatively formal and structured debate that are located within civil society), these opinions can be shaped and elaborated into a sophisticated political discourse, rather than remaining the expression of arbitrary preferences or being moulded into a unanimous 'public opinion'.

Another implication of Arendt's stress on the spatial quality of politics has to do with the question of how a collection of distinct individuals can be united to form a political community. For Arendt the unity that may be achieved in a political community is neither the result of religious or ethnic affinity, nor the expression of some common value system. Rather, the unity in question can be attained by sharing a public space and a set of political institutions, and engaging in the practices and activities which are characteristic of that space and those institutions. As Christopher Lasch has remarked in an essay clearly indebted to Arendt, the assumption that 'shared values, not political institutions or a common political language, provide the only source of social cohesion . . . represents a radical break from many of the republican principles on which this country was founded'.[32] What unites people in a political community is therefore not some set of common values, but the world they set up in common, the spaces they inhabit together, the institutions and practices which they share as citizens. As Canovan puts it, individuals can be united

> by the *world* which lies between them. All that is necessary is that they should have amongst them a common political world which they enter as citizens, and which they can hand on to their successors. It is the space between them that unites them, rather than some quality inside each of them[33]

or some set of common values and beliefs.

A further implication of Arendt's conception of the spatial quality of politics is that since politics is a public activity, one cannot be part of it without in some sense being present in a public space. To be engaged in politics means actively participating in the various public forums where the decisions affecting one's community are taken. Arendt's insistence on the importance of direct participation in politics has sometimes been interpreted to imply that individuals have an existential need for participation which they can only satisfy by engaging in public affairs. This actually represents a misunderstanding of Arendt's commitment to participatory politics, since it is based on what Canovan aptly calls a subjective or *person-centred*, rather than a public or *world-centred*, conception of politics. Although people may engage in political activity to fulfil their needs for involvement and participation, for Arendt it is not so much these personal needs as the *concerns* about the common world that constitute the substance and value of political action. Thus, as Canovan notes,

> while Arendt certainly did maintain that political participation was personally fulfilling, her fundamental argument for it was not only less

subjectivist but also more simple . . . it was that, since politics is something that needs a worldly location and can only happen in a public space, then if you are not present in such a space you are simply not engaged in politics.[34]

Public and private interests

This public or world-centred conception of politics lies also at the basis of Arendt's distinction between public and private interests. According to Arendt, political activity is not a means to an end, but an end in itself; one does not engage in political action simply to promote one's welfare, but to realize the principles intrinsic to political life, such as freedom, equality, justice, solidarity, courage, and excellence. Politics is a world with its own values and ends that are realized in public action and deliberation; it is, as Arendt says, 'concerned with the *world as such* and not with those who live in it'.[35] In a late essay entitled 'Public Rights and Private Interests' she discusses the difference between one's life as an individual and one's life as a citizen, between the life spent on one's own and the life spent in common with others. As she writes:

> Throughout his life man moves constantly in two different orders of existence: he moves within what is his *own* and he also moves in a sphere that is common to him and his fellow men. The 'public good', the concerns of the citizen, is indeed the common good because it is located in the *world* which we have in common *without owning it*. Quite frequently, it will be antagonistic to whatever we may deem good to ourselves in our private existence.[36]

What Arendt is claiming is that our *public* interests as citizens are quite distinct from our *private* interests as individuals. The public interest cannot be automatically derived from our private interests: indeed, it is not the sum of private interests, nor their highest common denominator, nor even the total of enlightened self-interests.[37] In fact, it has little to do with our private interests, since it concerns the world that lies beyond the self, that was there before our birth and that will be there after our death, and that finds its embodiment in activities and institutions with their own intrinsic purposes which may be often at odds with our short-term and private interests.[38] As Arendt says, 'the self *qua* self cannot reckon in terms of long-range interest, i.e. the interest of a world that survives its inhabitants'.[39] The interests of the world are not the interests of individuals: they are the interests of the public realm which we share as citizens and which we can pursue and enjoy only by going beyond our own self-interest. As citizens we share that public realm and participate in its interests: but the interests belong to the public realm, to the realm that we have in common 'without owning it', to that realm which transcends our limited life-span and our limited private purposes.

Arendt provides an example of such public interests by examining the activity of serving on a jury. As jurors, the interests we are asked to uphold are the public interests of justice and fairness. These are not the interests of our private selves, nor do they coincide with our enlightened self-interest. They are the interests of a political community that regulates its affairs by means of constitutional laws and procedures. They are *public* interests transcending and outlasting the private interests that we may have as individuals. Indeed, the fairness and impartiality demanded of the citizens, Arendt notes, 'is resisted at every turn by the urgency of one's self-interests, which are always more urgent than the common good'.[40] The public interest in impartial justice which we share as jurors may interfere with our private affairs: it often involves inconvenience, and could sometimes involve greater risks, as when one is asked to testify against a group of criminals who have threatened retribution. According to Arendt, the only compensation for the risks and sacrifices demanded by the public interest lies in what she calls the 'public happiness' of acting in concert as citizens in the public realm. Indeed, it is only through acting in the public realm and enjoying the freedom and happiness of common deliberation that we are able to discover our public interests and to transcend, when needed, our more limited private interests.[41]

A further illustration of Arendt's distinction between public and private interests is provided by her discussion of the question of civil disobedience. At the time of the protest movement against the Vietnam War and the struggle for civil rights for blacks in the 1960s, the legitimacy of civil disobedience was often discussed in terms drawn from exemplary cases of conscience, in particular, Socrates' refusal to escape from prison after being condemned to death by the Athenians, and Thoreau's refusal to pay taxes to a government that tolerated slavery and engaged in an expansionist war against Mexico. Arendt maintained that these examples of action undertaken for the sake of one's conscience were inappropriate to characterize the struggles and protests of the 1960s, since the latter were motivated not by a concern with the integrity of one's conscience, but by a concern with the injustices taking place in the world. Thoreau's stance, as set out in his famous essay 'On the Duty of Civil Disobedience', was to avoid being implicated in the actions of the US Government, rather than fighting actively for the abolition of slavery and foreign aggression. 'It is not a man's duty', he writes, 'to devote himself to the eradication of any, even the most enormous, wrong; he may still properly have other concerns to engage him; but it is his duty, at least, to wash his hands of it.'[42] Thoreau's concern, in other words, was to avoid self-reproach, to avoid being implicated in something he considered wrong, rather than fighting for the redress of injustice. Arendt's comment is the following:

Here, as elsewhere, conscience is unpolitical. It is not primarily interested in the world where the wrong is committed or in the consequences that the wrong will have for the future course of the world. It does not say, with Jefferson, 'I tremble *for my country* when I reflect that God is just; that His justice cannot sleep forever,' because it trembles for the individual self and its integrity.[43]

The rules of conscience are unpolitical, they concern the self's integrity and not the integrity of the world. They say: 'Beware of doing something that you will not be able to live with.'[44] As such, they may be effective during emergencies or when a particular atrocity is being committed, but they cannot serve as political standards; they are too much concerned with the self to serve as a basis for collective action aiming at the redress of injustice in the world.[45] One of the comments Arendt made about Rosa Luxemburg was that she 'was very much concerned with the *world* and not at all concerned with herself'. She had engaged in political action because 'she could not stand the injustice *within the world*'. Thus, for Arendt, 'the decisive thing is whether your own motivation is clear – for the world – or for yourself, by which I mean for your soul'.[46] To be sure, Arendt did not dismiss the role of conscience altogether; in her lecture 'Thinking and Moral Considerations' and in *The Life of the Mind* she argued that conscience, as the inner dialogue of me and myself, can prevent individuals from committing or participating in atrocities.[47] Conscience, however, gives no positive prescriptions; it only tells us what *not* to do, what to avoid in our actions and dealings with others; its criterion for action is 'whether I shall be able to live with myself in peace when the time has come to think about my deeds and words'.[48] It is not something that can be taken for granted – many people lack it or are unable to feel self-reproach. It cannot be generalized – what I cannot live with may not bother another person's conscience, with the result that one person's conscience will stand against another person's conscience. And, as we have seen, it directs attention to the self rather than to the world. The counsels of conscience are therefore unpolitical. They can only be expressed in purely individual, subjective form. As Arendt writes:

> When Socrates stated that 'it is better to suffer wrong than to do wrong,' he clearly meant that it was better *for him*, just as it was better for him 'to be in disagreement with multitudes than, being one, to be in disagreement with himself.' Politically, on the contrary, what counts is that a wrong has been done.[49]

In sum, for Arendt there was a clear distinction to be made between the private, unpolitical stance of conscience and the public, political stance of actively caring for the affairs of the political community. Those who struggled for the extension of civil rights and the termination of the war in Vietnam were not trying to save their conscience; rather, they were struggling to improve their polity, to establish standards of universal justice and respect for national self-determination. They were acting as citizens rather than as individuals concerned with their own private integrity.[50]

Citizenship, agency, and collective identity

In the light of the preceding discussion, I would like now to turn to an examination of the connection between Arendt's conception of citizenship and the questions of political agency and collective identity. My aim in what follows is to argue that Arendt's participatory conception of citizenship and her theory of action provide the best starting points for addressing both the question of the constitution of collective identity and that concerning the conditions for the exercise of effective political agency.

Citizenship and collective identity

Let us then examine first the question of collective identity. In her book *Wittgenstein and Justice* Hanna Pitkin argues that one of the crucial questions at stake in political discourse is the creation of a collective identity, a '*we*' to which we can appeal when faced with the problem of deciding among alternative courses of action. In addressing the question 'What shall we do?' the 'we', she notes, is not given but must be constantly negotiated. Indeed, since in political discourse there is always disagreement about the possible courses of action, the identity of the 'we' that is going to be created through a specific form of collective action becomes the central question. As Pitkin puts it:

> In political discourse's problem of 'what shall we do?' the 'we' is always called into question. Part of the issue becomes, if we pursue this or that course of action open to us, who could affirm it, who could regard it as done in his name? Who will still be with 'us' if 'we' take this course of action?[51]

Thus

> Part of the knowledge revealed in political discourse is the scope and validity of the claim entered in saying 'we': i.e., who turns out to be willing and able to endorse that claim.[52]

Whenever we engage in action and political discourse we are thereby also engaging in the constitution of our collective identity, in the creation of a 'we' with which we are able to identify both ourselves and our actions. This process of identity-construction is never given once and for all, and is never unproblematic. Rather, it is a process of constant renegotiation and struggle, a process in which actors articulate and defend competing conceptions of

cultural and political identity, and competing conceptions of political legitimacy. As Habermas has noted, if a collective identity emerges in complex
societies,

> its form would be an identity, non-prejudiced in its content and indepen-
> dent of particular organizational types, of the community of those who
> engage in the *discursive* and *experimental* formation of an identity-
> related knowledge on the basis of a critical appropriation of tradition,
> as well as of the inputs from science, philosophy and the arts.[53]

In political terms this means that a collective identity under modern conditions can arise out of a process of public argumentation and debate in
which competing ideals of identity and political legitimacy are articulated,
contested, and refined.[54] From this standpoint, Arendt's participatory conception of citizenship assumes a particular relevance, since it articulates the
conditions for the establishment of collective identities. I would argue, in
fact, that once citizenship is viewed as the process of active deliberation
about competing identity projections, its value would reside in the possibility
of establishing forms of collective identity that can be acknowledged, tested,
and transformed in a discursive and democratic fashion.

Such a conception of citizenship would also be able to articulate what
Nancy Fraser has called 'the standpoint of the *collective concrete other*'.
By this term Fraser refers to the standpoint from which specific collective
identities are constructed on the basis of the specific narrative resources
and vocabularies of particular groups, such as women, blacks, and members
of oppressed classes. The standpoint of the collective concrete other, Fraser
writes, focuses on 'the specificity of the vocabularies available to individuals
and groups for the interpretation of their needs and for the definitions of
situations in which they encounter one another'. It would also focus on the
'specificity of the narrative resources available to individuals and groups
for the construction of individual life-stories [and of] group identities and
solidarities'.[55] From such a standpoint people are encountered 'less as
unique individuals than as members of groups or collectivities with culturally
specific identities, solidarities and forms of life . . . here one would abstract
both from unique individuality *and* from universal humanity to focalize the
intermediate zone of group identity'.[56] The norms that would govern the
interactions among such groups or collectivities would be 'neither norms
of intimacy such as love and care, nor those of formal institutions such as
rights and entitlements. Rather, they would be norms of collective solidarities
as expressed in shared but non-universal social practices.'[57] The value of
autonomy could then be formulated in terms that would not pit it against
solidarity; rather, to be autonomous would mean

> to be a member of a group or groups which have achieved a degree of
> collective control over the means of interpretation and communication

sufficient to enable one to participate on a par with members of other groups in moral and political deliberation.[58]

The achievement of autonomy could then be considered as one of the conditions necessary to the establishment of relations of equality, mutuality, and solidarity.

This formulation of the norms and values of citizenship from the standpoint of the 'collective concrete other' can be interpreted in my view as a fruitful extension of many of the themes articulated by Arendt's participatory conception of citizenship. The stress on *solidarity* rather than on care or compassion, on *respect* rather than on love or sympathy, and on *autonomy* as a precondition of solidarity, seems to express the same concerns that animated Arendt's conception of citizenship. Indeed, as Fraser remarks, an ethic of solidarity elaborated from the standpoint of the collective concrete other

> is superior to an ethic of care as a *political* ethic. It is the sort of ethic which is attuned to the contestatory activities of social movements struggling to forge narrative resources and vocabularies adequate to the expression of their self-interpreted needs. It is attuned also to collective struggles to deconstruct narrative forms and vocabularies of dominant groups and collectivities so as to show these are partial rather than genuinely shared, and are incapable of giving voice to the needs and hopes of subordinated groups. In short, an ethic of solidarity elaborated from the standpoint of the collective concrete other is more appropriate than an ethic of care for a feminist ethic, if we think of a feminist ethic as the ethic of a *social and political movement*.[59]

In this respect, Fraser concludes, an ethic of solidarity is 'just as appropriate as a *political* ethic for movements of lesbians, gays, blacks, hispanics, other people of color and subordinated classes'.[60] An ethic of solidarity is therefore not the prerogative of any specific group; rather, it is an ethic that can develop out of the struggles of all those groups who have been silenced or marginalized in the past, and who are now attempting to articulate new conceptions of cultural and political identity.[61]

Citizenship and political agency

The foregoing discussion has stressed the importance that political action and discourse have for the constitution of collective identities. In this section I would like to focus on a related theme, namely, the connection between political action, understood as the active engagement of citizens in the public realm, and the exercise of effective political agency. This connection represents in my view one of the central contributions of Arendt's theory of action, and underlies what I have called her 'participatory' conception of citizenship. According to Arendt, the active engagement of citizens in the determination of the affairs of their community provides them not only with the experience of public freedom and the joys of public happiness, but also with a sense of *political agency and efficacy*, the sense, in Jefferson's phrase, of being 'participators in government'. The importance of participation for political agency and efficacy is brought out clearly in the following passage from *On Revolution*. Commenting on Jefferson's proposal to institute a system of wards or local councils in which citizens would be able to have an effective share in political power, Arendt remarks that

> Jefferson called every government degenerate in which all powers were concentrated 'in the hands of the one, the few, the well-born or the many.' Hence, the ward system was not meant to strengthen the power of the many but the power of '*every one*' within the limits of his competence; and only by breaking up 'the many' into assemblies where *every one* could count and be counted upon 'shall we be as republican as a large society can be.' In terms of the safety of the citizens of the republic, the question was how to make everybody feel 'that he is a *participator* in the government of affairs, not merely at an election one day in the year, but every day.'[62]

In Arendt's view only the sharing of power that comes from civic engagement and common deliberation can provide each citizen with a sense of effective political agency. Arendt's strictures against representation must be understood in this light. She saw representation as a substitute for the direct involvement of the citizens, and as a means whereby the distinction between rulers and ruled could reassert itself. When representation becomes the substitute for direct democracy, the citizens can exercise their powers of political agency only at election day, and their capacities for deliberation and political insight are correspondingly weakened. Moreover, by encouraging the formation of a political elite, representation means that

> the age-old distinction between ruler and ruled . . . has asserted itself again; once more, the people are not admitted to the public realm, once more the business of government has become the privilege of the few, who alone may 'exercise their virtuous dispositions' . . . The result is that the people must either sink into lethargy . . . or preserve the spirit of resistance to whatever government they have elected, since the only power they retain is the 'reserve power of revolution.'[63]

As an alternative to a system of representation based on bureaucratic parties and state structures, Arendt proposed a federated system of councils where citizens could be actively engaged at various levels in the determination of their affairs. The relevance of Arendt's proposal for direct democracy lies in the connection it establishes between *active citizenship* and *effective political agency*. It is only by means of direct political participation, by engaging in common action and in public deliberation, that citizenship can be reaffirmed and political agency effectively exercised. As Pitkin and Shumer have remarked,

> even the most oppressed people sometimes rediscover within themselves the capacity to act. Democrats today must seek out and foster every opportunity for people to experience their own *effective agency* ... dependency and apathy must be attacked wherever people's experience centers. Yet such attacks remain incomplete unless they relate personal concerns to public issues, extend individual initiative into shared political action.[64]

In a similar vein, Sara Evans and Harry Boyte have highlighted the ways in which

> the dispossessed and powerless have again and again sought simultaneously to revive and remember older notions of democratic participation ... and ... given them new and deeper meanings and applications. Democracy, in these terms, means more than changing structures so as to make democracy possible. It means, also, schooling citizens in *citizenship* – that is, in the varied skills and values which are essential to sustaining effective participation.[65]

Viewed in this light, Arendt's conception of participatory democracy represents an attempt to reactivate the experience of citizenship and to articulate the conditions for the exercise of effective political agency. It is worth noting, moreover, that such a conception does not imply value homogeneity or value consensus, nor does it require the dedifferentiation of social spheres. Insofar as Arendt's participatory conception is based on the principle of *plurality*, it does not aim at the recovery or revitalization of some coherent value scheme, nor at the reintegration of different social spheres. As Benhabib has noted, on Arendt's participatory conception,

> the public sentiment which is encouraged is not reconciliation and harmony, but rather *political agency and efficacy*, namely, the sense that one has a say in the course of the economic, political, and civic conditions which define our lives together in the political community, and that what one does makes a difference. This can be achieved without value homogeneity among individuals, and without collapsing the various spheres into one another.[66]

Arendt's conception of participatory democracy does not, therefore, aim at value integration or at the dedifferentiation of social spheres; rather, it aims at reactivating the conditions for active citizenship and democratic self-determination. As she put it in a passage of *On Revolution*:

> If the ultimate end of the Revolution was freedom and the constitution of a public space where freedom could appear . . . then the elementary republics of the wards, the only tangible place where everyone could be free, actually were the end of the great republic . . . The basic assumption of the ward system, whether Jefferson knew it or not, was that no one could be called happy without his share in public business, that no one could be called free without his experience in public freedom, and that no one could be called either happy or free without participating and having a share in public power.[67]

Citizenship and political culture

The foregoing discussion has articulated Arendt's conception of citizenship around the issues of political agency and collective identity. In this last section I would like to explore the connection between Arendt's conception of participatory citizenship and the constitution of an active and democratic political culture. In her book *On Revolution* and in two essays contained in *Between Past and Future*[68] Arendt claimed that the possibility of reactivating the political capacity for impartial and responsible judgement depended upon the creation of public spaces for collective deliberation in which citizens could test and enlarge their opinions. As she put it:

> Opinions will rise wherever men communicate freely with one another and have the right to make their views public; but these views in their endless variety seem to stand also in need of purification and representation . . . Even though opinions are formed by individuals and must remain, as it were, their property, no single individual . . . can ever be equal to the task of sifting opinions, of passing them through the sieve of an intelligence which will separate the arbitrary and the merely idiosyncratic, and thus purify them into public views.[69]

Where an appropriate public space exists, these opinions can in fact be tested, enlarged, and transformed through a process of democratic debate and enlightenment. Democratic debate is indeed crucial to the formation of opinions that can claim more than subjective validity; individuals may hold personal opinions on many subject matters, but they can form *representative* opinions only by enlarging their standpoint to incorporate those of others. In the words of Arendt:

> Political thought is representative. I form an opinion by considering a given issue from different viewpoints, by making present to my mind

the standpoints of those who are absent; that is, I represent them . . .
The more people's standpoints I have present in my mind while I am
pondering a given issue, and the better I can imagine how I would feel
and think if I were in their place, the stronger will be my capacity for
representative thinking and the more valid my final conclusions, my
opinion.[70]

The capacity to form valid opinions requires therefore a public space where
individuals can test and purify their views through a process of public argumentation and debate. The same holds true for the formation of valid judgements: as 'the most political of man's mental abilities',[71] judgement can only
be exercised and tested in public, in the free and open exchange of opinions in
the public sphere. As Arendt says, judgement

cannot function in strict isolation or solitude; it needs the presence of
others 'in whose place' it must think, whose perspectives it must take
into consideration, and without whom it never has the opportunity to
operate at all. As logic, to be sound, depends on the presence of the
self, so judgment, to be valid, depends on the presence of others.[72]

As in the case of opinion, the validity of judgement depends on the ability
to think 'representatively', that is, from the standpoint of everyone else, so
that we are able to look at the world from a number of different perspectives.
And this ability, in turn, can only be acquired and tested in a public setting
where individuals have the opportunity to exchange their opinions and to
articulate their differences through democratic discourse. As Benhabib has
put it:

To think from the standpoint of everyone else entails sharing a public
culture such that everyone else can articulate indeed what they think
and what their perspectives are. The cultivation of one's moral imagination flourishes in such a culture in which the self-centered perspective of
the individual is constantly challenged by the multiplicity and diversity
of perspectives that constitute public life.[73]

In this respect, she argues, the cultivation of enlarged thought 'politically
requires the creation of institutions and practices whereby the voice and
the perspective of others, often unknown to us, can become expressed in
their own right'.[74] The creation and cultivation of a public culture of democratic citizenship that guarantees to everyone the right to opinion and action
is therefore essential to the flourishing of the capacity to articulate and
acknowledge the perspectives of others.

Conclusion

In this chapter I have argued that Arendt's conception of citizenship can be articulated around three major themes, namely, the *public sphere, political agency* and *collective identity*, and *political culture*.

With respect to the first theme, after having analysed Arendt's understanding of the public sphere, I have highlighted three of its major features: its artificial or constructed quality, its spatiality, and the distinction between public and private interests.

With respect to the second theme, I have argued that Arendt's participatory conception of citizenship provides the best starting point for addressing both the question of the constitution of collective identity and that concerning the conditions for the exercise of effective political agency. Drawing on some of the arguments of Pitkin and Habermas, I have shown the connection between the practice of citizenship and the constitution of collective identities. I have then examined Arendt's conception of participatory democracy and stressed the links between active citizenship and effective political agency. I have also argued that Arendt's conception of participatory democracy does not imply value homogeneity or the dedifferentiation of social spheres.

Finally, with respect to the third theme, I have explored the connection between citizenship and political culture, and have argued that the ability of citizens to enlarge their opinions and to test their judgements can only flourish in a public culture of democratic participation that guarantees to everyone the right to action and opinion.

These three themes, I would argue, are highly relevant to the present discussion on the nature and scope of democratic citizenship. The practice of citizenship depends in fact on the reactivation of a public sphere where individuals can act collectively and engage in common deliberation about all matters affecting the political community. Second, the practice of citizenship is essential to the constitution of a public identity based on the values of solidarity, autonomy, and the acknowledgment of difference. Participatory citizenship is also essential to the attainment of effective political agency, since it enables each individual to have some impact on the decisions that affect the well-being of the community. Finally, the practice of democratic citizenship is crucial for the enlargement of political opinion and the testing of one's judgement, and represents in this respect an essential element in the constitution of a vibrant and democratic political culture.

Notes

The following abbreviations will be used:

OT: *The Origins of Totalitarianism*, New York: Harcourt Brace Jovanovich, 1973.
HC: *The Human Condition*, Chicago: The University of Chicago Press, 1958.
BPF: *Between Past and Future*, New York: Viking Press, 1968.

OR: *On Revolution*, New York: Viking Press, 1965.
MDT: *Men in Dark Times*, New York: Harcourt Brace Jovanovich, 1968.
CR: *Crises of the Republic*, New York: Harcourt Brace Jovanovich, 1972.
LM: *The Life of the Mind*, New York: Harcourt Brace Jovanovich, 1978.
RPW: *Hannah Arendt: The Recovery of the Public World*, M.A. Hill (ed.), New York: St. Martin's Press, 1979.

 1 HC, p. 50.
 2 HC, p. 51.
 3 HC, p. 199.
 4 HC, p. 199.
 5 HC, p. 52.
 6 HC, p. 52.
 7 HC, p. 52.
 8 HC, pp. 52–3.
 9 HC, p. 55.
10 HC, p. 135.
11 BPF, p. 95.
12 HC, p. 173.
13 HC, p. 55.
14 M. Canovan, 'Politics as Culture: Hannah Arendt and the Public Realm', *History of Political Thought*, vol. 6, no. 3 (Winter 1985), pp. 617–42.
15 For Arendt's rejection of the concept of human nature, see HC, pp. 10–11.
16 Cf. M. Oakeshott, *Hobbes on Civil Association* (Oxford: Basil Blackwell, 1975), p. 7.
17 See HC, p. 215; OT, p. 234; OR, pp. 30–1.
18 See OT, pp. 290–302, esp. pp. 295–6.
19 See OT, p. 296.
20 Cf. E. Young-Bruehl, *Hannah Arendt: For Love of the World* (New Haven: Yale University Press, 1982), p. xiv; L. Botstein, 'Liberating the Pariah: Politics, The Jews, and Hannah Arendt', *Salmagundi* no. 60 (Spring–Summer 1983), pp. 73–106; F. Feher, 'The Pariah and the Citizen: On Arendt's Political Theory', *Thesis Eleven*, no. 15, 1986, pp. 15–29.
21 Hannah Arendt, *The Jew as Pariah*, R. Feldman (ed.) (New York: Grove Press, 1978).
22 Cf. C. Pateman, *Participation and Democratic Theory* (Cambridge: Cambridge University Press, 1970); *Participation in Politics*, J. R. Pennock and J. W. Chapman (eds) (New York: Atherton, 1975); B. Barber, *Strong Democracy: Participatory Politics for a New Age* (Berkeley: University of California Press, 1984).
23 MDT, p. 13.
24 MDT, p. 16.
25 MDT, p. 25.
26 M. Canovan, 'Politics as Culture: Hannah Arendt and the Public Realm', op. cit., p. 632.
27 See OR, p. 253.
28 Cf. H. Pitkin and S. Shumer, 'On Participation', *Democracy*, vol. 2, no. 4 (Fall 1982), pp. 43–54, esp. pp. 47–8.
29 See OR, pp. 227–8.
30 See BPF, pp. 220–1.
31 OR, p. 227.
32 C. Lasch, 'The Communitarian Critique of Liberalism', *Soundings*, vol. 69, no. 1–2 (Spring–Summer 1986), p. 64.

33 M. Canovan, 'Politics as Culture: Hannah Arendt and the Public Realm', op. cit., p. 634 (emphasis mine).
34 Ibid., p. 635.
35 H. Arendt, 'Freedom and Politics', in *Freedom and Serfdom: An Anthology of Western Thought*, A. Hunold (ed.) (Dordrecht: D. Reidel, 1961), p. 200 (emphasis mine).
36 H. Arendt, 'Public Rights and Private Interests', in *Small Comforts for Hard Times: Humanists on Public Policy*, M. Mooney and F. Stuber (eds) (New York: Columbia University Press, 1977), p. 104.
37 See CR, p. 175.
38 Cf. M. Markus, 'The "Anti-Feminism" of Hannah Arendt', *Thesis Eleven*, no. 17, 1987, pp. 76–87.
39 CR, p. 175.
40 H. Arendt, 'Public Rights and Private Interests', op. cit., p. 105.
41 Ibid., p. 106.
42 H. D. Thoreau, 'On the Duty of Civil Disobedience', quoted in CR, p. 60.
43 CR, pp. 60–1.
44 CR, p. 64.
45 Arendt believed that the morality of conscience was too private and subjective to serve as a valid standard for political action. In place of conscience she advocated the political principle of active citizenship.
46 RPW, p. 311.
47 H. Arendt, 'Thinking and Moral Considerations: A Lecture', *Social Research*, vol. 51, no. 1 (Spring 1984), pp. 7–37; LM, *Thinking*, pp. 190–3.
48 LM, *Thinking*, p. 191.
49 CR, p. 62.
50 Canovan argues that for Arendt the important difference was between 'living as a private individual with a conscience, and living together with others in a public world for which all are jointly responsible' ('Politics as Culture: Hannah Arendt and the Public Realm', op. cit., p. 639).
51 H. Pitkin, *Wittgenstein and Justice* (Berkeley: University of California Press, 1972), p. 208.
52 Ibid.
53 J. Habermas, 'On Social Identity', *Telos*, no. 19 (Spring 1974), p. 102.
54 Cf. C. Mouffe, 'Rawls: Political Philosophy without Politics', *Philosophy and Social Criticism*, vol. 13, no. 2 (Summer 1988), pp. 105–23, esp. pp. 116–17.
55 Nancy Fraser, 'Toward a Discourse Ethic of Solidarity', *Praxis International*, vol. 5, no. 4 (January 1986), p. 428.
56 Ibid.
57 Ibid.
58 Ibid.
59 Ibid., pp. 428–9 (last emphasis mine).
60 N. Fraser, 'Toward a Discourse Ethic of Solidarity', op. cit., p. 429 (emphasis mine).
61 For a discussion of Arendt's attitude to the questions raised by the women's movement, see M. Markus, 'The "Anti-Feminism" of Hannah Arendt', op. cit.
62 OR, p. 254 (emphases mine).
63 OR, pp. 237–8.
64 H. Pitkin and S. Shumer, 'On Participation', op. cit., p. 52 (emphasis mine).
65 S. Evans and H. Boyte, *Free Spaces: The Sources of Democratic Change in America* (New York: Harper & Row, 1986), p. 17 (emphasis mine).
66 S. Benhabib, 'Autonomy, Modernity, and Community: Communitarianism and Critical Social Theory in Dialogue', in A. Honneth, T. McCarthy, C. Offe and A.

Wellmer (eds), *Zwischenbetrachtungen im Prozess der Aufklärung* (Frankfurt: Suhrkamp, 1989), p. 389.
67 OR, p. 255.
68 'The Crisis in Culture' and 'Truth and Politics', in BPF, pp. 197–226, pp. 227–64.
69 OR, p. 227.
70 BPF, p. 241.
71 H. Arendt, 'Thinking and Moral Considerations', op. cit., p. 36.
72 BPF, pp. 220–1.
73 S. Benhabib, 'Judgment and the Moral Foundations of Politics in Arendt's Thought', *Political Theory*, vol. 16, no. 1 (February 1988), pp. 47–8.
74 Ibid., p. 47.

Part 2

Legal perspectives

6 The civility of law: between public and private[1]

Christine Sypnowich

In 1929 Virginia Woolf coined the powerful phrase 'a room of one's own' to argue that women, like men, are entitled to a sphere to develop their capacities and pursue their goals.[2] In so doing, she drew on an idea fundamental to the modern age: privacy. The idea that the individual is entitled to a private domain, immune from interference, pervades the politics, economics and culture of modernity. Its importance for modern individuals is such that our living space is configured with several senses of privacy in mind: the locked door of the bathroom behind which one attends to the body; the study, sometimes called the 'den' to which one retreats for solitary contemplation, or the ideal of one bedroom per child to encourage children to develop into autonomous selves. Privacy is perhaps one of the first abstract concepts that children learn, and a child's interest in it is usually commended as a sign of maturity. We assume we will have opportunities for privacy in everyday life, and the invasion of privacy is a horror that we trust we will seldom encounter.

The political institutions with which we protect privacy, such as individual rights and the rule of law, are of recent vintage, however. They are complex and fragile. This is particularly the case in the face of developments in contemporary political theory which challenge the conception of a divide between the public and the private. In this chapter I examine the idea of privacy and how it is attacked on putatively progressive grounds. I note that there are certain respects in which the private must be intruded upon for social justice to be achieved. I take issue, however, with ideas such as an 'ethic of care' and the 'politics of recognition' which threaten to collapse the divide between public and private in their insistence that personal relations be the model for political life. I argue that we should understand legal institutions as deploying an 'ethic of civility' that respects a distinction between the private and the public, a distinction upon which the pursuit of justice depends.

The institutions of privacy

In his book on the family, *Centuries of Childhood*, the French historian Philippe Ariès gives a fascinating account of everyday life in pre-modern times, when even the layout of the family house attested to the diluted sense of the private. He reports that the bedroom did not exist as a separate chamber until the eighteenth century; individuals were seldom allowed the luxury of retreating from family life, and the family, in turn, was submerged in the community, its festivals, codes and relations.[3] Whilst privacy concerns the intimate and the personal, it requires a reconfiguring of the public realm for it to exist. It is thus, perhaps paradoxically, a political value, and as such emerged in the modern era with liberalism and its emphasis on individual freedom. Privacy is also an economic value, and the capitalist economies that have accompanied liberal political orders employ the private in two ways: first, with the idea of 'laissez-faire' and the requirement that the state not intrude on self-interested market activities; and second, with the idea of the consumer, an 'ordinary person' with a private domain to furnish and enjoy. With modernity, then, the conception of the private individual emerged, a conception that was clearly a social artifact, the product of shifting relations among people, and enforced by societal rules and structures.

Why do we value privacy?

This question might be best addressed by considering some examples.

The Neys family go on a camping holiday in the woods of northern Ontario. Determined to get the most secluded spot in the campground, they rise before dawn to beat the other campers, and upon arrival tour the park, depositing a child plus sleeping bag to reserve choice sites before making their final selection.

Jill comes home to find the police investigating a break-in. The burglar was frightened away by a barking dog, so nothing was taken. Nonetheless, Jill is upset, both fearful and depressed, for several days.

Mary is wearing a dress her colleague Eleanor much admires, but Eleanor refrains from making a compliment, deciding that such a remark, however positive, is too personal.

Patrick, who is heterosexual, accompanies his homosexual brother to a gay bar. While there he sights Francis, a neighbour with whom he is on friendly terms. Patrick decides, however, that the considerate thing to do is to pretend he does not see Francis.

Jacob is annoyed with the naughty behaviour of his young son, Michael, whilst they travel on a city bus. Feeling awkward about a public rebuke, however, Jacob decides – for both their sakes – to scold Michael when they get home.

Peter, a cigarette-smoker, is enraged by a law requiring that tobacco companies print health warnings on cigarette packages. He decides to remove this intrusion into his personal affairs by keeping cigarettes in his own containers.

Karma discovers that from the desk in her study she looks right into the newly built shower of her neighbour, Mr. Brown. Karma is in a quandary. She is offended by the recurring view of Mr. Brown's ablutions, but she fears embarrassing or offending him in turn if she raises the issue.

These examples all involve the idea of protecting privacy. The holidaying family, the break-in victim, the solicitous colleague, the heterosexual neighbour, the chastising father, the beleaguered smoker and the offended scholar, all seek to avoid either involving themselves in others' affairs, or having others involved in their own. But there is much that is different from one case to the next. In some cases the involvement in question is a minimal matter of not being observed. This is at issue in the Neys family's efforts to find a secluded camp-site, and in Jacob's wariness about scolding in public. Privacy in the sense of not disclosing oneself can shade into the idea of restricting others' knowledge about oneself, preventing others from acquiring or seeking personal information.[4] Not wanting strangers to know about one's personal affairs is at issue in Jill's feeling of invasion after an attempted burglary. One also respects another's privacy when, having inadvertently obtained a view or some knowledge, one seeks to avoid drawing attention to it, as in the case of Patrick and his gay neighbour. In the case of the Neys family, should they turn out to be in view of other campers, it would be especially important for their privacy that their neighbours not watch them in an obvious way. It is not only the disclosing of oneself which is at issue; in the case of Karma, her view of her neighbour constituted an invasion of her own privacy. (Mr. Brown's privacy is being infringed, too, of course; indeed, that Karma cannot help but infringe it makes the situation especially intolerable for her.)

The examples point to a second sense of privacy, which goes beyond knowing about someone's personal affairs to taking an active, or meddling, interest in them, in a way that threatens the individual's independence. Eleanor, the solicitous colleague, is concerned that she keep her opinions to herself, since volunteering them would be presuming an intimacy with Mary that does not obtain. Jacob is perhaps worried that onlookers would meddle should he rebuke his son in public. Patrick might fear that Francis would find any greeting in the gay bar, however solicitous, to be interfering with his private life. The preoccupations of the Neys family could be connected with this second sense of privacy (suppose they are 'hippies' who want to ward off public disapproval). Jill is perhaps haunted by the possibility that the burglar snooped amongst her most intimate possessions in a way that might inhibit her enjoyment of private pursuits.[5] Karma's case illustrates the fragility of one's sense of independence. To use a contemporary turn of phrase, she feels her 'space' is invaded, even if the 'invader' is unaware that his actions affect anyone else. Finally, Peter's case against the cigarette law is squarely based on a defence of his independence.

Of course, respect for privacy is based on more than our interests in controlling visual access or knowledge about oneself, or the broader idea of being independent of others.[6] Our interest in privacy after all overlaps with a diversity of interests, such as an interest in liberty, property, security of person, or our interest in avoiding a cluster of harms such as humiliation, distress or embarrassment. Given privacy's entanglement with other values, it is understandable that some philosophers, such as Judith Jarvis Thomson, have balked at the idea of a right to privacy, arguing that any such right really is a group of rights of other kinds, such as the right to property.[7] Nonetheless, that privacy is a distinctive value is not thereby disproven; rather, the difficulties of privacy perhaps serve only to illustrate the salutary common sense that not all we value can be formulated in terms of rights. Invasions of privacy might not violate anything as robust as a 'right to privacy'. But if privacy cannot always be coherently conceptualised as a right, this probably means that its violation as a right is simply the limiting case of a general value that can be abridged in minor as well as major ways.[8] And where other rights are at issue, their importance often rests on their role in protecting privacy. I might shout, 'this is private property!' to someone taking a short-cut across my garden, but my concern will likely be for the private, not the property.

That 'private property, no trespassing' comes to mind in discussions of privacy might help us to zero in on the meaning and value of privacy, even if we are sceptical that it can be fully captured by rights-talk such as property rights. Privacy often suggests the idea of boundaries not to be crossed, exemplified by Virginia Woolf's room of her own. The question of the integrity of a personal domain is explicit in the campground and break-in examples. Of course, as some of our examples show, invasions of privacy can refer to more intangible boundary-crossings such as the making of certain remarks, exhibitionism or displays. But crossing a boundary of some kind still seems pertinent, even if we need to conceive it abstractly. Thomas Scanlon claims that privacy is a 'zone' or 'territory' which can be 'invaded' not only when one's property is stolen but also when one's personal effects are viewed or when intrusive personal remarks are uttered.[9] This spatial sense to privacy is invoked in much of our language about social relations. Indeed, as we saw earlier, the word 'space' pervades common parlance about privacy. Consider too, that someone with whom we share the private is 'close' to us; a relation we do not know well is 'distant'; an acquaintance who presumes intimacy is called 'forward'; some meetings are referred to as 'behind closed doors'.

Privacy and the state

Our conceptions of society, government and the economy also invoke the idea of boundaries and territory, public and private sectors, open societies and private persons. The remark of Pierre Trudeau, as Canada's Justice

Minister in 1967, that 'the state has no place in the bedrooms of the nation', captured an essential idea: certain aspects of life are the prerogative of the individual and should be safe from political interference.[10] The bedroom has come to symbolise the quintessentially private, an exclusive domain sheltered from social and political purview. Trudeau's remark affirms that there is no public interest at issue in the matter of sexual relations between consenting adults, and, therefore, if public institutions are to play any role at all, it is to safeguard the private from public surveillance or intervention. The private stands as a domain that, assuming the absence of politically defined harms, has no relevance to the state or one's fellow citizens. This idea of irrelevance can also shade into a sense of the offensiveness of disclosure. Thus individuals, in turn, have an obligation to keep some aspects of their lives private, borne out by our example of the unwanted view of the showering neighbour. Couching this in terms of an individual's obligation to maintain his or her privacy would be misleading, since the obligation is in essence about respecting the privacy of others. That is, it is out of respect for my privacy that I ask you not to conduct an orgy in the park, however willing you are to forfeit your own privacy.

There is also a more positive argument to be made on behalf of privacy than the idea of 'none of your/my business'. Privacy also involves a recognising of the great relevance for the individual of his or her unimpeded sphere of action. Mill invoked the wrong of interference, and the irrelevance for others of most people's actions, but he also provided an argument about the positive good of individuals developing themselves without impediment, first, because it contributes to their happiness, and second, because it contributes to their betterment, and thus, if only by example, to the betterment of others. Human progress, he argued, stands to gain from radical 'experiments in living', if the experiments and experimenters are left alone.[11] A domain of privacy is a constituent of freedom, a condition for different kinds of social relationships,[12] and it is because we value it that we might opt for institutions like individual ownership of property.

The institutions for respecting privacy are, of course, varied. There is a plethora of privacy-respecting cultural practices, such as knocking on a closed door; avoiding inquiries about sensitive topics; even (a perverse one, in some people's minds) refraining from looking over the shoulder of strangers to read their newspapers. Again, they involve a sense of boundaries that ought not to be crossed. The divide between public and private is manifest in the fact that whilst peering through a shop window is encouraged, peering through the window of someone's residence is a ground for prosecution.

Of course, maintaining one's privacy in the face of nosy neighbours is of a different order from protecting a private domain from the intrusions of the state. In a liberal democratic society the former is a more frequent concern, but the latter a more important one. Because the state by definition enjoys sovereignty over its citizens, and thus possesses a monopoly of putatively legitimate coercion, the state's invasions of privacy are potentially very harmful to those concerned. There are a number of ways in which the state's power is checked for the sake of individuals' privacy. Property rights, whilst usually conceived in terms of market exchanges and the accumulation of capital, also refer to the more mundane but highly prized personal property which the state cannot invade or appropriate except under very special circumstances. Rights to freedom of conscience, opinion, association and expression involve respect for the citizen's privacy from the state. Legal rights that protect the individual from arbitrary arrest, lack of legal counsel, or an unfair trial, also provide the means for precisely demarcating the private realm from the public. These rights can be spelled out in constitutions or statutes or embedded in common law, or assured by some combination of the three.

For legal institutions to protect privacy, they must embody the ideal of the rule of law.[13] At its most basic, the rule of law refers to the idea that law should meet certain procedural requirements so that the individual is enabled to obey it. The requirements of the rule of law are first, that law be general. Law must take the form of rules that are by definition directed to more than a particular situation or individual. The rule of law also requires that law be certain, clearly expressed, open, and adequately publicised. A legal system should also be internally consistent, so that particular laws do not conflict with each other. In addition, law must be prospective, directed only at behaviour which takes place after it is enacted; retroactive law, which prosecutes for actions taken before the law was made, prevents people from taking the requirements of the law into account when planning their affairs. The practical effect of these principles is to set limits to the discretion of legislators, administrators, judges and the police. The rule of law ensures that these different agencies of governance are kept separate, so that political interference in legal affairs, for example, and the arbitrary power which is its result, are impermissible. The rule of law also aims to regulate internally the sphere of action of each of these functions of government. Detention without charge, arbitrary decrees, conviction without sufficient evidence, unduly harsh punishment: all would constitute violations of the standards of consistency and coherence integral to a system of law.

Law and legal conduct that failed to meet the standards of the rule of law would fail in their very function as constituents of a code of behaviour that individuals can consult when deciding how to act. Since the rule of law ensures that law's intrusions on the private should not be arbitrary or unpredictable, we need to know where the boundary between public and private is drawn in order for our privacy to be protected; it is thus essential that the actions of public officials are regulated so that the public–private distinction is a reliable one.

For John Locke, one of the first exponents of the rule of law, the chief advantage of civil society over the state of nature is the assurance of 'established, settled, known law', applied by a judge who is both 'known and indifferent', who does not produce judgments that are 'varied in particular cases, but to have one rule for rich and poor, for the favourite at court, and the country man at plough'. The impersonal tenor of Locke's ideal persists in what is probably the most pervasive image of justice, that of a blindfolded woman weighing scales, as though it is the scales, rather than the woman, who renders judicial decisions.[14] In fact, of course, the law is drafted, and subsequently applied, by people. It is as people, with particular interests, needs and aims, that we are motivated by the rule of law and its dictates. It is nonetheless also true that the rule of law aims to rein in or check human foibles in the administration of justice. The rule of law seeks to render the law impartial, abstract, neutral, general, universal – all of these words indicating something of the transcendent, even if it is a procedural rather than substantive set of standards which would transcend the hurly-burly of human affairs. The personal, the domain of privacy, thus seems to depend on a legal order set, in some sense, above everyday persons.

The connection between the rule of law and privacy might seem historical, rather than logical or conceptual. Consider the idea of a society that has the rule of law but also has a diminished sense of privacy. One can imagine a radically communal society, characterised by nudism and California-style open therapy, and eschewing private residences or closed doors. There seems no reason to suppose that such a society could not also be characterised by strict observance of the procedural requirements of the rule of law. The rule of law does not demand privacy. What of the converse: does privacy require the rule of law? We might be able to conceive of a society where privacy is respected but the rule of law is not. In such a society, however, privacy would in fact be vulnerable. Right-wing dictatorships or racist regimes with market economics, for example, have a model of privacy in place, but it is unevenly assured. Indeed, we might suspect that the rule of law is inadequately instantiated precisely in order to invade the privacy of certain people: so-called subversives or sub-citizens. In apartheid South Africa, the absence of procedural justice as embodied in the pass laws, intrusive surveillance and political trials, for example, deprived certain categories of South Africans the enjoyment of privacy.[15] And in Pinochet's Chile, privacy was an uncertain value for opponents of the regime who risked being searched, seized and arrested without the benefit of due process. On the basis of these considerations I submit a more radical conceptual claim, that in a society where public power is unconstrained by the rule of law, privacy is insecure.

It would be an overstatement to say that there would be no privacy without the rule of law; after all, just as a matter of practicality, seclusion cannot be entirely obliterated even in putatively 'totalitarian' societies. In fact, people probably retreat into the private all the more in a society characterised by procedural injustice. Consider the symbolic importance of gathering in the kitchen, 'na kukhne', for political conversation in Soviet Russia, even though Russians were acutely aware that surveillance could intrude the home (it was a common belief, no doubt erroneous, that all telephones were bugged).[16] Nonetheless, insofar as privacy is particularly significant as a zone of non-interference from the state, it is incontrovertible that the rule of law is essential for such privacy.

The private is political: privacy and equality

Thus far we have presented privacy, and its ally, the rule of law, as unequivocally valuable. But there have been many criticisms of both. Egalitarians in particular attack the public–private divide, regulated by the rule of law, that characterises modern liberal societies and the normative theories of liberalism. The idea that equality is in some sense in tension with privacy is a disturbing possibility. I will thus consider how an egalitarian position raises some important considerations about how we conceive of privacy, concluding, however, that privacy *per se* is rarely what is in fact at issue in many radical arguments, and that on those few occasions where it is, the critique is unpersuasive.

Is the idea of privacy in tension with the pursuit of equality? Certainly if intrinsic to the idea of privacy is an unqualified title to private property, immune to interference, then the conflict with egalitarian arrangements that seek to redistribute wealth is obvious. Historically the idea of personal freedom has been couched in terms of implying a right to the accumulation of private property. And we have noted that a claim to property and a claim to privacy may in certain cases overlap. But the connection is not a necessary one. Whilst some idea of a personal domain is essential for privacy to be respected, such a domain need not be owned. A peeping Tom invades the privacy of a guest or housesitter as much as that of the owner or tenant. As Scanlon argues against Thomson's property-based view, 'ownership is relevant in determining the boundaries of our zone of privacy, but its relevance is determined by norms whose basis lies in our interest in privacy, not in the notion of ownership.'[17]

Although ownership *per se* is not essential to privacy, titles to property are a way of expressing the claim to privacy. Private property is an important means of constituting the inviolable zone or territory that attaches to the person whose privacy is at stake. We might elect to protect privacy by means of private property, not just in the form of personal effects, but also, perhaps, a place of residence. It is interesting that the privacy argument for private property is in fact seldom made; most defences of private property derive their arguments from the idea of freedom to accumulate wealth, or the efficiencies of a market system. I would suggest, too, that the privacy argument is unique in its compatibility with serious restrictions on the extent of ownership. The role of personal property in protecting privacy does not mean we need be cowed by large property claims. Such claims, that is, claims to capital, returns on investment, income, and so forth, are not necessary to secure privacy, nor are they even rightly characterised as private.

Indeed, what distinguishes these larger forms of property is their public nature, in the way they are produced and exchanged, and in the interests they affect. It is too much a concession to inequality for socialists to accept the idea of some inevitable affinity between privacy and a laissez-faire economy. The links between privacy and the inequalities of private property are historical, not conceptual. There is thus no contradiction between respecting individuals' privacy whilst redistributing wealth to further equality (though there may be practical matters about redistribution that involve tampering with the private). Indeed, wealth might be redistributed to further equality of privacy. Given the importance of privacy for individuals' well-being, egalitarians should avoid latching on to right-wing views about the erosion of privacy in an equal society.

Egalitarians make another objection to the idea of privacy that follows, indirectly, from their concerns about property. The objection centres on the type of culture that obtains where privacy is valued and rule of law is deployed to protect it. On this view, privacy and the rule of law are the trappings of a defective society, a society characterised by unjust property relations. In such a society, it is argued, privacy and the rule of law contribute to a culture characterised at best by anonymity and at worst by selfishness. Where we govern our relations with each other by the criteria of a proceduralist ethics, careful to respect the boundaries of each individual's personal domain, we will have forfeited the more rewarding bonds of community, solidarity and spontaneous fellow-feeling. Moreover, the causal relation might go the other way around: in the absence of community, people might desire privacy as an escape, seeking, as Christopher Lasch said of the family, a 'haven in a heartless world'.[18] This might be dubbed the 'utopia' objection. It has its roots in classical socialist writings that envision a society that, in abolishing private property, has removed the obstacles to true community.

Even if one aspires to a society defined by equality and community, however, one would still need the certainty and predictability of the rule of law if only to mediate, with fairness and respect, precisely these egalitarian and communitarian arrangements. As for the idea of transcending privacy, I think our discussion of the value of this idea gives grounds for believing that a society which has forfeited privacy might also have forfeited its claim to being a utopia. On this point the privacy-seekers of apartheid South Africa and Pinochet's Chile, however much they looked forward to an egalitarian society, would have agreed.

To the extent that the egalitarian's suspicion of privacy and the rule of law is, if not warranted, historically understandable, it would follow that there is a special need for establishing such institutions in an egalitarian society. If a society, in its institutions, practices and culture, endeavours to secure material equality and substantive justice, it will particularly need to attend to the rule of law to ensure that it does not run afoul of the demands of regularity and proceduralism which render a legal system fair and just in a minimal but important sense. Similarly, if socialism is a society that aspires to greater fellow-feeling, community and a sense of the common good, then it will also need to be vigilant that these ideals do not displace the idea that individuals are entitled to a personal domain, immune to interference.

The personal is political: privacy and difference

So far the egalitarian objection has been cast in the traditional terrain of property, social class and distributive justice. But it may be that the greatest challenge to the idea of privacy comes, not from socialists, but from advocates on behalf of women, racial or cultural minorities, whose claims have taken the centre of the egalitarian stage in recent debates. There is some overlap with the socialist arguments; these critics, too, point to the injustice that is hidden within the putatively private. To that extent, some of the same counter-arguments apply about privacy's value. To recall Woolf, the case for equality between the sexes involves an affirmation of the idea of privacy as something important for both men and women. Cultural minorities may be appealing for the right to practise traditions and customs in a personal domain without prejudicing their options in the domain of the public. Here, too, their claims can be put in terms of an extension of the idea of privacy, rather than a repudiation of it.

There are difficulties, however. The socialist case can be put in terms of reducing the ambit of the private to meet the demands of redistribution, without jeopardising altogether the idea of a personal domain; the market is thus a quasi-public sphere with unjust power relations, yet the idea of a personal domain, a sphere beyond the market, remains. But feminists after Woolf have presented a different kind of case, one that targets the idea of the personal itself. The slogan 'the personal is political' evokes the idea that it is the most intimate of settings that are riddled with injustice, and thus that egalitarians ought to probe and reconstitute such settings. Accordingly, feminists have often lambasted the 'public–private distinction' for turning a blind eye – the blindfolded eye of unsisterly justice, perhaps? – to the oppression of the traditional family. As Carole Pateman puts it:

> The fundamental assumption is that the patriarchal separation of the private/natural sphere from the public/civil realm is irrelevant to political life. . . . A (house)wife remains in the private domestic sphere, but the unequal relations of domestic life are 'naturally so' and thus do not detract from the universal equality of the public world.[19]

Is the idea of privacy thereby impugned as in some sense irredeemably sexist? Pateman suggests this when she speaks of the separation of private and public as 'an ideological mystification of liberal–patriarchal reality'.[20] It may nonetheless be possible to tackle the injustices of the personal whilst affirming the liberal value of privacy. Indeed, Will Kymlicka has argued that there is a conceptual confusion at work in the feminist scorn for the divide between the public and the private. The contempt is well placed if it is directed at a view that there should be no public scrutiny of harms practised in the private. But to enjoy privacy does not mean being immune from public regulation; most murders are committed 'in private', after all. Again, the historical link between two senses of private should not lead us to believe that there must be a conceptual link. There is certainly a historical connection between the idea of privacy and the idea that husbands enjoy a prerogative over wives. But the patriarchal concept of the private as a domain of natural authority, immune to political scrutiny, can be given up without abandoning a concept of the private as a sphere of freedom important to all individuals, men and women.[21] Indeed, the Western family has historically evolved from the patriarchal version to the other, egalitarian one. Instead of 'a head with more or less personally integral appendages, like arms and legs', the family is now conceived as an 'association of mutually dependent persons having a special kind of involvement with each other', an involvement which admits of limits so that family members can each have concerns that are private in respect to other members.[22]

Recent variants of feminism have taken another tack against the public–private distinction to challenge the integrity of the divide between the two domains. Here the move reverses the previous one. Instead of the private being brought under the jurisdiction of the public, it is now suggested that the public ought to be oriented by the values of the private. This is in essence the position of the 'ethic of care', where it is argued that the proceduralism of the public is a traditionally masculine orientation that ought to be comple- mented by a feminine orientation of affective nurture and concern. The argu- ment might be interpreted as a call to give public recognition to a beleaguered female perspective, without necessarily attending to the content of that perspective. The ethic of care is identified as the morality of the private, and insofar as women have historically been relegated to the private, to care of loved ones in the home, then it is also (perhaps contingently) a feminine ethic. 'It's the girls' turn', the argument might go, an instance of what Foucault called the 'insurrection of subjugated knowledges' whose claim lies simply in the fact of their subjugation.[23]

The argument also concerns the substance of this ethic, however, the idea being that what Carol Gilligan called 'a different voice' has special virtues. According to Gilligan, women have a psychological history different from men's that produces 'a different sense of experience'.

> Since the reality of connection is experienced by women as given rather than freely contracted, they arrive at an understanding of life that reflects the limits of autonomy and control. As a result, women's development delineates the path not only to a less violent life but also to a maturity realised through interdependence and taking care. . . . While an ethic of justice proceeds from the premise of equality – that everyone should be

treated the same – an ethic of care rests on the premise of nonviolence – that no one should be hurt.[24]

This voice attends to the particular, perceives the connectedness of human beings with each other, takes a posture of care and nurture, and is concerned about outcomes: at odds with the rule-bound, formalistic procedures of impartial justice. The idea of a distinctive female voice of care is akin to the idea of 'maternal thinking' developed by Sara Ruddick, which she offers as a feature of women's 'cultures, traditions, and inquiries which we should insist upon bringing to the public world'.[25] The ethic of care, it is argued, will better meet people's needs, and it will also foster a community of fellow-feeling, sympathy and mutual regard which the rule of law, in its impersonal, abstract approach, cannot supply. The ethic of care thus invokes some of the socialist ideas about a society of fellowship and community, beyond justice. This ideal is connected to the hostility to legalism, since it involves a notion of sympathetic and sociable persons who relate to each other transparently, unmediated by political and legal institutions, unbounded by impersonal rules. Indeed, some feminist legal theorists have sought to revise concepts of law in light of this anti-legalism. Jennifer Nedelsky, for example, has argued that we 'reconceive rights as relationship' to better reflect 'the ways in which our essential humanity is neither possible nor comprehensible without the network of relationships of which it is part'.[26]

The case is further supported by arguments made on behalf of 'difference' more generally. These arguments point to the disadvantaged position of members of minority groups of a variety of kinds, ranging from race, sexual orientation, ethnicity, or disability, to repudiate both privacy and proceduralism. Iris Marion Young, the most prominent exponent of this view, targets the 'civil public' which 'expresses the universal and impartial point of view of reason, standing opposed to and expelling desire, sentiment, and the particularity of needs and interests'.[27] The ideal of privacy, it is charged, relegates certain minority interests and concerns to the non-public, and law's role in regulating the private undermines its claim to universalism and generality. To counter such traditional approaches, Young counsels that we deny 'a social division between public and private spheres, each with different kinds of institutions, activities and human attributes'. Two principles are adduced. First, that 'no persons, actions or aspects of a person's life should be forced into privacy', and second, that 'no social institutions or practices should be excluded a priori from being a proper subject for public discussion and expression'.[28] The import of these critiques, I think, is to challenge the very idea of a private domain. They suggest that the political be structured and modelled on the personal, and that the personal in its essence resists the procedural. Thus both the idea of privacy and the institutions of procedural justice are under attack.

In what follows I will defend both. My defence will have three parts. First, I will consider the complexities of two examples of difference to suggest that privacy is in fact essential to the demands of minority groups. Second, I will note the special vulnerabilities that disclosure of the private can present. Finally, I will offer a more nuanced characterisation of the ideas of privacy and the rule of law which draws upon the idea of civility.

A Room of One's Own

What is at issue in 'opening up privacy' for members of minority groups in liberal society? There is a plethora of examples to draw on, but let's consider two, paradigmatic ones: persons of non-Christian religious faith and persons of a homosexual orientation. First, non-Christian religious observances are typically not accommodated in workplaces and public institutions. The work-week and shopping hours have been organised around the Christian calendar, and non-Christian ceremonial dress is often precluded by dress codes and uniforms. Second, homosexual relationships are typically discriminated against in the customs and laws guiding sexual unions, in access to professions such as teaching, and in public culture and social life more generally. These two cases, whilst quite different from each other, suffer a common fate as 'the different': their practices are relegated to the private; as a result, gays and non-Christians are not only denied social resources but are rendered invisible and illegitimate. Young's charge that the problem is difficult to perceive in the liberal order characterised by privacy and proceduralism thus demands to be taken seriously.

However, it may be that these cases indicate not that we should abandon privacy or proceduralism but that we should apply these ideals more consistently, so that the divide between public and private does not carve up society in ways that are prejudicial to members of minority groups. Our historical–conceptual distinction is again useful. For there is again an obvious historical link between such prejudicial divisions and the very concepts of public and private, but no necessary conceptual one. Indeed, the history is now being remade to achieve a consistent application of the concept. As Kymlicka notes, judicial decisions have ordered that workplaces accommodate religious minorities, finding that uniforms whose design posed no difficulty for Christian beliefs should simply be adjusted for the private beliefs of other religions.[29] The case of religious observances should be understood not in terms of exposing or incorporating the private but in terms of protecting and accommodating it. No Canadian Muslim is calling for Ramadam to be a state holiday, nor do Jews want all shops closed on Saturdays; rather, they seek to be able to enjoy their holidays without enduring costs that members of the majority do not.

Analogously, gay rights movements have devoted their energies, with some success, to securing the same public recognition of their relationships as are enjoyed by heterosexuals, with an appeal to the idea that the precise character of private attachments is irrelevant to the state. Homosexuals still face enormous prejudice at the social level, so that, for example, public displays of affection remain risky. Young is right to stress the neglected realm of culture here. But at issue is that the ideas of public and private should be applied to homosexuals as it is to members of the majority sexual orientation: gays, too, should be free, not only to enjoy a domain of privacy, but also to hold hands, kiss goodbye and so forth when in view of others. If we are to go beyond tolerance to acceptance, then the ideas of public and private are essential as constituents of human well-being whatever one's sexual orientation.

More problematic is the claim that homosexual sex reconfigures the public, so that public displays of not just affection but sexual activity ought to be permitted. 'Queer politics' thus suggests a bigger challenge to the idea of the private. Even here, though, the challenge is not to all facets of the private – even the most exhibitionist among us would not welcome state officials arriving without notice at one's home. Moreover, it is, after all, a challenge issued not by all homosexuals, nor is it restricted to them, since there are heterosexuals who also favour such ideas. At this point our culture is opposed to such displays for the reasons we noted at the outset of our discussion, for reasons of others' privacy. It may be that, like Victorian bathing costumes, our views about what is 'decent' for public display will one day be revised. But for now we should not be side-tracked by a subversive sexual taste to abandon the public–private distinction that is for most people crucial to their personal freedom.

Being a member of a minority group might be in some sense an inevitable disadvantage for which one can never be fully compensated; there are, as John Rawls says, 'sociological facts of the matter' which dictate that some ways of life will be more subscribed to than others.[30] And, like partakers of a variety of minority views, cultural minorities may have to resign themselves to their sociological fate, at some level, so long as they do not suffer bigotry or persecution.[31]

A second consideration is the special vulnerabilities that disclosure of the private can present. There is a cultural lag on such issues as ethnicity, race and sexual orientation, so that despite legal advances members of minority groups still face bigotry or violence. Members of minority groups may have much to lose by the revelations that Young proposes. Indeed, Young's remarks remind one, doubtless contrary to her intentions, of the controversial cases of non-consensual 'outing' of gays. Of course, Young's object is precisely the cultural oppression that stops members of minority groups from being open about their beliefs and practices, and she is right to underscore our collective responsibility to remedy such oppression. But it is no solution to the discrimination of the public domain to whittle away the protection of the private. However much we progress in fostering a public culture of openness in Western liberal societies, we must understand that whether or not one discloses publicly one's sexual orientation or religious beliefs will ultimately be a matter of personal choice. It is not for political theorists to decide whether life in the closet should be up for 'discussion'.

Erving Goffman's work underscores the risk we all feel, however subtly, in the public domain, our vigilance in warding off danger, however minor, in our encounters with others. In a sense, it is intrinsic to society that the public is not characterised by loving care. This is not because the public is a Hobbesian world devoid of consideration for others, but because it is consideration of a distanced kind, based on the 'intricacies of mutual trust presupposed in public order'. In public we seek to preserve the integrity of what Goffman calls a personal 'surround'; something that is threatened not just by the pickpocket or flasher, but also by the overly solicitous or familiar.[32] Care is inappropriate in this domain because it lacks the background conditions of intimacy and knowledge of the other. We lack, that is, the depth of feeling for strangers that care requires, and we are too unacquainted with each other to know what care would consist of. Moreover, in a society of inequality and discrimination, care may be an unlikely prospect. In Ibsen's famous play, lacking 'a room of her own', Dora flees the 'Doll's House' precisely to be rid of the suffocating, ill-judged care of her patronising husband. Care is of no help here; indeed, it is too implicated in conditions of oppression. Even were we to greatly diminish inegalitarian attitudes, there would still be conflicts of interest that render care difficult to muster in matters of public concern. Moreover, if we take seriously the Marxist insight about the structural conflicts of interest between people with different material positions, then care in the abstract looks idealistic indeed. In such a context, to contend, as does Nedelsky, that legal institutions such as rights somehow be the expression of care and relationship, risks a naïve understanding of the nature of the public domain.

Civility and the rule of law

Of course, a society where people are wholly indifferent to each other's needs or interests would be difficult to characterise as a society at all. So, whilst I have argued against importing dimensions of the private into the public, this does not mean that the ethical relations of the private have no instantiation whatever in the public. Some kind of regard for our fellow-citizens is essential not just for public order but also for justice, equality and the very protection of the private itself. The kind of regard I have in mind is civility.

Civility is an interesting word. Its root is the Latin word for city, and thus, as one historian of etiquette notes, it represented the reverse of 'crude country behaviour'.[33] Its source in the city also underscores that it only comes to have relevance in a setting where relations are more impersonal, where we encounter people who are neither friend nor foe. 'Neighbourliness' is the spirit of civility, and the slogan 'good fences make good neighbours' is particularly apt, since civility rests on demarcating the private spaces of individuals, rather than overcoming them. Civility is thus at issue precisely in the impersonal yet nonetheless social relations of citizens. The community to which the civil citizen belongs is clearly a modern one, its relations looser than those of the classical model of the ancient Greek polis.[34] Civility is the form of care appropriate for public life, distinct from the care of the intimate or private realm. Indeed, the care to which civility refers is perhaps best understood in the more muted sense of regard.

The idea that the civil is demarcated from the uncouth or savage is explicitly deployed in early liberal theories. Hobbes and Locke invoke 'civil society' as the polity that emerges once a more primitive state of nature has been forsworn. Rousseau's idea of 'civic virtue' involved over-throwing that civil society for a more ambitious political community. Hegel, another communitarian, reinstates civil society as the social realm between family and state; it is structured largely by market activity but also by a variety of voluntary associations of various kinds, and imbued with a moral consciousness more impersonal than that of the family. Hegel, of course, contrasted the ethical life of civil society with the superior morality of the state.[35] But he also noted the importance of the former in fostering the latter; civic virtue is thus initiated, if not fulfilled, in civil society.

In civil society one engages with others in a spirit of reciprocity and fair dealings. One shows not love or even respect, attitudes appropriate for those with whom one has some bond, be they family or friends, nation or state. Instead, the civil citizen shows consideration for others. Civic virtue encompasses a deeper commitment owed to one's community or nation, but civility is an important facet of it. It is the foundation for just dealings among citizens. As Leslie Green has argued, civility is a basic civic virtue, lesser in importance than the virtue of obedience, but easier to justify and defend, since it retains the sense of independent judgement about state insti-tutions, whilst recognising state authority.[36] It is so pervasive as to be almost invisible, perhaps an unacknowledged condition of such liberal virtues as tolerance, fairness, openness and lawfulness.[37]

Mark Kingwell has made an important argument for civility in politics. Kingwell's interest in civility, he says, is as a 'vibrant and politically engaged set of conversational practices, all of them governed by a commitment to self-restraint and sensitivity'.[38] He astutely observes:

> genuine respect is too strong a value to demand . . . in a deeply pluralistic society. The relative advantage of civility is that it does not ask partici-pants to do anything more than treat political interlocutors *as if* they were worthy of respect and understanding, keeping their private thoughts to themselves.[39]

Kingwell emphasises the role of consensus in supporting principles of justice, but argues that consensus depends on 'civil constraints' on the dialogue that negotiates moral differences. In some witty examples of the role of evasion to assuage tender feelings, Kingwell qualifies the role of sincerity in accounts of communication such as that of Habermas. He notes that 'codified versions of civility' operate in the domain of legal procedure, but he counters such 'rarefied realms' to his ideal of 'vigorous public debate in as many places as possible'.[40]

I think there is, however, something rarefied about Kingwell's account, precisely because of its focus on polite speech. Politeness is indisputably important in many interpersonal dealings, amongst both friends and strangers. But it is unclear what work it does in its manifestation as a constraint on conversation in the political domain. Ideas of free speech involve, as Salman Rushdie insisted, 'the freedom to offend', a freedom that, he argued, is not bestowed and received in an exchange of politeness. Freedom, he said, is 'taken, not given'.[41] 'Holding one's tongue' is easy to defend when it comes to expressing one's opinion of a friend's ugly haircut; it is less clear what role it might have when there are conflicting political interests, conditions of inequality, or controversies over the distribution of power at stake. The emphasis on disclosure by theorists of difference is attuned to precisely these concerns. Of course, in most democratic societies where freedom of speech is protected, there are proscriptions against some forms: libel, slander, hatred or incitement to violence. But such restraints are considered to be exceptions, to be exercised carefully and infrequently, because of the importance of maintaining precisely the publicity of the public domain.[42] To render public debate akin to the conversation at a polite dinner party is to run foul of that crucial public–private distinction that serves not only to safeguard privacy but to enable public measures of social reform. Moreover, such a rendering would be uncivil. In politics, the civil thing to do is to be candid, to speak frankly. The guile of the politician is no token of esteem; it is a sign of disrespect. And where there is deceit, there is mistrust; precisely the unstable, privacy-jeopardising context that the rule of law seeks to prevent.

Lest we think that the freedom of discussion is a freedom valued only by the privileged,[43] consider how causes on behalf of the disadvantaged, expressed in protests, strikes, and marches, historically have been suppressed by reference to society's need for 'civility'.[44] Kingwell anticipates these worries about freedom of speech and political quietism. But his response is to hover between a view of civility as a set of impersonal rules and as a means of expressing care and concern. He calls for a society of tact, tolerance and distance rather than a 'deeply corporate' one, but at the same time he claims that civility will enable understanding and community.[45] It thus sometimes seems that his model, contrary to his intentions, is more apposite for the intimate relations of siblings than for the impersonal ties of citizens.

Deborah Cameron has persuasively argued that efforts at 'verbal hygiene', that seek to isolate language from the points of view of speakers or the context in which they speak, are both futile and at odds with the project of communication.[46] This is an argument she directs against the traditionalists, who seek to preserve language from change, e.g. the introduction of gender-neutral terms. But it is also an argument that should be directed against the camp Cameron aims to defend: the radical verbal hygienists, who seek to purify language to reach some transparent, 'politically correct' medium, devoid of a historical legacy of conflicts of interest and struggles over power. Cameron commends the radicals for making the meaning and use of words 'a matter of contestation',[47] but in a sense, this contestation is short term; their aim is, like that of the traditionalists, the purification of language. If speech in the public domain is the vehicle for articulating interests and values, conflicts and accords, then it is inevitably ridden with interminable contestation. Cameron is critical of the idea of civility in speech. But 'political correctness' is difficult to understand except as another example of misplaced civility.

The burdens of civility here become evident. Insofar as civility has connections with formalised rules of etiquette, it might be deemed a form of regard that is petty and trivial at best, snobbish and callous at worst. Elaborate rituals that daunt the unschooled seem to underscore gaps between the advantaged and the disadvantaged. Derision of snobbishness is familiar. The author of an 1895 manual on etiquette put it well when he mocked those who denounce rules of etiquette as 'trammels and shackles': 'let them be cast off or burst through, say they; let everyone do as he likes, let all behave as they like, we are in a free country, why should we not wipe our mouths upon the tablecloth if we please?'[48] Such views, like the idea of openness in communication of the so-called 'California school', have in mind that rules of politeness are class-bound impediments to social interaction.[49] They overlook, however, the accessibility of the modern idea of civility. In the history of etiquette, it was when liberal societies became more democratic, their class structure more porous and mobile, that rules of deportment began to have a mass appeal. After all, if etiquette were the province of the elect, there would have been no point in offering advice on the subject.

Early twentieth-century America, that society so set off from Old World status and rank, was a particularly fertile ground for advisors on parlour civility, from Emily Post to Miss Manners to Amy Vanderbilt.[50] The 'simplicity of manners' Judith Shklar praises as the 'great achievement of democracy' in America was deemed consistent with some pointers on the placement of table napkins.[51] Civility was perhaps still construed as a mark of superiority that some might have easier access to than others (consider how the author of that 1895 manual was referred to simply as 'A Member of the Aristocracy'), but it was a mark others could earn. Moreover, manuals were at pains to emphasise that snobbery is not good manners, that, as Shklar points out, far from a mark of superiority, snobbishness is in fact a sign of being 'ill bred'.[52] Insofar as the core of civil behaviour, as stressed by the manuals, is the simple principle, 'consideration towards others', then it is quite rightly touted as 'indispensable' to society.[53]

How can we have both civility and openness? A lot of the answer is provided by my claim that civility should not be interpreted as imposing politeness restraints on political discourse, that civility instead dictates honesty in the public domain. There are institutional constraints, however, which are necessary for free speech to flourish. A civil society assures the speakers that speech, however provocative, will not in fact provoke, or be the prelude to, harmful action. Civility is thus embedded in the institutional framework for open discussion. Robert's rules of order and standards of parliamentary decorum provide conditions of civility precisely in order to facilitate the contestation, even belligerence, that features in frank and open debate. This is illustrated by the incivility of contemporary Russia, a society that aspires, so far surprisingly unsuccessfully, to be democratic. On the television news one evening the world watched a member of the Russian Parliament grab a fellow parliamentarian by the throat. Such an act was not an example of freedom of expression, unfettered by civil niceties. It was the opposite: an act impeding freedom of expression, and the consensus and social improvement that such consensus aims to achieve. Certainty and predictability in the context in which one conducts one's affairs are important, both for the private individual and the participant in public debate. A civil context, assured by political and legal institutions, provides conditions of trust that enable frank discussion.

One such institution is the rule of law, that virtue of a legal system we identified as essential to the protection of privacy. For Locke, the rule of law gives institutional embodiment to the trust that obtains between an accountable government and its citizenry. As opposed to the idea of decorum in speech, civility in the law respects individuals' freedom to operate as they choose; it dictates that neither state nor individual can take an interest in the conduct of individuals except under suitably formulated laws and legislation. The clue to Russia's difficulties in democratising its culture and institutions is in large part that culture's low regard for both privacy and procedural justice. Democracy will inevitably founder so long as there is not a stable procedural context within which open debate can be conducted. The rule of law exemplifies the civility that the state owes its citizens, the foundation of trust necessary for the citizen to conduct his or her public and private business, with the assurance that, under normal circumstances, the business of one domain will not be brought to bear on that of the other.

Conceiving civility as a virtue of institutions rather than modes of conversation has the advantage, too, of avoiding charges of ethnocentrism.[54] After all, there are a myriad of ways in which members of one culture will differ from members of another in how they engage in polite speech. Conversational politeness is beset by cultural conventions which can be divisive in an ethnically diverse society. It may be suspected that the standards of politeness which prevail in such circumstances will be those of the dominant (Anglo) culture, undercutting the civil enterprise itself. Conceiving civility as a property of institutions evades such difficulties.

The rule of law is unmistakably Anglo-Saxon in its origins, but it is not a convention specific to such people. The rule of law has moral and political value such that philosophical argument can be adduced to justify it. And its value is such that cultures other than Britain have adopted or sought to adopt it. This institutional focus permits us to judge the assault in the Russian Parliament, for example, as uncivil in a moral sense without at the same time asking of Russians that they converse as Britons do. Charges of cultural insensitivity are perhaps impossible to dispatch altogether, but they can be allayed.

Civility nonetheless may seem too thin a basis for the active contributions to the welfare of others that are called for by egalitarians of all stripes. The needy cannot live off civility, no matter how politely they beg. It is incontrovertible that civility is not a sufficient condition for equality. I hope to have shown, however, that the institutional embodiment of civility in the rule of law is of value for egalitarians, for two reasons. First, only in the regulated public provided by the civility of law can open debate make progress towards a consensus on equality. Second, the rule of law ensures that our efforts at such progress do not run afoul of the distinction between public and private which is so crucial for privacy.[55] The public–private divide, regulated by the rule of law, seeks to ward off the stifling misguided solicitations of the doll's house and to protect the precious privacy of a room of one's own, for men and women, majorities and minorities.

Protecting the private does not mean, of course, that the nature of that domain is beneath notice. In seeking to render the public domain more faithful to the virtues of the rule of law, we are inevitably led to ideas of substantive justice which address the unfairness obscured by previous, inegalitarian claims to privacy. Seemingly empty formalistic rules, we have noted, are in fact an important source of fairness, in their scrupulous attention to same treatment for all citizens. Moreover, they are in fact rooted in an idea of equal citizenship, an idea that has historically been widened and deepened to involve ideas of social justice and material equality. And the egalitarian society is one that protects privacy not as a 'cover' for privilege, abuses of power or inequitable property holdings, but as a fundamental human interest of all citizens.

Not only is the rule of law important for equality; equality is important for the rule of law. There is reason to believe that the rule of law functions better in an egalitarian society. 'Buying justice' arises, after all, in even the most uncorrupt legal systems, when some have more income than others. Expert legal counsel beyond most people's means, upper-class judges, scares about robbery and theft – all are particularly symptomatic of a society with a gap between rich and poor.[56] Where that gap is greatest, and the political order marshalled to entrench it, the legal system risks becoming corrupt and the public order most vulnerable to intrusive crossings of the public and private. In such societies, those who seek to remedy the gap know this well, but so too do affluent, liberal visitors who have been the object of persistent and distressing appeals for commerce or charity in poverty-stricken streets.[57] Systems founded on inequality produce a number of social forces that threaten privacy.

Privacy and the rule of law exist as ideals precisely because of the difficulties that beset them, forces of arbitrariness or intrusiveness that emerge even when we are seeking to do right by our neighbours and fellow-citizens. Such forces may be accidental, or they may be concerted, based on a view of privacy and the rule of law as obstacles to more ambitious political ideals. I have argued that in the face of cultural diversity, respect for privacy that is genuine and consistent is especially important. The dilemma of difference is precisely that the different are other than us, distanced from our concerns and thus unable to call upon our care or concern in any intimate sense. And yet of course the different are us, too: self and other, us and them, all are human beings who require fair treatment. Thus we aim to design institutions so that we need not rely on the precarious attentions of particular persons. The rule of law is one such institution which helps ensure that we are accorded worth and dignity in the domain of the public, that we are included and counted as citizens. But the rule of law also seeks to leave us unimpeded and unseen in our particular personal domains, according us respect as private persons. We might say that, in light of the preceding argument, the rule of law directs government to be civil to its citizens, to treat citizens with a concern which, unlike the care of intimates – or inmates – is generalised and abstract, unintrusive and aloof. As our cases of privacy in everyday life made clear, often the civil thing to do is to refrain, rather than attend. In its instantiation in the rule of law, civility retains that sense of safeguarding boundaries. It reminds us that arguments for equality should ward off utopian appeals to transparency and community which dismiss privacy as a relic of oppression and alienation. The civility of the rule of law keeps the public and private in place, and demarcates one from the other.

Notes

1 I wish to thank David Bakhurst for excellent advice on several drafts of this chapter. Thanks are also owed to my father, Peter Sypnowich, whose defence of privacy fell on deaf ears so many years ago, and who kindly provided invaluable copy-editing suggestions. I am also grateful to the Social Sciences and Humanities Research Council of Canada for generously funding my research.
2 Woolf, *A Room of One's Own*, Harcourt Brace Jovanovich, New York, 1989.
3 Philippe Ariès, *Centuries of Childhood: A Social History of Family Life*, transl. Robert Baldick, Vintage, New York, 1962, 394–404.
4 So Alan Ryan defines privacy in 'Private Selves and Public Parts', in S.I. Benn and G.F. Gaus, eds, *Public and Private in Social Life*, Croom Helm, London 1983. It is also the definition which has been prominent in Western jurisprudence: for example, the Canadian Protection of Privacy Act of 1973 referred only to disclosure of information, making it an offence to intercept a private communication without having a person's consent or without being authorised to do so.

5 See Judith Jarvis Thomson, 'The Right to Privacy', *Philosophy and Public Affairs*, 4(4), Summer 1975, 299.

6 American jurisprudence, however, reflects this approach, having gone beyond the famous but rather broad idea of being 'let alone', to a bipartite conception, with one in tort law, focusing on the individual's interests in non-disclosure, and the other in constitutional law, focusing on the idea of autonomy. See Judith Wagner DeCew, *In Pursuit of Privacy: Law, Ethics and the Rise of Technology*, Cornell University Press, Ithaca, NY, 1997, chs 1–2.

7 See Thomson, *ibid*. As we shall see, privacy is at issue even where private property is not. A sense of personal domain need not require direct ownership, as Thomas Scanlon argues in his excellent reply, 'Thomson on Privacy', *Philosophy and Public Affairs*, 2(2), 1975, 318–21.

8 Ferdinand Schoeman, 'Privacy: Philosophical Dimensions of the Literature', in Schoeman, ed., *Philosophical Dimensions of Privacy*, Cambridge University Press, Cambridge, 1984, 4–5.

9 *Ibid.*, 316–17.

10 In Britain the 1957 Report of the Wolfenden Committee on Homosexual Offences and Prostitution in Britain similarly claimed that 'there must remain a realm of private morality which is, in brief and crude terms, not the law's business'. This is discussed in Simon Lee, *Law and Morals*, Oxford University Press, Oxford, 1986, 20.

11 John Stuart Mill, *On Liberty*, in *John Stuart Mill: A Selection of His Works*, John Robson (ed.), Macmillan, Toronto, 1966, ch. 3.

12 This point is well made by James Rachels, 'Why Privacy is Important', *Philosophy and Public Affairs*, 2(2), Summer 1975.

13 I discuss the rule of law in ch. 3 of my book, *The Concept of Socialist Law*, Clarendon Press, Oxford, 1990.

14 Indeed, that justice is represented by a woman in this early symbol, before women could vote or own property, let alone act as lawyers or judges, attests to the irrelevance of the corporeal person who holds the scales. Judith Shklar makes much of an earlier image of justice in Giotto's picture in the Arena Chapel in Padua. *La Giustizia* is not blindfolded, but her benign, expressionless face does suggest, Shklar says, that 'she may not be a real person at all'; *The Faces of Injustice*, Yale University Press, New Haven, 1990, 103.

15 For an excellent discussion of the rule of law during the apartheid era in South Africa, in light of the hearings of the Truth and Reconciliation Commission, see David Dyzenhaus, *Judging the Judges, Judging Ourselves* (forthcoming). See also his *Hard Cases in Wicked Legal Systems: South African Law in the Perspective of Legal Philosophy*, Clarendon Press, Oxford, 1991.

16 I am grateful to David Bakhurst for this example.

17 Scanlon, 'Thomson on Privacy', 318.

18 Ferdinand Schoeman notes this criticism, referring to the idea that privacy functions to 'protect people from an imperfect social world'; 'Privacy and Intimate Information', *Philosophical Dimensions of Privacy*, op. cit., 403–4.

19 *The Sexual Contract*, Stanford University Press, Stanford, California, 1988, 13, 117. See also Pateman, 'Feminist Critiques of the Public/Private Dichotomy', in S.I. Benn and G.F. Gaus, eds, *Public and Private in Social Life*, Croom Helm, London, 1983.

20 *Ibid.*, 295.

21 Will Kymlicka, *Contemporary Political Philosophy*, Oxford University Press, Oxford, 1990, 247–62.

22 S.I. Benn and G.F. Gaus, 'The Liberal Conception of the Public and the Private', in Benn and Gaus eds, *Public and Private in Social Life*, 38, 45–46,

54–5. For an interesting discussion of the absence of privacy within the family in ancient Greece, see Arlene Saxonhouse, 'Classical Greek Conceptions of Public and Private', in *Public and Private in Social Life*, op. cit.

23 Michel Foucault, 'Two Lectures', *Power/Knowledge*, Pantheon, New York, 1980, 81.

24 C. Gilligan, *In A Different Voice*, Harvard University Press, Cambridge, Mass., 172–4.

25 S. Ruddick, 'Maternal Thinking', *Feminist Studies*, 6, 2, 1980, 345.

26 J. Nedelsky, 'Reconceiving Rights as Relationship', *Review of Constitutional Studies*, vol. 1, no. 1, 1993, 12.

27 *Justice and the Politics of Difference*, Princeton University Press, Princeton, 1990, 108.

28 *Ibid.*, 120.

29 Will Kymlicka, *Multicultural Citizenship*, Oxford University Press, Oxford 1995, 114–15. It is worth reflecting that in imperial India the equivalent of the 'mounties' (the Royal Canadian Mounted Police) wore martial turbans as part of their uniform.

30 *Political Liberalism*, Columbia University Press, New York, 1993, 193.

31 It may be important to distinguish between immigrant groups and their descendants, on the one hand, and on the other, national minorities, such as aboriginal people, the Scots in Britain or the Quebecois in Canada. In the latter case there will be questions of historical entitlement and records of oppression which provide a better basis for remedying disadvantage. I address these issues in 'Equality and Nationality', *Politics and Society*, vol. 24, no. 2, June 1996, and 'The Culture of Citizenship' (forthcoming).

32 Erving Goffman, *Relations in Public*, Harper and Row, New York, 1971, 331, 252.

33 Esther B. Aresty, *The Best Behavior: the Course of Good Manners – from Antiquity to the Present – as Seen through Courtesy and Etiquette Books*, Simon and Schuster, New York, 1970, 10.

34 Clifford Orwin, 'Civility, Citizenship and Liberal Democracy', in Edward C. Banfield (ed.), *Civility and Citizenship in Liberal Democratic Societies*, Paragon House, New York, 1992, 84–5.

35 Hegel, *Philosophy of Right*, trans. and annotated T.M. Knox, Oxford University Press, Oxford, 1978.

36 Green, *The Authority of the State*, Clarendon Press, Oxford, 1988, ch. 9.

37 Such as those enumerated in William Galston, *Liberal Purposes*, Cambridge University Press, Cambridge, 1991.

38 Kingwell, *A Civil Tongue: Justice, Dialogue and the Politics of Pluralism*, Pennsylvania State University Press, University Park, Penn., 1995, 26.

39 *Ibid.*, 247.

40 *Ibid.*, 249.

41 Rushdie, 'In Good Faith', *The Independent*, London, 11 February 1990. Contrast with Bhikhu Parekh's sympathy for the British Muslim community's complaint about the lack of civility of Rushdie's novel. See 'The Rushdie Affair', *Political Studies*, vol. 38 (1990), 695–709.

42 Robert A. Goldwin, 'Rights, Citizenship and Civility', in Banfield, ed., *Civility and Citizenship*, op. cit., 50–4.

43 This is implied by Bhikhu Parekh in 'The Rushdie Affair'.

44 This is well illustrated by Edward Shils's complaints that trade unions, the unemployed, 'the criminal and delinquent class', 'the consumption of narcotics as well as the practice of homosexuality', contribute to patterns of conduct which are 'almost wholly uncivil in [their] disruptive intrusions into domestic

and economic private life'; 'Civility and Civil Society', in Banfield, ed., *Civility and Citizenship*, op. cit., 12–14.

45 Compare Kingwell, *A Civil Tongue*, at 226, 174 and at 230, 249.
46 *Verbal Hygiene*, Routledge, London, 1995, 74.
47 *Ibid.*, 164.
48 A Member of the Aristocracy, *Manners and Rules of Good Society*, Frederick Warne and Co., 21st edn, London and New York, 1895, 2.
49 Kingwell, *A Civil Tongue*, op. cit., 241.
50 Aresty, *The Best Behavior*, op. cit., chs 35, 36.
51 J. Shklar, *Ordinary Vices*, Harvard University Press, Cambridge, Mass., 1984, 136–7.
52 *Ibid.*, 136.
53 *The Best Behavior*, 294; *Manners and Rules of Good Society*, 3, 4.
54 The role of politeness in the context of cultural diversity is a recurring theme in Kingwell's discussion.
55 For an interesting discussion of the relation between civility and truthfulness see Steven Shapin, *A Social History of Truth: Civility and Science in Seventeenth-Century England*, Chicago University Press, Chicago, 1994, ch. 1.
56 I elaborate on this point in ch. 3 of *The Concept of Socialist Law*.
57 See *ibid.*, 332–3.

7 Is privacy a legal duty?

Reconsidering private right and public virtue in the domain of intimacy

Jean L. Cohen

> Another instinct which is very natural to democracies and very dangerous, is a
> tendency to despise individual rights and take little account of them . . . Our
> fathers were always prone to make improper use of the idea that private rights
> should be respected, and we are by nature inclined to exaggerate the opposite
> view, that the interest of the individual should always give way to the interest
> of the many.
>
> Alexis de Tocqueville, *Democracy in America*, pp. 699–701

Introduction

Modern republican political theory has always had an ambivalent relationship to privacy. Most theorists in this tradition insist on the importance of
a clear demarcation between public and private. Both Tocqueville and
Arendt (the two most important nineteenth- and twentieth-century exem-
plars) argued that rights which institutionalize and protect the private
sphere are a basic precondition for an adequately demarcated and autonomous public sphere. They counter the danger specific to egalitarian forms
of republican government, namely, the inherent tendency of public power
to expand and to trespass on private interests.[1]

Nevertheless, republican theorists were far more preoccupied with the
opposite risk of civil privatism. Recall Tocqueville's prescient warnings
about the potential effects of an acquisitive and expanding commercialism
(and egoistic individualism) on civic virtue in an egalitarian democratic
society. The danger of corruption of representative organs by powerful private
interests was a key concern of his. Hannah Arendt's analysis of the rise of the
social and her fears regarding the impact of the corresponding deepening and
expansion of intimacy on public life parallels Tocqueville's. With respect to
the latter, she explicitly noted two additional dangers: first, the citizen's
deepening experience of private happiness in the domain of intimacy could
seduce him away from public life. Second, the preoccupations of the intimate
domain could invade the public sphere, replacing interest in the *res publica*
with personal concerns of the self, leading to general indiscretion and to

the degradation of the public into a mere social space. Republican theory, in short, was concerned less with the intrinsic goods that privacy protects than with its 'external face': its role in demarcating public space.

The contemporary neo-republican revival in political and legal theory has resurrected much of this rhetoric.[2] Jean Elsthain's marriage of Arendtian republicanism with her own particular version of communitarianism is a particularly striking case in point, as her most recent book, *Democracy on Trial*, witnesses.[3] Elsthain marshals a discourse of public space, civic virtue, responsibility and duty in an effort to defend the distinction between public and private against what she calls 'the politics of displacement'. This is a version of identity politics which makes everything private public, including one's sexual practices, and which gives precedence to one's private (group) identity and desires over public ends and purposes.[4] Echoing Arendt's critique of the rise of the social and the blurring of distinctions, Elsthain insists on the importance of maintaining clear boundaries.

Accordingly, she argues that certain issues, actions, and talk – in particular regarding sexuality, the intimate aspects of the body and the self – are essentially private. Against the narcissism of relentless self-disclosure, she advocates silence, secrecy, discretion. Citing Arendt, she affirms the importance of shame and concealment regarding the 'body's functions, passions and desires'.[5] Indeed, in the context of a discussion of 'gay liberation', she insists upon a duty of privacy (that she calls civility) vis-à-vis desire, intimacy and sexuality.

She does so in order to distinguish between acceptable and unacceptable claims for 'gay rights'. Accordingly, an acceptable civil rights agenda would revolve around the claim that society has no business scrutinizing or intruding on the private sexual preferences of gays and lesbians. But, she insists, these groups would have to accept a 'duty of civility' in return for privacy protection, and refrain from 'flaunting' their sexuality and desires in public. Moreover, in her view, demands for public legitimation of a 'gay lifestyle' or 'homosexual ethos' (allegedly the credo of 'gay liberationists'), are utterly unacceptable. No one has the right to public or state-induced acknowledgement of the worth of his or her ethical values, beliefs, or habits. Indeed, demands for public validation of minority sexual identities blur the distinction between the personal and the political, the private and the public. They lead to 'shameless', narcissistic public disclosures of one's own orientations and sometimes forced disclosures ('outings') of others'. These things should not intrude into civic life. Elsthain thus reproduces the standard republican strategy for securing (reinstating) a clear and distinct boundary between the public and private: by mapping an analytic distinction (public and private) onto institutional spheres of life (domestic–private sphere/political–public sphere) she constructs an essentialized and rigid *dichotomy* based on a sort of phenomenological essentialism which has the effect of silencing and excluding not only issues but the people associated with them from the public realm, even if that is not her intention.[6] Her arguments for privacy do, and are meant to, privatize. They are, moreover, only apparently impartial: heterosexuals are not asked to keep their sexual orientation private/secret. *Their* intimate choices are celebrated in public through state-sponsored or state-acknowledged institutional forms (marriage) denied to homosexuals.

The neo-republican discourse of boundaries and distinctions is a response to real problems but I will argue that this way of reinstating the boundary between public and private is deeply misguided and politically suspect. One cannot develop a convincing demarcation between private and public without rethinking *both* sides of the boundary. Truly epochal changes in the last quarter of the twentieth century impacting particularly on the 'domain of intimacy' have made the reconceptualization of the boundary between public and private, of what it is that personal privacy rights should protect, their function as well as the justification for such rights, a pressing theoretical and political issue. Shifting gender relations, processes of individualization, the massive entry of married women into the labour force, new bio-technologies along with the destandardization of labour, the decentring of marriage, the demotion of reproductive sex from the moral to the ethical level and the corresponding pluralization of forms of life are only a few of the processes at work here.[7] Challenges by social groups to discrimination, repression and stigma on the basis of gender or sexual 'identities' are part of this conundrum.

We cannot address the really difficult conceptual and political issues regarding the 'domain of intimacy' and the types of personal autonomy and privacy appropriate to it if we simply try to ressurect the myth (itself never innocent) of a natural pre-political sphere or essentially private concerns. Nor can legal issues be adjudicated from this perspective as if nothing had changed and as if the liberal paradigm that informed juridification of this domain in the past could simply be revived.

We have to confront the hard questions of what mode of legal regulation and which forms of constitutionalization of rights could and should protect a plurality of forms of intimate association from intolerant majorities while avoiding both the disintegrative effects of over-regulation and the unjust effects of 'non-regulation'. But before such questions can be meaningfully posed, clarity regarding the intrinsic goods that privacy rights protect is indispensable.

Instead of reifying definitions, the way to begin is by asking what conception and scope of privacy and personal decisional autonomy citizens must grant one another in the domain of intimacy (in the form of privacy rights) if everyone is recognized as an equal moral person meriting equal concern and respect *and* as an equal citizens with fair opportunities for voice in the public domain. One can then proceed to rethink the forms of privacy required for just and rewarding intimate relationships to flourish and the personal autonomy that we want and need in and for such relations.

I thus shift perspectives and try to reconceptualize what Arendt once called the 'non-privative' aspects of privacy. The strategy of my privacy analysis goes in a different direction from the neo-republican approach. Instead of focusing on the privative dimensions of privacy, I try to develop a conception of the goods that privacy rights ought to protect without falling into dichotomous or essentialist thinking. From this perspective, I show that the attempt to restore the link between the idea of a right to privacy and notions of shame, silence and secrecy is an example of what Tocqueville called an 'improper use of the idea of privacy rights'. The most serious incivilities in public life are tied to injustice, not to indiscretion. In particular, and *pace* Elsthain, it is the injustice of denying full privacy rights to gays and lesbians for their intimate associations (along with attempts to exclude them from the public realm and the denial of equal protection of the law) that ought to be our target, not the sometimes foolish and unfortunate responses (the politics of displacement) that such injustice leads to. Finally, I will try to show that when properly construed, the right to privacy need not lead to privatization either in the republican sense of the abandonment of public for private happiness, or in the sense of silencing and depoliticizing the issues or bearers of such rights.

I proceed by addressing the most recent attempt to impose a 'duty of privacy' on to gays and lesbians, namely the 'new' military policy regarding homosexuality, put into place during the first Clinton administration. I shall discuss the legal backdrop that made such a policy plausible. I hope in the process to provide an alternative to what I take to be the unfortunate and politically dangerous linkage of privacy rights with the obligation to conceal – a connection made both by advocates (like Elsthain) and by critics (especially within the gay and lesbian movement) of privacy analysis.

The 'New Military Policy': privacy protection for gays?

Almost immediately upon being elected to his first term, President Bill Clinton announced that he would fulfil his 1992 campaign promise to lift the ban on gays and lesbians in the armed forces.[8] President Clinton sought a policy that would end discrimination in the military based on sexual orientation.

Things did not turn out quite the way the new Administration assumed they would. The heated debate within and outside the Government occasioned by this announcement clearly came as a surprise.[9] Indeed, the campaign promise led to a prolonged, open controversy during the first six months of the Clinton presidency that has re-emerged periodically during his second term as well.[10] Once the mobilization among the citizenry against it[11] was reinforced by the criticisms of the Joint Chiefs of Staff and by Sam Nunn, head of the Senate Armed Services Committee, simply rescinding the ban by executive order became politically impossible. Instead, the Administration, the Joint Chiefs of Staff and Congress reached a compromise, apparently designed to protect the privacy of gay people as well as discipline and morale in the military.[12] The 'compromise', summed up in the phrase 'Don't ask, don't tell, don't pursue', has been codified into law by Congress.[13]

The Joint Chiefs of Staff had staunchly defended the military policy in place at the time of Clinton's statement. That policy involved both a pro-hibition on acts of consensual sodomy and an outright ban of homosexuals from service.[14] It required the investigation and discharge of anyone evincing homosexual desire, identity, or acts.[15] Since the early 1980s, the US armed services have accordingly excluded and expelled homosexuals from their ranks.[16] Standard military procedure entailed the questioning of recruits as to whether they were homosexuals and the rejection of those who said yes.

The new 'compromise' policy seems to do away with all this. It lifts the ban against gay men and lesbians from entering into military service.[17] It forbids the interrogation of recruits as to their sexual orientation, and disallows the dismissal of military personnel for 'alleged' homosexual feelings or identity. Apparently, no longer will men and women be excluded from military service on the basis of their response to questions posed by officials about their sexual orientation; nor will they be subjected to surveillance and dismissal on the basis of their sexual status alone.[18] Apparently the 'privacy' of gays and lesbians is thereby respected while their sexual status is removed as a basis for discriminatory treatment.

But only apparently. For the 'compromise' dimension in the new policy resides in the fact that military personnel continue to be susceptible to inves-tigation and discharge for 'homosexual conduct'. Instead of focusing on sexual status, orientation, or 'same-sex' desire, the new policy forbids 'only' homosexual acts. A great deal hinges, of course, on just what counts as a 'homosexual act'. The conception of such conduct in the new guidelines is rather broad: it includes not only same-sex marriage, and same-sex sodomy, but also same-sex handholding and kissing as well as a speech act of 'coming out' or *publicly* stating that one is a homosexual.[19] To be sure, the new rules specify that 'mere confession' of one's homosexual orientation would not be a sufficient ground for drumming a service member out of the military. But such a 'confession' *is* considered a sufficient basis to begin an investigation into whether the individual engages in homosexual behaviour![20] Moreover, the military will discharge a member who makes a public statement that he or she is a *practising* homosexual or a bisexual. In effect, 'homosexual conduct' is made so elastic a concept that it can be 'stretched into virtual equivalence with homosexual status'.[21]

Thus the 'measure of personal freedom' secured by the new rules is ambig-uous. One is assured of freedom from investigation by the authorities, one's 'privacy' is protected, only on the condition of silence and secrecy. That is the upshot of the 'don't ask, don't tell, don't pursue' compromise. Small wonder that many have construed this policy as an alarming attempt, disclaimers notwithstanding, to force gays and lesbians back into the closet of privacy.[22]

The new policy has important implications particularly for the theoretical understanding and normative assessment of the right to privacy that transcend its limited application (it applies only to the military). It reveals quite clearly in my view the weaknesses of the neo-republican approach described above. But it is also worth addressing because it seems to confirm the worst suspicions of many scholars critical of privacy analysis, regarding the dangers of invoking privacy for the purpose of securing relief to homosexuals and lesbians from surveillance, persecution, and discrimination. Surely the military's concession of privacy (don't ask, don't tell) to homosexuals – or rather, its seeming imposition of privacy upon them – reinforces the stigma attached to them without affording much protection against harassment or ultimate expulsion from its ranks.

This assessment is undoubtedly correct. Nevertheless, I want to argue that the new policy reveals the importance rather than the uselessness or even danger of claiming privacy rights. Far from confirming the critics' views as to its risks, I will maintain that the policy makes the opposite case. For, despite appearances, it is predicated on the *denial* and not on the granting of the most basic privacy rights to homosexuals and lesbians as a group. Indeed, I argue that the policy must be understood against the backdrop of the 1986 Supreme Court ruling in *Bowers v. Hardwick* that no fundamental privacy right attaches protectively to 'homosexual sodomy'.[23] The *Hardwick* ruling thus affirmed the constitutionality of laws criminalizing consensual sexual conduct among adults, thereby considerably restricting the protective reach of privacy analysis. It was this opinion that constructed the terrain on which the military's ostensible focus on homosexual 'conduct' rather than 'status' could make sense.[24] The shift from status to conduct, so pivotal in the new policy, is inconceivable outside a social and legal context in which the proscription of sexual conduct is made to serve as the vehicle for discrimination on the basis of sexual orientation.

Accordingly I take the new policy and the debate it has generated as an opportunity to clarify the difference between having the legal protection afforded by constitutional privacy rights and being forced into 'privacy' – into secrecy (into the closet) – and exposed to harassment and discrimination in their absence. It will be my thesis that in addition to constituting a grave injustice, the denial of privacy protection for acts of 'homosexual sodomy' plays a pivotal role in legitimating the legal and extra-legal discriminatory practices against homosexuals and lesbians in a wide range of institutions including, but hardly restricted to, the military. The importance of clarifying the concept of a right to privacy and the value of fighting for it should become apparent as the discussion proceeds.

The right to privacy and the 'Epistemology of the Closet'

While criticism of the idea of a constitutional right to privacy has become something of a cottage industry, two arguments have emerged with respect to gay and lesbian rights which are distinctive.[25] The first maintains that by invoking privacy rights in order to secure legal protection against persecution on the basis of their sexual activity, gays and lesbians become trapped into what Eve Sedgwick has called in a recent book the *Epistemology of the Closet*.[26] The second insists that the privacy paradigm is at best incapable of securing equality or political empowerment for gays or lesbians, and at worst serves as a roadblock to such goals.[27]

In her now classic essay of the same title, Sedgwick states that: 'The closet is the defining structure for gay oppression in this century.'[28] By this she means that given the social stigma and legal sanctions attached to it, gay (and lesbian) sexuality has the status of a shameful, highly significant secret even when it is revealed publicly and openly affirmed.[29] It is not possible in such a context for gays to avoid having to make (and remake) the rather unattractive choice between disclosure and secrecy regarding their sexual orientation and practices. Unfortunately, as Sedgwick correctly notes, neither alternative breaks the oppressive construction (the epistemology of the closet) within which gay sexuality and/or identity is situated; rather it places homosexuals and lesbians in a painful and harmful double bind. In an environment saturated with homophobic attitudes and laws, one can either go public ('come out') thereby risking condemnation and discrimination, or remain private, conceal one's sexuality and thus become complicitous with the negative evaluations attached to it.

The logic of 'self-disclosure' inherent in the first option has, perforce, the form of an open secret – an admission, a confession, in public that 'I am one of them' – a member of a despised social category. One thereby becomes visible but hardly protected, uninjured or unburdened. Self-disclosure does little to allay the vulnerabilities attached to gay/lesbian identity. Nor does it mitigate the stress of information-management that burdens gays and lesbians. Moreover, the price of 'coming out' is often that one has to adopt (confess to) an identity that under other circumstances one would not necessarily embrace as the 'deep truth' of oneself.

On the other hand, the privacy afforded by remaining in the closet (the second option) is equivocal, to say the least. For it seems to presuppose that there is something shameful about one's sexual desires, conduct, and intimate relationships that should be kept secret. Thus, both disclosure (confession) and silence are part of the 'epistemology of the closet'. Both involve strategies of adaptation to a legal and social context that makes the shameful secret, whether or not it is told, the defining feature of 'gay life'. Both entail the obvious harms of furtiveness, shame, denial and/or a very risky and expensive 'self-revelation'.[30] For 'going public' or 'choosing' silence are two flawed alternatives constructed by a legal and social context in which a particular mode of intimate relationships and sexuality – heterosexual marriage – is (re-)centred as the norm and the standard to which one must either conform or from which one must deviate.

That is why so many legal and political theorists concerned with 'gay rights' opt for abandoning the discourse of privacy.[31] In the best recent statement of this position, Kendall Thomas has argued that privacy analysis reinforces the epistemology of the closet.[32] Gays and lesbians do at times invoke privacy as a tactic to avoid being forced out of the closet (exposed), yet for them, '. . . the closet is less a refuge than a prison-house'.[33] If for heterosexuals the value of claiming a privacy right is that it can be used to provide a space for self-discovery and self-direction, gay men and lesbians invoke it to protect against the dangers of disclosure.[34] Indeed, on Thomas's view, there is a 'structural' link between privacy and secrecy, between the closet and shame, that obtains in the broader context of homophobia, and marks the difference in the meaning of privacy rights for homosexuals.[35] Accordingly, Thomas concludes that the privacy paradigm is a trap, for it serves as a cornerstone of the very structure of domination it purports to protect against.[36]

The second argument invoked against the privacy paradigm is related to the first. It consists of the apparently straightforward claim that it is a strategic error to focus on gaining privacy protection for gay sex because this can yield neither equality nor power to gays and lesbians. Personal privacy rights cannot undo the stigma attached to gay identity. Nor can they end discrimination against gays and lesbians as a group. Thus, to couch the issue of gay oppression as a matter of sexual liberty, i.e. as an issue of Constitutional privacy rights, is to misconstrue what is at stake: '. . . as though political empowerment were a matter of getting the cops back on the street where they belong and sexuality back into the impermeable space (the bedroom) where *it* belongs . . .'.[37]

According to the critics, this approach trivializes the issue of toleration that confronts gays and lesbians. To frame the problem of gay oppression as a privacy issue is to presume that what is at stake is forbearance for idiosyncratic personal sexual taste, rather than equality and power for gays as a group. Privacy analysis, in short, depoliticizes the problem.

Even worse, the conception of toleration that goes with privacy analysis not only does nothing to undermine the stigma associated with the tolerated group's 'identity' or status, it seems to presuppose and reinforce it.[38] In other words, a privacy right interpreted as a liberty right to engage in various forms of consensual sex out of public view would, in a homophobic context, go hand in hand with the compulsion to secrecy and thereby reinforce individual shame along with the denigration of gays as a group. It certainly does nothing to undermine the public disdain for homosexuality, on this reading. Hence the charge that 'liberal privacy' affords toleration of gay and lesbian individuals on the condition of privatization (the injunction/warning to be 'discreet' about your sexual preferences in public) and depoliticization. Since prejudice against gays/lesbians and the denial of equal concern for and respect to them because of their sexual orientation is usually the motive behind laws and policies regulating their sexual conduct, to focus on privacy is to forgo the real terrain of contestation.[39] Issues of equality, power and respect, not personal privacy, are at stake in such laws whether or not they are articulated in neutral terms or mention sexual orientation explicitly.

I believe that these critiques of privacy analysis are convincing, but only against a particular conception of privacy. The critics are misguided, however, when they target the very concept of privacy rights. In that case they are based on two conceptual mistakes: (1) the confusion of a right to privacy with a duty of privacy; and (2) the failure to distinguish between the *concept* of a right to privacy and various *conceptions* of what that right entails and signifies, and what it can accomplish. Those who assume that invoking privacy rights would lock gays into the closet mistake what it means to have a right to privacy with what I consider to be an unfairly, because selectively imposed (be it through social or legal sanction) 'duty of privacy'. It is the 'duty' and not the right that is structurally linked to secrecy, shame, silencing and depoliticization, especially when it is imposed only on particular groups, as is the case with the 'new military policy'. Confusion over the difference between rights and duties goes hand in hand with the failure on the part of most privacy critics to distinguish between the *concept* of a right to privacy and a particular *conception* of privacy.[40] The first is, in my view, indispensable to any modern understanding of freedom. There are, however, *conceptions* of privacy that are unacceptable and which contribute to inequality or the denial of freedom to certain social categories. But before these can be properly identified, clarity about the distinction is necessary.

The new military policy *is* a textbook example of the conception of privacy appropriately described as the 'epistemology of the closet' and of the sham of a purportedly 'liberal' and 'tolerant' public policy that forces privatization and secrecy onto certain groups. The operative conception of privacy here is that of secrecy about what one does at home, self-effacement ('discretion') in public: just what neo-republicans seem to advocate. But, as Sedgwick herself has shown, these dynamics come into play precisely in a context in which the privacy *rights* (along with certain speech, associational and equality rights) of gays and lesbians have been *denied* constitutional protection.[41] The military policy does not concede such rights, rather it offers an exchange – we won't pursue you into your bedrooms on the condition of silence and concealment of your sexuality. This (rather disingenuous) offer of non-interrogation and non-harassment is made conditional on acceptance of a duty of privacy; rights have nothing to do with it. Indeed, what I am calling here the 'duty of privacy' is not the correlative of the right to privacy in the usual sense. Rather the form it has taken, ('don't tell') is predicated on the absence of key privacy rights for those on whom it is imposed. Under constitutional privacy doctrine, to say that a matter is private means that it is presumptively immune from legal prohibition and that the *decisional autonomy of the individual* in the matter is protected.[42] This means that the decision whether or not to reveal one's private affairs in public is also protected.[43] The *concept* of a right to privacy securing decisional autonomy in the domain of intimacy thus includes, along with the right to associate intimately and sexually with adult partners of your choice (freedom of intimate association), the right to say and be who you are in public without risking either your dispositional control over information, access to the self, the body, or the claim to have your individual integrity respected and recognized. In other words, if certain conduct, information or relationships are constitutionally protected as private, it does not follow that society may mandate that they be kept secret! On the contrary, if the relevant intimate relationships, sexual acts, object choices, bedrooms, etc. of homosexuals and lesbians were protected by constitutionalized privacy rights, government would be powerless to impose special requirements of secrecy or silence about them. *Full privacy rights entail freedom from the obligation to conceal as well as informational privacy, i.e. the choice not to reveal or have revealed one's personal affairs.*[44] In this sense it entails 'communicative liberty'.

This becomes obvious as soon as one reflects upon what it is precisely that the obligation of privacy conceptualized as silence/secrecy entailed in the 'don't ask, don't tell, don't pursue' policy involves. Let us be very clear. The 'duty' at stake here is not that one refrain, out of mutual consideration for each other's 'privacy', from engaging in sexual intercourse or sexual acts visibly and openly in public. Since sex acts are coded as intimate in our society, since additionally we have cultural taboos on nudity, everyone is presumed to owe to everyone else a duty of civility which involves refraining from violating these taboos. That is what strictures about public decency supposedly enforce.

Whatever we might think of such 'rules of civility', they are not at issue here.[45] But then, what is? The obligation of privacy imposed in the 'don't ask, don't tell' policy explicitly enjoins *speech and expression* about sex acts, and, despite disclaimers, insists upon 'discretion' regarding sexual orientation and desire – a 'duty' imposed selectively and exclusively on homosexuals and lesbians. To be more specific, people are required to refrain from indicating in any way that they have, do, or might engage in acts of sexual intimacy *with others of the same sex*. The 'duty of privacy' here refers to speech about acts when linked to homosexual (or lesbian) orientation, not to the public or private performance of the acts.

The new policy makes no distinction at all between public and private conduct, between acts engaged in, on or off duty, on or off base. It is one thing to forbid genital sexual activity between individuals on base or on duty, something apparently well within the province of military authority. It is quite another to attempt to regulate speech about what one does in private or off base in a non-official capacity, especially when such regulations are applied only to a particular group. No such obligation of secrecy, no such 'duty of privacy' is imposed on heterosexuals. So far as I am aware there has never been a case in which a legal duty to be discreet about legal action has been selectively imposed on any group by regulatory action.[46]

The question to ask in this context is how the imposition of such an obviously discriminatory obligation on to a minority is legally possible. In addition to the violation of personal autonomy, there are obvious first amendment issues involved here, not to mention anti-discrimination principles. Indeed, two recent Supreme Court rulings (the *Watkins* and *Meinhold* cases) have held that homosexuals as *persons*, i.e. as a particular kind of person, are entitled to Constitutional protection under the Equal Protection Clause, and that the (former) policy of the US Army and the Department of Defense of discharging service members merely for admitting that they were homosexual, violates Constitutional anti-discrimination principles.[47] Hence the 'new' military policy that no longer cites homosexual status as a reason for interrogation, investigation or discharge.

What, then, does it cite? We already have the answer: 'conduct' and its voluntary disclosure are the issue. But in order to understand what that means, we must turn to another context, and look at the Supreme Court decision which ruled that 'homosexual conduct' could be criminalized without violating the constitution. Only then can we begin to see what function the selective denial of privacy rights plays in the official oppression of gays and lesbians.

As already indicated, I contend that the revised military policy must be understood against the historical, social-psychological, normative and legal context constituted by the 1986 Supreme Court decision in *Bowers v. Hardwick*.[48] In that decision, the Court ruled that the Constitution does not confer a right of privacy that extends to 'homosexual sodomy' regardless of whether it is consensual or practised in the privacy of one's home. Indeed the Court maintained that the fundamental privacy rights of homosexuals were in no way violated by the anti-sodomy statute under consideration. It is this ruling that is the condition of possibility of the *new* military policy, in my view. For had the Court not affirmed the constitutionality of the *criminalization* of 'homosexual sodomy', it would hardly have been possible for the military to simultaneously accept gays and lesbians into the service and yet punish them for committing 'homosexual acts' off base and in private, while exposing them to interrogation and likely dishonourable discharge, if they 'flaunt', i.e. express, their sexual orientation in public or engage in speech about same-sex acts. Unless something called 'homosexual sodomy' were denied constitutional privacy protection, unless it were legal for states to criminalize and attach very harsh penalties to it, the military would be hard put to justify discharging homosexuals and lesbians, and only these categories of individuals, for committing it or for speaking about it![49]

If one reflects that shortly after the *Hardwick* ruling, *Watkins* and *Meinhold* were decided, it seems rather clear that the focus on criminalizable 'homosexual acts' provided the military with a constitutionally safe route to target and regulate the behaviour of a particular group without, as it were, having to name names.[50] The focus on conduct serves admirably to accomplish what the old emphasis on status can do no longer.

And yet my last sentence should signal that the situation is somewhat complex. After all, most anti-sodomy statutes, including the one at issue in *Hardwick* and in the military code, are neutral vis-à-vis the gender of the persons committing the forbidden acts.[51] How, then, could *Hardwick* provide the implicit justification for regulating the conduct of homosexuals and lesbians exclusively?

I discuss this decision in detail in a longer version of this chapter.[52] For a provisional answer to the question, let me invoke Janet Halley's suggestive analysis of the 'deep equivocation' between acts and identities in statutes criminalizing sodomy.[53] This equivocation derives from the tendency so prevalent today to construe sodomy as a metonym for homosexual personhood. Reproduced and raised, as it were, to constitutional principle in *Hardwick*, it supplies the ground for targeting and policing the sexual behaviour of gays and lesbians through gender-neutral law. The trick is accomplished by articulating sexual preference (homosexuality) on to criminalized acts (sodomy), and criminalized acts on to identities (the homosexual as personage). A vicious rhetorical circle ensues that becomes the basis for the construction of an inferior group identity ('homosexual sodomites') and for the denial of basic rights to individuals associated with the respective group. This is a two-level process. The first level involves the formation (from above) of the identity category and its alleged meaning; the second level involves the process by which an individual is designated (often by others' discretionary power) as a member of the group and is assigned the relevant identity.[54] It is the Supreme Court's identity politics in this case that is suspect and open in my view to the charge of injustice.

The criminalization of sodomy today plays a crucial role in the generation of stigmatized sexual-orientation identities.[55] To be sure, discrimination on the basis of homosexual preference (and status) exists in states that do not have anti-sodomy statutes and in countries that have abolished them, as the example of the United Kingdom shows.[56] Nevertheless, criminalization certainly makes it easier to construe those associated with the outlawed acts as unworthy of equal concern and respect. It is not only that people with a particular group identity are targeted for prejudicial and discriminatory treatment by such rhetorical means. Rather, the problem is that under the cover of neutrality, law (and state policy) in part *constitutes and renders visible and vulnerable* the very identity (the 'homosexual sodomite') it simultaneously stigmatizes as criminal and abnormal, for engaging in the acts it outlaws.

In re-examining the *Hardwick* ruling, I show that although the critics of privacy are correct to argue that what is at stake in the struggle of gays and lesbians against oppression is not simply sexual liberation, they are wrong to suggest that we jettison privacy analysis. If it is true that gaining the protective shield of privacy rights to cover 'gay sex' (whatever that is) will not of itself deliver full equality or power to homosexuals and lesbians, the denial of this shield has and continues to play a central role in supporting official and unofficial oppression, surveillance, and discrimination against them.

However, the critics are also wrong to belittle the importance of a privacy right protecting the freedom of intimate association among consenting adults providing no other principles of justice are violated. Whatever their original function, today harsh sex laws, even if unenforced, serve not only to deny certain liberties but also to construct, impose and codify sexual identities, norms and hierarchies.[57] State laws that criminalize or regulate the choice of sexual act and partners obviously restrict decisional autonomy in what many consider to be an intensely personal and ethically important domain of life. They also take the discretionary power of identification, of the naming and locating of individuals within group identities, out of the hands of the individuals themselves and place it into the hands of the state. The right not to have an identity imposed upon one which one cannot affirm and embrace – a right, in my view, that is, along with autonomy issues, at the centre of contemporary privacy jurisprudence, is thereby violated. If the law constructs the subject before the law, then it is certainly worth the effort to have some input into the legal construction of sexual subjects.[58]

Insisting on privacy rights for gays and lesbians, *pace* Sedgwick, is thus not a matter of getting sex back into the impermeable space of the bedroom, but of challenging the role that sex law plays in regulating all individuals, in unfairly privileging certain forms of intimate association over others, and in oppressing specific categories of people without even naming the categories. The decriminalization of sodomy statutes will not yield the full panoply of rights that gays and lesbians need but it would pull the rug out from under the rhetorical/legal construction of gays and lesbians as a tendentially *criminal* population undeserving of the same rights as others. The current military policy ostensibly focusing on conduct rather than status, would thereby lose its raison d'être. Affording privacy protection to cover the sexual choices and intimate associations of homosexuals and lesbians would abolish many of the inequalities established and reinforced by sex law including rigid gender norms and hierarchies. Moreover, it would constitute an enormous symbolic victory for it would indicate that the law no longer construes homosexuals as so different (i.e. inferior) that they may be denied basic rights and be subject to a degree of surveillance and administrative/police intrusion in their personal lives which would not be tolerated if imposed on, say, heterosexual men.

Accordingly, the privacy argument for striking down anti-sodomy statutes involves far more than the protection of idiosyncratic sexual tastes. It does not ignore the political stakes of the issue. On the contrary, it is one of the stakes, because it is aimed at abolishing the pretext for the denial of equal liberty (freedom of intimate association and privacy) to individuals on the basis of their sexual choices/orientation. Creating a legal context in which gays and lesbians enjoy full privacy rights would thus be an important step towards undermining the epistemology of the closet which is based on denial of such rights. It would also help to expand and ensure privacy rights in the domain of intimacy for everyone. Let me briefly turn to the *Hardwick* opinion to make this point.

The construction of a stigmatized identity: the majority opinion in *Hardwick*

As many have pointed out, the *Hardwick* case seemed to offer a textbook example of privacy issues.[59] Michael Hardwick was arrested for engaging in consensual sexual conduct with another (male) adult in the privacy of his own home.[60] All three of the central dimensions of constitutional privacy analysis considered standard since *Griswold* seemed to come into play here: the spatial (sanctity of the home as a protected private space); the relational (protection for intimate personal relationships); and the decisional (freedom of choice as to intimate (adult) partners and intimacies between them).[61] That is why the case appeared to fall squarely in line with the Court's privacy jurisprudence.[62] And yet in a 5–4 decision, the majority denied that previous privacy cases were *in any way* relevant to the case at hand. Why and on what grounds?

Hardwick challenged a gender-neutral sodomy statute on its face. The Georgia law stated that: 'A person commits the offense of sodomy when he performs or submits to any sexual act involving the sex organs of one person and the mouth or anus of another.'[63] The Court, however, maintained that 'The issue presented is whether the Federal Constitution confers a fundamental right upon *homosexuals* to engage in sodomy and hence invalidates the laws of the many States that still make such conduct illegal and have done so for a very long time' (my emphasis).[64] To the majority, the fact that *Hardwick* was caught engaging in sodomy *with another male* was the central pivot of the case.

In his vigorous dissent, Justice Blackmun radically disagreed with this characterization. He insisted that the case was not about a fundamental right to engage in 'homosexual sodomy' at all. Rather, it concerned a number of more general rights which had been protected under the rubric of privacy, including the right to control the nature of one's intimate associations with others, the right to conduct intimate relationships in the privacy of one's own home, and the 'right to be let alone' in order to be able to decide for oneself whether to engage in particular forms of consensual sexual activity in private.[65] As Justice Stevens also pointed out in his dissenting opinion, not only is the Georgia statute at issue not limited to homosexuals, it does not even mention them. Instead, it expresses the 'traditional view' that sodomy is an immoral kind of conduct and the gender of those engaged in it is irrelevant.

Accordingly, a proper analysis of the Georgia statute's constitutionality requires consideration of two questions: first, whether a state may totally prohibit the described *conduct* by means of a neutral law applying without exception, and second, if not, whether the State may save the statute by announcing that it will only enforce the law against homosexuals?[66] Stevens believed that under *Griswold* and its progeny, states may not totally prohibit the conduct proscribed by the Georgia criminal code.[67] Indeed, he reminds the Court that the Georgia Attorney General conceded that Georgia's statute would be unconstitutional if applied to a married couple, because of the 'right of marital privacy' as identified by the Court in *Griswold*![68]

A careful reading of the majority opinion shows that it was cleverly designed to anticipate, finesse, and trump precisely these sorts of arguments.[69] The Court defined the issue presented by the Georgia statute as whether the Federal Constitution confers a fundamental right upon homosexuals to engage in sodomy, and hence invalidates the laws of many states that still make 'such conduct' illegal.[70] But it left it unclear whether the term 'such' in 'such conduct' referred to sodomy or to homosexuality. This equivocation in the meaning of 'homosexual sodomy' allowed the Court to deny privacy protection in this 'most private of privacy cases' in part by masking an indefensible antipathy (its own) to a group in the form of a 'moral' aversion to what the group allegedly does.[71] The strategy of the majority opinion was to play upon the ambiguity in the very meaning of the concept 'homosexual sodomy', to 'erect a wall of difference' between the case before it and the line of earlier cases in which certain fundamental rights in the 'domain of intimacy' were deemed to be protected under privacy jurisprudence.[72]

Justice White set aside the privacy precedents by defining the rights at stake in earlier cases as having to do with *family, marriage* and *procreation*.[73] He then insisted that '. . . none of the rights announced in those cases bears *any* resemblance to the claimed constitutional right of homosexuals to engage in *acts* of sodomy that is asserted in this case. No connection between family, marriage, or procreation on the one hand and homosexual activity on the other has been demonstrated . . .' (my emphasis).[74]

The rhetorical function of combining the focus on identity and acts under the rubric 'homosexual sodomy' served two purposes. First, it enabled the majority to rely on the fact that the Court has not explicitly questioned the right of states to forbid particular sexual acts. Indeed, Justice White points out that many forms of voluntary sexual conduct between adults are prohibited, including adultery, incest and other 'sexual crimes'.[75]

Accordingly the idea that privacy precedents '. . . stand for the proposition that any kind of private sexual conduct between consenting adults is constitutionally insulated from state proscription is insupportable'.[76] Only if the previous privacy cases were interpreted *broadly* would they cover *Hardwick*'s case.[77] Speaking for the majority of the Court, White asserted that 'We are unwilling to start down that road.'[78]

The second purpose the focus on 'homosexual conduct' served was to enable the Court to evoke disgust vis-à-vis particular sexual acts (sodomy) deemed immoral in the past, and then to attach this disgust to the persons who are today habitually associated with the commitment of such acts (i.e., homosexuals). Justice Burger's concurring opinion devotes itself entirely to this task. Paraphrasing Blackstone, he states that sodomy has long been deemed an 'infamous crime against nature', an offence of 'deeper malignity' than rape, a heinous act, 'the very mention of which is a disgrace to human nature' and 'a crime not fit to be named'.[79] He concludes that to deem the 'act' of *homosexual sodomy* to be a fundamental right would be to cast aside 'millennia of moral teaching'.[80]

The slippage of the rhetoric of acts into the rhetoric of identity thus attaches the stigma associated with allegedly immoral and hence justifiably criminalized acts on to the persona of a specific group: homosexuals. The group is thereby constructed as radically different, indeed as a criminally inclined class, requiring differential treatment by the law. The homosexual sodomite is rendered visible, perpetually open to surveillance. At the same time, heterosexual sodomy is erased from view. Here is the place to locate the legal context for the epistemology of the closet and identity politics.

The establishment of radical difference and the legal reinforcement of the privileged status of heterosexual marriage as the only acceptable form of intimacy is the real point of White's assertion that 'no connection between family, marriage, or procreation on the one hand and homosexual activity on the other has been demonstrated'.[81]

It is worth pointing out that the appeal to tradition and to historical attitudes regarding the 'immorality' of a practice is hardly sufficient to save a law from constitutional attack, as the example of miscegenation law shows.[82] Moreover, by the time of the decision, half of the states had repealed their sodomy statutes, and in that half of the states that did not repeal them, the laws were no longer being enforced unless there were aggravating circumstances.[83] This would seem to indicate that the alleged historical consensus regarding the immorality of *sodomy* had dissolved, along with the will to punish 'offenders' as criminals.[84]

But this has to mean that what really drives the entire argumentation is not the 'ancient', 'traditional' or 'religious/moral' disgust for certain sex acts, but rather an antipathy to homosexual object-preference. As Richard Posner has aptly put it, it is the fact that men lust after other men, and not the form in which this lust is expressed, that marks homosexuality as being *profoundly different* from heterosexuality in the minds of the majority of the justices.

The Court in *Hardwick* drew on social constructions of homosexual identity as radically different and inferior, in short, as 'other', that had been readily available in psychological, medical, sociological and moral discourses since the nineteenth century. But the reproduction of such constructions in the legal text was not mere mimesis. Rather, with the concept of 'homosexual sodomy' we have a clear example of the legal construction of the subject before the law. Indeed the category served to create and re-create a stigmatized group identity just when those sorts of constructions were in the process of being abandoned and just when the stigma attached to homosexuality and the 'deployment of sexuality' was being openly challenged.[85] It continues to provide a pretext for differential (greater surveillance and regulation, reduced rights) (mis-)treatment of individuals associated with that identity. Indeed, if 'homosexual sodomy' simultaneously constitutes both criminal behaviour and a criminal class, then, at least on some influential interpretations, the equal protection clause must allow the states and the federal government a broad scope for treating it differently from heterosexuality even when 'expressed' in physically similar acts.[86]

Conclusion

It might seem naive to argue for the extension of constitutional privacy protection to cover consensual adult intimacy, in light of what we know about the partially constructed and politically contested terrain of sexuality, of intimate association, of rights in general, and of the right to privacy in particular.[87] But this holds true only for one model of privacy. If we distinguish the *concept* of a right to privacy from various *conceptions* of privacy, we can acknowledge the constitutive character of the former and the constructed, historically variable character of the latter. We can be quite aware of the political implications of each and argue *on that basis* for constitutionally protected privacy rights and for a specific conception of privacy to shield previously uncovered activities and relations.

The *concept* of a right to personal privacy particularly regarding intimate association involves the dispositional autonomy over personal boundaries, wherever these are drawn. This means that the individual rights-holder is construed as an ethically competent subject with respect to what are considered to be 'personal matters', and then granted a certain leeway to organize her own conduct in relation to this 'legally constituted' presumptively protected terrain.[88] Such rights do not imply that the decisional autonomy accorded to individuals must be exercised in a certain way or in certain circumscribed 'private' places. Constituted as the rights-holder, it is up to the individual to choose whether, how, and where to exercise her legally acknowledged agency.

In conferring a right to personal privacy, moreover, the law constitutes and protects a structure of recognition whereby the claim to individual integrity (personal inviolability, a bounded self, agency) of the natural person is acknowledged and the expectation that others will respect it is institutionalized.[89] In other words, the concept of a right to personal privacy affirms the importance of *intersubjectively* recognized personal *boundaries* – and places presumptive dispositional control over practice and disclosure within whatever is socially construed as the personal in the hands of the individuals involved.

As such, a right to privacy is 'dualistic': it faces in two directions. On the one side, the ideas of decisional autonomy, control over access, and informational privacy bring the notion of a boundary into play. Accordingly, decisional autonomy implies control over access to the self, freedom of choice to enter and exit intimate relationships, along with the liberty to withdraw certain concerns, motives, personal decisions, from public scrutiny. The latter aspect involves the 'negative' dimension of what I have called 'communicative liberty': the absence of any legal obligation either to reveal or to justify one's personal choices in the same terms that everyone else would accept.[90] One has, as it were, the right to be different in this domain. The state may not require me to reveal my reasons for acting in the domain in which I have the right to act on my own reasons.

But privacy rights also face outward: they are exercised in public as well as in 'private' spaces.[91] From this optic, what is at stake is the right to decide with which 'socially constructed identities' one will identify, and which dimensions of one's personal 'identity' one wishes to present in different fora. A second dimension of communicative liberty is tied to this aspect of personal autonomy, namely, the right to present aspects of oneself, one's way of life, one's projects in public, as a claim for recognition. Accordingly the state may not require that I conceal my identity, my desires, my personal choices or the reasons I have for making them. In protecting personal autonomy, privacy rights also entail the right to speak and present who one is in public, ascribing discretionary power over how to present oneself to the individual.[92] Thus it is only apparently paradoxical that a privacy right ensuring personal decisional autonomy over certain concerns entitles one to think and to be what one chooses and to announce it to the world, thereby ensuring a right to public expression as well.

Of course just where and how the boundaries of personal privacy are drawn is a public and political question. The concept of a right to privacy does not dictate any particular conception of what should be private or where the boundary should be drawn. In this regard it is, as are all other basic rights (to speech, to equality) indeterminate. That is why one cannot answer the question of 'application' by an analysis of concepts, normative or constitutional.[93] Just what should come under privacy coverage and who gets such protection depends on shifting cultural understandings, changing perceptions of threats to individual integrity, new interpretations of what are deemed personal and ethical as distinct from moral issues and, of course, on the constellation of power and the particular context in which the issue arises. Whether acts or relationships get cast as matters of morality and criminal law, or as questions of an individual's or group's form of life and thus as a matter of personal choice depends on the outcome of such struggles.

But this does not mean that nothing is ever settled. Simply because one cannot analytically deduce a normative conception of what privacy rights should cover does not mean one has to abandon privacy analysis on the grounds that the whole issue is 'political', and that all line-drawing and every assertion of a fundamental right is 'arbitrary'. Rather, one must start *in medias res*, for the normative boundary between public and private is always already drawn. It is also contested. Indeed, privacy rights are (recursively) a condition of the possibility of democratic contestation. To the degree to which they protect self-determination (mental autonomy) against domination, and afford at least a minimum degree of personal security, they enable one to be an autonomous participant in the contestation over where to draw the boundaries. 'Hard cases' involve contested *conceptions* of where the boundaries should be drawn. Nevertheless, the moral weight of the *concept* of a 'fundamental' right to personal privacy is presupposed in each claim.[94] *The questions to ask are:*

1 What is at stake in the highly politicized struggle over which forms of intimacy to include under privacy protection; and
2 Why is this battle going on now?

It should be clear from the above that today it is the overall *conception* of privacy vis-à-vis the 'domain' of intimacy that is at stake. The line of decisions beginning with *Griswold* focused on intimate relationships and sexuality as partially constitutive of intimacy. The debate ever since has been over whether this decision and its progeny are to be interpreted narrowly as protecting (and privileging) only heterosexual marital relationships, the 'traditional' (patriarchal, heterosexual) family construed as an entity or broadly as protecting the freedom of intimate association and all that it entails irrespective of marital status or gender. The conception that I argue for in this chapter construes the individual as the bearer of personal privacy rights and all intimate relationships between consenting adults as presumptively meriting protection from unwarranted intrusion or regulation by the state or third parties with one proviso: that the demands of justice are not violated within the relationship. This approach presumes, as did Justice Blackmun, that '. . . in a Nation as diverse as ours, . . . there may be many "right" ways of conducting those relationships and that much of the richness of a relationship will come from the freedom an individual has to *choose* the form and nature of these intensely personal bonds'.[95]

Indeed the interpretive dispute indicates both that the old consensus on the moral privileging of reproductive sex within traditional marriage is deeply shaken (otherwise there would be no open contest) and that sexuality has become politically and ethically important. The previously hegemonic form of intimate association – monogamous, heterosexual, permanent, patriarchal marriage with its rigid gender norms and hierarchies and explicit homophobia – has been decentred, and a pluralization of forms of intimacy demanding equal treatment has occurred.[96] Presumptive gender equality and claims to equal citizenship for all is the background terrain for the contemporary disputes over regulating intimacy. The battle is between those trying to reinstate the former model regardless of the amount of repression necessary to do so, and those defending pluralization and gender equality.

But the dispute also involves a challenge to the version of the medical model of sexuality that constructs perverse sexual identities and ascribes them to the perpetrators of 'abnormal' and/or 'immoral' sexual acts. It is this model which informs current efforts to revitalize laws criminalizing sodomy as the majority opinion in *Hardwick* patently demonstrates.

Here is where one must look in order to answer the second question. For the historically specific 'deployment of sexuality', so brilliantly analysed by Foucault helped construct the terrain on which it is now being challenged.[97] As Foucault pointed out, the appearance in psychiatry, jurisprudence and literature of a whole series of discourses on the species and subspecies of homosexuality (and other 'perversions') facilitated a strong advance of social controls into this area, '. . . but it also made possible the formation of a "reverse" discourse: homosexuality began to speak in its own behalf, to demand that its legitimacy . . . be acknowledged . . .'.[98]

Accordingly, new forms of sexual politics have emerged on the terrain developed historically through the deployment of sexuality, some of which challenge the very presuppositions of that deployment. In part, the political struggle has taken the form of a demand for a specific range of rights.[99] When such demands are articulated by those whose sexuality is considered deviant or whose sexual identity is deemed pathological, they clearly are meant to challenge such evaluations. In other words, these claims involve an effort to shift 'different' sexualities and acts from the status of 'immorality' and 'pathology' to the status of personal expression and ethical choice (to be protected by privacy rights). Particular sex acts, touchings, and object choices would thereby lose their moral salience while the ethical issues raised by the plurality of intimate relationships would become more visible.

In my view, what should replace the 'moral' and medicalized assessment of sex acts and object choices is an egalitarian morality of intimate relationships. The criteria undergirding the regulation of adult intimacy should not be where one is touched or by whom, but rather whether or not the relationships or encounters *between adults* are consensual, reciprocal, egalitarian, with real exit opportunities and do not involve subjugation or domination, or forced, fraudulent, violent, oppressive, abusive, exploitative acts, etc. Every adult on this approach should be construed by law to be an ethically competent, responsible legal subject whose personal autonomy merits protection in this domain. The burden of proof should shift to the shoulders of those who would criminalize or stigmatize through law certain forms of intimate association or sexual choices. They would have to show that the proscribed relationships fit the second rather than the first category. If they cannot do so, then privacy rights protecting personal autonomy and the freedom of intimate association should trump any effort on the part of the state to proscribe, persecute, force disclosure or silence a particular form of intimacy. Liberty in this domain must, of course, be equal liberty. The majority cannot grant itself freedoms which it denies to others.

Of course, this formulation does not mean that the right to privacy is a natural right or that the state cannot intervene into a particular domain of social life to protect other rights, or to provide for the worth of the right it has acknowledged. Nor does it entail the idea of a natural pre-political sphere cordoned off from state action. The state and regulatory regimes are involved in the domain of intimate association even when the decisional autonomy of the individual is acknowledged. What is needed is a way to think of fundamental constitutionalized privacy rights protecting intimate relationships without relying on a logic that construes acts as constitutive of identity and without resurrecting the myth of a natural private sphere 'beyond' justice.

Conceptions of legitimate private intimate relationships vary with prevailing cultural models of gender identity, and the relative thickness or thinness of our ethical understanding of personal identity. Constitutional regimes and legal paradigms influence and are affected by these conceptions. My sense is that current struggles over the meaning of privacy rights and the proliferation of hard cases in the domain of intimate association indicate that we need to rethink core assumptions of the liberal legal paradigm. This paradigm assumes that there are natural spheres of personal autonomy (and deep sexual identities slumbering within the individual) that should be liberated from repression, shielded from state intrusion and left to private orderings once the law has ensured against force or fraud. Freedom of intimate association protected by privacy is thus assimilated to freedom of contract. Liberty on this model is negative liberty – i.e. freedom from external constraint (physical or moral) on the self-determination of the will.

Accordingly, on the liberal legal paradigm, liberty and law, personal freedom and state regulation are placed in a zero sum relationship: the only way to ensure personal liberty is to limit the scope of state action vis-à-vis a private domain wherein the individual is sovereign. Privacy analysis is construed as a way to keep the state out. This conception of personal freedom as negative liberty and the opposition between law and freedom was first developed by Hobbes and has haunted liberal political and legal theory ever since. It contributes to the misleading conception of privacy rights as protecting a natural domain of individual freedom, sovereign self-determination and associational autonomy that lies outside power, politics, law, state action and is beyond regulation.

My argument for extending constitutional privacy protection to cover consensual forms of intimate association among adults regardless of their sexual orientation should not be construed as a call to extend the immunities once enjoyed exclusively by the male head of heterosexual patriarchal households to all intimate associations. Nor do I want to assimilate freedom of association to freedom of contract, regulated only to prevent forced or fraudulent terms of entry or exit. As already indicated above, the public/private line must go right through intimate association: privacy as decisional autonomy to enter and control intimate associations by the intimate associates themselves cannot shield these associations from the demands of justice. For we know all too well that the 'domain of intimacy' involves gender and sexual relations that are socially and legally constructed, often involve differentials in power and resources, and can reproduce social hierarchies of status and other sorts of structural inequalities and forms of domination. Intimate associations cannot be free if privacy shields them from legal protection against internal forms of oppression.

But we are not doomed to the liberal conception of freedom. Once we see that the freedom protected by privacy rights vis-à-vis intimate association is broader than negative liberty, once it is acknowledged that privacy as decisional autonomy protecting personal liberty must include freedom from oppression, from domination, and real exit options, the paradoxes of regulating intimacy can be resolved. For these forms of freedom can only be guaranteed through law. 'Negative liberty' in the sense of freedom of choice and freedom from constraint regarding entry and exit into intimate associations for adults is of course part of what is meant by the freedom of intimate association, protected by constitutional privacy rights. But this can and must be disassociated from untenable dimensions of the liberal legal paradigm, in particular from the image of a private sphere beyond justice. Negative liberty is necessary but not sufficient to protect freedom in this domain. A key dimension of freedom at stake in the freedom of intimate association is the right to be free from personal oppression and domination by intimate associates. Freedom from instrumentalization to another's purposes (from being treated as a means *only*) is also crucial to personal liberty. Coming to us from the republican tradition of political theory this conception of personal autonomy can and should inform privacy analysis, and guide state regulation in this domain. Far from being in a zero-sum relationship with the law, personal freedom understood in this way *requires* legal regulation to ensure that intimate associations conform to the basic principles of justice and to ensure that they apply to everyone equally. On the republican view, the law can *create* personal liberty by protecting against the resources or *dominium* of those who would otherwise have arbitrary power over their associates.[100] Privacy rights protecting the freedom of intimate association must involve protection of freedom as non-domination within such associations and thus they involve state action and appropriate forms of regulation.

But this need not mean that we must bring the heavy hand of the law to bear on intimate association through *direct substantive regulatory measures* aimed at undoing inequalities of resources or power or at *imposing one substantive conception of 'good intimacy' on to all relationships*. If the liberal paradigm involves an overly narrow conception of liberty that ignores inequalities and oppression within intimate association, an unabashed interventionist approach fails to take personal autonomy and privacy seriously. It is the effects of power that regulation protects against by ensuring the personal freedom of each intimate associate.

The drastic changes in gender relations, including individualization and pluralization in the domain of intimacy among other areas of civil society, thus require a more nuanced approach – typified by what some have called a 'reflexive' paradigm of law.[101] Such an approach would proceed from the constructed character of private intimate relations as well as the reflexive structure of individual identities.[102] Constitutionalization on this model must be understood as constituting the domain of intimacy in a suitable institutional form such that normatively directed processes of adjustment and self-correction to secure personal liberty are possible.[103] In other words, one should understand constitutional privacy rights as constitutive of the personal autonomy that it protects and as fostering self-regulating autonomous intimate relationships structured so as to equalize the bargaining power, voice and standing of the partners and to protect against oppression and injustice. Social autonomy would be supported but not through adaptation to alleged natural orders and not by taking prior distributions of power and prestige as given but through the regulation of self-regulating intimate associations to ensure a just distribution of rights and competencies – freedom as non-domination – of the intimate associates themselves. The appropriate form of juridification of such 'constructed' private intimate relations would thus have a triple task: to avoid both the disintegrative effects of overly intrusive regulation and the unjust effects of 'non-intervention' while providing normative and institutional resources that enable secure, rewarding and autonomous intimate relationships to develop. Privacy as decisional autonomy regarding entry, exit, and the conduct of intimate association must go together with freedom from oppression within such associations, otherwise the autonomy of the partners is overturned.

Let me conclude. Properly interpreted, appeals to personal privacy in the domain of intimacy involve both choice regarding a range of activity and an 'endorsement constraint': the right not to have an identity imposed on one by the state which one cannot freely affirm and embrace. Whatever the source of one's sexual orientation, the notion of personal autonomy leaves it up to the individual whether or not to construe sexual desires or acts as defining the core of one's identity.[104] The choice of affiliating with the relevant group-identity should also be an individual one. Accordingly, legal imposition of an unwanted identity constitutes a real harm regardless of its social status.[105]

Needless to say, the harm is especially great if the identity so imposed is a stigmatized one. The *Hardwick* opinion articulated an interpretation of gay identity as perverse and immoral, and construed it to be inherently a set of criminalizable sexual acts. This legal construction provided the pretext for denying a wide range of other rights to the people falling into the stigmatized identity category. The 'new military policy' is an example. On its own, the *Hardwick* decision has a 'chilling effect' regarding public speech about one's sexual conduct if one is gay. It also undermines the chances to develop secure and rewarding intimate relationships that deviate from the heterosexual norm. The military has made the chilling effect into public policy, imposing a 'duty of privacy' regarding sexual desire and conduct selectively on to one particular category of individuals. Both dimensions of 'communicative liberty' discussed above are thereby violated for the targeted group.

Had the privacy rights of gays and lesbians been acknowledged instead of denied in *Hardwick*, the military would have had to find some other route for accomplishing its goal – unequal treatment of gays and lesbians.

The point is not that privacy secures gay rights or liberation. Only if voice and equal protection are secured, can the low social status of a group identity be challenged, and equal dignity prevail over the shame, secrecy and fear attached to previously disdained forms of life. But privacy, understood on the reflexive model of constitutional rights, serves to protect individuals from having an identity, whatever its social status, ascribed to them which they do not endorse or with which they wish only partially and sporadically to identify, and that without coercion and without risking being 'totalized' as essentially this or that. It also facilitates the development of rewarding and just intimate relationships. Were this to be acknowledged in full, it would go a long way towards undermining the epistemology of the closet.

Notes

1 Hannah Arendt, *On Revolution* (New York: Viking Press) 1965, p. 252. Arendt saw the Bill of Rights in the American Constitution as the most exhaustive legal bulwark ever contrived in modern times for the protection of the private realm against public power. Yet she viewed the decentring of property rights in the twentieth century with deep foreboding, fearing that the boundary between public and private was thereby fatally weakened. See Jean L. Cohen, 'Redescribing Privacy: Identity, Difference and the Abortion Controversy', *Columbia Journal of Gender and Law* 1992, pp. 105–12 for a discussion.

2 See Michael Sandel, *Democracy's Discontent* (Cambridge, Mass.: Harvard University Press) 1996; Robert Bellah, *Habits of the Heart* (Berkeley: University of California Press) 1985; Mary Ann Glendon, *Rights Talk* (New York: Free Press) 1991.

3 Elsthain, Jean Bethke, *Democracy on Trial* (New York: Basic Books) 1995.

4 Elsthain, *Democracy on Trial*, p. 52.

5 *Democracy on Trial*, pp. 55–7.

6 Here Elsthain follows Arendt. Arendt accomplished this by a conceptual manoeuvre that mapped an analytic distinction (public and private) on to quasi-ontologized categories of action (labour and work) and then on to institutional spheres of life (domestic–private sphere/political–public sphere). Here too the result was the construction of an essentialized and rigid dichotomy.

7 Ulrich Beck, *Risk Society* (Newbury Park, Ca.: Sage) 1986.

8 See Adam Pertman, 'Clinton May Provide Fusion of Politics, Policy', *Boston Globe*, 30 Oct. 1992, at A1; Jane M. Adams, 'Gay Man Returns to Navy Service: Clinton Stands by Opening of Military to Homosexuals', *Boston Globe*, 13 Nov. 1992, at A1. Cf. Gwen Ifill, 'Clinton Accepts Delay in Lifting Military Gay Ban, *New York Times*, 30 Jan. 1993, at A8. (Reporting Clinton's post-electoral news conference discussing his charge to the Secretary of Defense to formulate a new policy.)

The military ban has been in place since 1943 when the military issued final regulations banning lesbians and gays from all of its branches. These regulations have remained by and large unchanged until now. See Randy Shilts,

Conduct Unbecoming: Gays and Lesbians in the U.S. Military (New York: St. Martin's Press) 1993, p. 17.

9 It is worth noting that all NATO countries except Britain allow gays and lesbians into the military. Recently, in 1999, the European Court of Justice ordered Britain to do so, invoking the *privacy right* of gays and lesbians. Canada's 1992 decision to revoke its military ban caused little controversy. Thus Clinton was not so wrong to assume that his proposal would not cause much dismay. This is so especially given the results of the 1992 Pentagon-commissioned Rand Corporation study of the military ban. The Rand study concluded that 'the ban could be dropped without damaging the order, discipline, and individual behavior necessary to maintain cohesion, and performance'. Cited in Craig A. Rimmerman, 'Promise Unfulfilled: Clinton's Failure to Overturn the Military Ban on Gays and Lesbians', paper delivered at APSA 1–4 Sept. 1994 meeting in New York City, pp. 4–5. The report was released in August 1993. See also Bruce Bawer, *A Place at the Table: The Gay Individual in American Society* (New York: Poseidon Press) 1993, p. 50.

10 A study by the Servicemembers Legal Defense Network in 1996 found that the new military policy in practice was 'as bad, if not worse than its predecessors', and that witch hunts for gays were still common (*New York Times*, 3 March 1996 at E7). Legal challenges continue to be made to the policy. Indeed it has become something of a political football continuously challenged in the courts and linked to complex political manoeuvres by various contending parties. It has certainly not, however, disappeared.

11 Orchestrated by the religious right. See Bruce Bawer, *A Place at the Table*, op. cit., p. 60, and Rimmerman, op. cit., p. 6.

12 Also party to the compromise was Sam Nunn, then chair of the Senate Armed Services Committee. For reports on the political process leading to the Department of Defense Directive, see Gwen Ifill, 'White House Backs 2-Step Plan to End Military's Gay Ban', *New York Times*, 27 Jan. 1993 at A1 (reporting President Clinton's suspension of the old military policy requiring investigation and discharge of anyone evincing homosexual desire or acts). See also 'Excerpts From the News Conferences by Clinton and Nunn', *New York Times*, 30 Jan. 1993 at A8 (discussing Clinton's charge to the Secretary of Defense to formulate a new policy acceptable to military leaders). See also Eric Schmitt, 'President's Policy on Gay Troops is Backed in Vote of Senate Panel', *New York Times*, 24 July 1993 at A7. See generally Bruce Bawer, *A Place at the Table*, op. cit., pp. 59–60.

13 10 U.S.C. # 654 (1994). After the brouhaha Clinton offered a compromise with his July 1993 'Don't Ask, Don't Tell' proposal. For details see Rimmerman, 'Promise Unfulfilled', op. cit., p. 708. Rimmerman points out that it was initially Clinton's purpose to issue the new policy as an executive order to undo the old ban which was itself enforced through an executive order. However, upon Sam Nunn's prodding, a modified version of the Clinton proposal was codified into law by the United States Congress, thus making it much more difficult for opponents of the ban to offer serious reforms in the future. Any policy change would now require congressional consent. Nunn's congressional manoeuvre enabled specifics of the Clinton plan to take effect but also codified into law a broad policy statement rejecting the notion of accepting gays without provisos in the military. Rimmerman, op. cit., p. 8.

14 It is worth noting that military courts have been willing to state frankly that sodomy statutes apply to consensual heterosexual conduct. Cited in Janet E. Halley, 'Reasoning About Sodomy: Act and Identity in and after *Bowers v. Hardwick*, 79 *Virginia Law Review* 1721, 1777, October 1993 (citing *United*

142   *Jean L. Cohen*

States v. Henderson, 34 M.J. 174 (C.M.A. 1992); *United States v. Fagg*, 34 M.J. 179 (C.M.A.) cert. denied, 113 S. CT. 92 (1992)).

15 See Patricia Cain, 'Litigating for Lesbian and Gay Rights: A Legal History', 79 *Virginia Law Review*, 1551, 1595–1600 (1993) (discussing cases of expulsion).

16 Anne Goldstein, 'Reasoning About Homosexuality: A Commentary on Janet Halley's "Reasoning about Sodomy: Act and Identity in and after *Bowers v. Hardwick*"', 79 *Virginia Law Review* 1781, at p. 484. The former US army regulation on the books from 1981–1993 required exclusion of any 'homosexual' defined as 'a person, regardless of sex, who engages in, desires to engage in, or intends to engage in homosexual acts'. Andrew Koppelman, 'Why Discrimination against Lesbians and Gays is Sex Discrimination', 69 *New York University Law Review* 197, 265 (1994) quoting Army regulation (AR) 635–200 #15–2(a). The rule is status-based since it exempted those who have been involved in an isolated homosexual act they regretted. Earlier regulations apparently focused on conduct and status. See Randy Shilts, *Conduct Unbecoming*, op. cit.

17 See 'The Pentagon's New Policy Guidelines on Homosexuals in the Military', *New York Times*, 20 July 1993, at A16.

18 As it was earlier. Although the term 'sexual status' usually refers to whether one is male or female, I use it here to refer to sexual orientation. It will become clear further on that the distinction between status and conduct is important in the legal decisions concerning homosexuals. However, as the term 'sexual orientation status' is cumbersome, I have chosen to use 'status' *tout court* to refer to orientation as distinct from conduct.

19 See 'The Pentagon's New Policy Guidelines on Homosexuals in The Military', *New York Times*, 20 July 1993 at A16. Defining 'homosexual conduct' as 'a homosexual act, a statement that the member is homosexual or bisexual, or a marriage or attempted marriage to someone of the same gender'. The Congressional legislation states that military cohesion and morale are threatened by 'the presence in the armed forces of persons who demonstrate a propensity or intent to engage in homosexual acts would create an unacceptable risk to the high standards of morale, good order and discipline, and unit cohesion that are the essence of military capability', 10 U.S.C.A. #654 a (15) West 1994.

20 See Anne Goldstein, 'Reasoning About Homosexuality', op. cit., pp. 485–8.

21 Ibid.

22 Bruce Baker, *A Place at the Table: the Gay Individual in American Society*, op. cit., p. 61, has argued that 'This compromise . . . would essentially write into law the institution of the closet . . .'

23 *Bowers v. Hardwick*, 478 U.S. 186 (1986).

24 See Patricia Cain, 'Litigating for Gay and Lesbian Rights', op. cit., pp. 1596–600.

25 In an earlier piece I have addressed feminist and communitarian critiques of privacy doctrine with respect to the abortion controversy. Here I address a set of distinctive arguments that have been raised in the context of debates over sexual orientation and sexual autonomy. See Jean L. Cohen, 'Redescribing Privacy: Identity, Difference and the Abortion Controversy', *Columbia Journal of Gender and Law*, vol. 3, 1992, no. 1, pp. 43–117.

26 Eve Kosofsky Sedgwick, *Epistemology of the Closet* (Berkeley, Ca.: University of California Press) 1990.

27 Ibid., p. 71. See also Janet Halley, 'The Politics of the Closet: Towards Equal Protection for Gay, Lesbian and Bisexual Identity', op. cit., pp. 915–76.

28 Sedgwick, *Epistemology*, p. 71.

29 The reign of the telling secret expresses the epistemology of the closet in her view: 'Even an out gay person deals daily with interlocutors about whom she doesn't know whether they know or not; it is equally difficult to guess for any given interlocutor whether, if they did know, the knowledge would seem very important. Nor – at the most basic level – is it unaccountable that someone who wanted a job, custody or visiting rights, insurance, protection from violence . . . from insulting scrutiny . . . could deliberately choose to remain in or to re-enter the closet in some or all segments of their life. The gay closet is not a feature only of the lives of gay people. But for many gay people it is still the fundamental feature of social life . . .' Sedgwick, *Epistemology*, p. 68.

30 See Phillip Brian Harper, 'Private Affairs: Race, Sex, Property and Persons', in *GLQ: a Journal of Lesbian and Gay Studies*, vol. 1, no. 2, p. 118, for a discussion of 'the social function of secrecy' as concealing not knowledge but the knowledge of knowledge.

31 'Notes: The Constitutional Status of Sexual Orientation: Homosexuality as a Suspect Classification', 98 *Harvard Law Review* (1985), pp. 1285, 1297, and Janet Halley, 'The Politics of the Closet: Towards Equal Protection for Gay, Lesbian and Bisexual Identity', op. cit., pp. 915–76; Kendall Thomas, 'Beyond the Privacy Principle', *Columbia Law Review*, vol. 92, no. 6, October 1992, pp. 1431–516; Andrew Koppelman, 'Why Discrimination Against Lesbians and Gays is Sex Discrimination', *New York University Law Review*, vol. 69, 1994, 101–93.

32 Thomas, 'Beyond the Privacy Principle', op. cit., pp. 1455–6.

33 Thomas, ibid., p. 1455.

34 Thomas seems to admit the importance of privacy rights when he states that 'I believe that each of the three components of privacy articulates distinctive and important dimensions of the moral conditions and consequences of sexual intimacy . . . efforts to identify and secure a sphere of protected places, intimate and emotional engagements, and individual autonomy generate helpful insights about the conditions without which a concrete personal sexual morality is impossible', ibid., p. 1456. Nevertheless he rejects privacy jurisprudence vis-à-vis sodomy statutes and for protecting the rights of homosexuals. See also Kendall Thomas, 'The Eclipse of Reason: A Rhetorical Reading of *Bowers v. Hardwick*', 79 *Virginia Law Review*, 1805.

35 Thomas, 'Beyond the Privacy Principle', p. 1455.

36 Ibid., p. 1456.

37 See Sedgwick, op. cit., p. 71.

38 For critiques of liberal tolerance along these line see the essays by Robert Paul Wolff, Barrington Moore Jr. and Herbert Marcuse, *A Critique of Pure Tolerance* (Boston, Mass.: Beacon Press) 1965. For a more recent discussion arguing that liberalism tolerates diversity through the depoliticizing and taming of difference, see Kirstie McClure, 'Diversity, Difference and the Limits of Toleration', *Political Theory* 18, 3 August 1990, pp. 361–92. For a theory of toleration that focuses on equality analysis see Elisabetta Galeotti, 'Citizenship and Equality: The Place of Toleration', *Political Theory* 21, 4, November 1993, pp. 585—605.

39 I rely here on the reader's common sense regarding the role played by prejudice against homosexuals in much law targeting their sexuality.

40 For this distinction see Ronald Dworkin, *Taking Rights Seriously* (Cambridge, Mass.: Harvard University Press) 1978, pp. 134–6.

41 Sedgwick, *Epistemology*, pp. 69–70.

42 For a discussion of the new privacy doctrine see Jean L. Cohen, 'Redescribing Privacy', op. cit., pp.1–92.

43 See Jean L. Cohen, 'Zur Neubeschreibung der Privatsphäre', in Christoph Menke and Martin Seel, eds, *Zur Verteidigung der Vernunft gegen ihre Liebhaber und Verächter* (Frankfurt am Main: Suhrkamp Verlag) 1993, pp. 300–32. Informational privacy goes with decisional autonomy here.

44 Both outing and enforced concealment or seclusion would violate such a privacy right.

45 See Lawrence Tribe, *American Constitutional Law*, 2nd edn (New York: The Foundation Press, Inc.) 1988, pp. 1424–5 arguing that the regulation of sexual activity in public must be distinguished from that dealing with sexual conduct at home or in private. See footnote 36, page 1425 for citations of relevant cases.

46 Sodomy is not protected behaviour and in some states it is illegal. But surely it would be paradoxical, to say the least, to impose a duty through policy or statutes to be discreet about illegal conduct! Of course I am not talking about officials guarding state secrets. The state can insist on silence and discretion on the part of officials of the CIA or FBI, for example. Moreover, private individuals can make contracts that stipulate non-disclosure. Needless to say these examples do not undermine my general claim.

47 See *Watkins v. United States Army* 847 F2d 1329, 1335–40 (9th Cir. 1988); *Meinhold v. United States Dept of Defense* 808 F. Supp. 1455, 1458 (C.D. Cal 1993). For a cogent discussion of older and more recent military cases regarding homosexuals see Patricia Cain, 'Litigating', op. cit., pp. 1596–600.

48 *Bowers v. Hardwick*, 478 U.S. 186 (1986). For discussions of the status of sodomy statutes before and after *Hardwick* on the state level, see Janet Halley, 'Reasoning about Sodomy', op. cit., at 1774–6.

49 To date no straights were interrogated by the military for consensual sodomy or for other sex crimes like visiting prostitutes. See the article by Hanna Rosin, 'The Ban Plays On', *The New Republic*, 2 May 1994, pp. 11–13.

   It is certainly true that the military can justify policies that regulate conduct even if it were protected by the Constitution for civilian life. It could invoke 'military' reasons for its policies regarding specific groups such as the importance of maintaining 'esprit de corps' or military discipline in the barracks. In the past such arguments were invoked in order to keep women out of the military and to keep blacks in special units segregated from whites. This nevertheless does not undermine my point regarding the *new* policy, namely that its alleged focusing on conduct and discretion is a thin disguise for targeting homosexual status. In many respects the old policy was more honest.

50 Clearly it is not the acts but the status of those committing them that interests the military. For if the issue really is the commitment of a criminalizable *act* (sodomy), and not one's sexual preference or identity, why is it that *only* homosexuals and lesbians are the subject of the new policy of 'don't ask, don't tell, don't pursue'?

51 See Halley, 'Reasoning about Sodomy', pp. 457–8 for statistics. On her reading only five state statutes specifically target sodomy between persons of the same sex.

52 Jean L. Cohen, 'Is There a Duty of Privacy? Law, Sexual Orientation and the Construction of Identity', *Texas Journal of Women and the Law*, vol. 6, Fall 1996, issue 1, pp. 47–129. This paper will also appear in a substantially altered version as Chapter 2 in Jean L. Cohen, *Rethinking Sex, Law, Privacy and the Constitutional Dilemmas of Regulating Intimacy* (Princeton: Princeton University Press, forthcoming).

53 Janet E. Halley, 'Reasoning about Sodomy', op. cit.
54 See Dan Ortiz, 'Creating Controversy: Essentialism and Constructivism and the Politics of Gay Identity', 79 *Virginia Law Review* 1833, October 1993.
55 Originally anti-sodomy laws did not play that role: rather they juridified a Christian moral world view and were intended to ensure that married couples engaged in reproductive sex. Since the late eighteenth century and what Foucault has called the 'deployment of sexuality' such laws have undergone a change in function; now they construct and stigmatize a sexual identity: the homosexual sodomite. See M. Foucault, *The History of Sexuality*, vol. 1 (New York: Vintage Books) 1990; Janet Halley, 'Reasoning about Sodomy', op. cit., p. 1. Indeed one could follow Gayle Rubin, 'Thinking Sex: Notes for a Radical Theory of the Politics of Sexuality', in Carol S. Vance, ed., *Pleasure and Danger* (London: Routledge and Kegan Paul) 1984, pp. 267–319, and make the general point that harsh sex law creates sexual-identity hierarchies. Others add to this argument the claim that harsh sex law serves to reinforce gender hierarchies and patriarchal norms. See Sylvia Law, 'Homosexuality and the Social Meaning of Gender', 1988 *Wisconsin Law Review* 187 (arguing that the legal and cultural disapprobation of homosexual behaviour is a reaction to the violation of gender norms and not simply to the violation of norms of sexual behaviour). See also Susan Moller Okin, 'Sexual Orientation and Gender: Dichotomizing Differences', paper presented at the 'Democracy and Difference' conference sponsored by the Conference for the Study of Political Thought (CSPT) at Yale University, New Haven, Conn., 16–18 April 1993. For a slightly different argument to the effect that sodomy statutes violate the constitutional bar on sex discrimination when they target relations between members of the same sex see Andrew Koppelman, 'Note The Miscegenation Analogy: Sodomy Laws as Sex Discrimination', 98 *Yale Law Journal* 145 (1988) and Koppelman, 'Why Discrimination Against Lesbians and Gays is Sex Discrimination', op. cit.
56 This point is argued forcefully by Anne Goldstein, 'Reasoning About Homosexuality', op. cit.
57 Gayle Rubin, 'Thinking Sex: Notes for a Radical Theory of the Politics of Sexuality', in Carol S. Vance, ed., op. cit., pp. 267–319.
58 See Judith Butler, *Gender Trouble* (New York: Routledge) 1990, p. 2.
59 See L. Tribe, *American Constitutional Law*, op. cit., pp. 1421–35, and Kendall Thomas, 'Beyond the Pleasure Principle', op. cit., p. 1437.
60 For a discussion of the details of the case, see Kendall Thomas, ibid., pp. 1436–43. See also Patricia Cain, 'Litigating for Lesbian and Gay Rights', pp. 1587–95 for a discussion of sodomy cases and their impact prior to and including the *Hardwick* ruling.
61 *Griswold v. Connecticut*, 381 U.S. 478, 485 (1965). See Kendall Thomas, 'Beyond the Pleasure Principle', op. cit., pp. 1444–8. See also Justice Blackmun's dissent in *Hardwick*, op. cit., pp. 2850–1 citing cases for protecting certain decisions and spaces. See also Vincent Samar, *The Right to Privacy: Gays, Lesbians and the Constitution* (Philadelphia: Temple University Press) 1991, pp. 26–42, for a discussion of three types of privacy rights.
62 In *Griswold*, 479, 485 the U.S. Supreme Court first recognized the constitutional right to personal privacy and found it to apply to the right of married couples to use contraceptives. *Eisenstadt v. Baird*, 405 U.S. 438 extended this right to non-married individuals and *Roe v. Wade*, 410 U.S. 113 (1973) concluded that a woman's right to decide upon an abortion was constitutionally protected as part of her constitutional right to privacy. This is the line of privacy

jurisprudence which seemed to be applicable, absent prejudice, to intimate personal choices of single homosexuals as well as single heterosexuals.

63 Ga. Code Ann. # 16-6-2 (1984) quoted in *Hardwick*, 478 U.S. at 188 n. 1. This statute imposed a very harsh penalty for acts of sodomy: '. . . a person convicted of the offense of sodomy shall be punished by imprisonment for not less than one, nor more than 20 years . . .', idem, para. 16-6-2b.

64 *Bowers v. Hardwick*, 478 U.S. at 190.

65 Ibid., at 199.

66 Ibid. (Blackmun, J. dissenting).

67 Ibid. at 200 (Blackmun, J. dissenting).

68 Ibid., at 186, 214–15 (Stevens, J. disssenting). The statute does not even mention homosexuals.

69 It helped a great deal that a lower court had denied standing to a married heterosexual couple who also wanted to challenge the Georgia law and had joined suit with Michael Hardwick. See Janet Halley, 'Reasoning about Sodomy', op. cit., pp. 425–50. I rely on her analysis a great deal in this section of the chapter.

70 *Bowers v. Hardwick*, 478 U.S. at 186, 190.

71 See Ronald Dworkin, 'The Forum of Principle', 56 *New York University Law Review* 469, 513–14 (1981).

72 See Kendall Thomas, 'Eclipse of Reason: A Rhetorical Reading of *Bowers v. Hardwick*', 79 *Virginia Law Review* 1805, 1829 (1993).

73 *Bowers v. Hardwick*, 478 U.S. 191 (1986). Noting that the Court's majority understand family, marriage and legitimate intimate relationships as involving heterosexuals and monogamy.

74 Ibid., at 190.

75 Ibid., at 195–6. But see 209 n. 4 (Blackmun, J. dissenting) noting that the problem with adultery and incest is not the specific form of sexual touching involved but the proscribed sexual relationships with particular sorts of partners. I do not believe that laws criminalizing adultery are defensible today. Laws regulating incest merit a more complex analysis.

76 *Hardwick*, 478 U.S. at 191.

77 Ibid., at 196. This is an interpretation consistent with the letter of the law although not with the spirit of privacy jurisprudence since *Griswold*. As Richard Posner states, it certainly is not compelled by precedent. See Posner, *Sex and Reason*, op. cit., p. 344.

For an early argument that the Court never intended to articulate a fundamental right of sexual freedom, but which nonetheless assumed that laws criminalizing sodomy and homosexuality would eventually be overturned by the Court because they serve no rational purpose, see Thomas Grey, 'Eros, Civilization and the Burger Court', *Law and Contemporary Problems*, vol. 43, no. 3, 1980, pp. 83–99. For the opposite view see David Richards, 'Sexual Autonomy and the Constitutional Right to Privacy: A Case Study in Human Rights and the Unwritten Constitution', 30 *Hastings Law Journal* 957, 958–64 (1979) (interpreting *Griswold* as extending the Constitution to protect sexual liberty as a basic human right).

78 *Hardwick* at 196. See K. Thomas, 'The Eclipse of Reason: A Rhetorical Reading of *Bowers v. Hardwick*', 78 *Virginia Law Review* 1805 (1993).

79 *Bowers v. Hardwick* at 197 (Burger, C.J. concurring).

80 Ibid., at 197.

81 Ibid., at 191. The purity of heterosexual relationships, the impurity of homosexual ones, and the invisibility of heterosexual sodomy are thereby secured.

82 Stevens states that '. . . the fact that the governing majority in the State has traditionally viewed a particular practice as immoral is not sufficient reason for upholding a law prohibiting the practice; neither history nor tradition could save a law prohibiting miscegenation from constitutional attack', *Hardwick*, 478 U.S. at 216 (Stevens, J. dissenting) (citing *Loving v. Virginia*, 388 U.S. 1 (1967) which struck down state laws criminalizing miscegenation). Moreover, as Justice Blackmun points out, traditional reasons for outlawing sodomy depended on Roman Catholic doctrine regarding forbidden, unnatural sex acts – hardly an appropriate foundation for secular law. He too cites *Loving* as an uncanny parallel to this case. See *Hardwick*, 478 U.S. 211 n. 5 (Blackmun dissenting).

83 See Richard Posner, *Sex and Reason*, op. cit., p. 344. See also Janet Halley, op. cit., Appendix B, pp. 456–8.

84 Ibid.

85 In 1973 The American Psychiatric Association removed homosexuality from its list of psychiatric disorders and resolved that 'homosexuality *per se* implies no impairment in judgement, stability, reliability, or general social or vocational capabilities'. It stated further that '. . . in the reasoned judgement of most American psychiatrists, homosexuality does not constitute any form of mental disease'. Similar resolutions were adopted in 1970, 1973, 1975 respectively by the American Anthropological Association, the American Bar Association, and the American Psychological Association. See Vincent J. Samar, *The Right to Privacy: Gays, Lesbians and the Constitution* (Philadelphia: Temple University Press) 1991, pp. 144–5.

86 This is a paraphrase of Posner, *Sex and Reason*, op. cit., p. 349.

87 In a longer version of this chapter I tried to show why libertarian (Richard Posner) and certain liberal (L. Tribe) 'personhood' arguments for overturning sodomy laws are flawed. I cannot go into this here. See Jean L. Cohen, 'Is There a Duty of Privacy', *Texas Journal of Women and the Law*, op. cit.

88 For a discussion of the idea that rights such as free speech or privacy are regulatory but also personally formative, granting to those deemed competent the chance to organize their action in the relevant domains, see Ian Hunter, David Saunders and Dugald Williamson, *On Pornography* (New York: St. Martin's Press) 1993, p. 206.

89 Ibid., pp. 95–6.

90 See Jean L. Cohen, 'Zur Neubeschreibung der Privatsphäre', in Christoph Menke and Martin Seel, eds, *Zur Verteidigung der Vernunft gegen ihre Liebhaber und Verächter* (Frankfurt: Suhrkamp Verlag) 1993, pp. 308–20.

91 For a perceptive discussion of my position, see Jodi Dean, *Solidarity of Strangers* (1996), pp. 165–7.

92 For a discussion of the political relevance of privacy, see Frank Michelman, 'Law's Republic', 97 *Yale Law Journal* 1493, pp. 1521–37 (arguing that privacy rights secure the autonomy of participants' public life and thus are democracy-reinforcing). See also Michelman, 'Private Personal but not Split: Radin versus Rorty', *Southern California Law Review*, vol. 63, no. 6, Sept. 1990, pp. 1783–95 arguing that what ought to be considered personal is a deeply political question.

93 Jean L. Cohen, 'Redescribing Privacy', op. cit., p. 113.

94 In this regard, Justice Blackmun and others were right to argue that there are both principle and precedent in privacy doctrine with implications (although no determinacy) for the domain of sexuality. Tribe agrees, *American Constitutional Law*, op. cit.

148   *Jean L. Cohen*

95 *Bowers v. Hardwick*, 478 U.S. 186, 205 (1986) (Blackmun, J. dissenting) citing Karst, K., 'The Freedom of Intimate Association', 89 *Yale Law Journal* 624, 637 (1980) and *Eisenstadt v. Baird*, 405 U.S. 438, 453 (1972); *Roe v. Wade*, 410 U.S. 113, 153 (1973).
96 Marriage is certainly no longer the master event that initiates sexual encounters, new households, or intimate association for one's lifetime.
97 Foucault, M., *The History of Sexuality*, vol. 1 (New York: Vintage Books) 1990.
98 Foucault, *History*, ibid., p. 101.
99 Ibid., p. 145:

> The 'right' to life, to one's body, to health, to happiness . . . and beyond all the oppressions or 'alienations', the 'right' to rediscover what one is and all that one can be, this 'right' – . . . was the political response to all these new procedures of power . . .

100 See Philip Pettit, *Republicanism: A Theory of Freedom and Government* (Oxford and New York: Oxford University Press) 1997 for a discussion of liberty construed as non-domination.
101 Guenter Teubner, 'Substantive and Reflexive Elements in Modern Law', *Law and Society Review*, vol. 17, no. 2 (1983), pp. 239–85; Jürgen Habermas, *Between Facts and Norms* (Cambridge, Mass.: MIT Press) 1996, pp. 388–446.
102 Anthony Giddens, *Modernity and Self-Identity* (Stanford, Cal.: University of California Press) 1991; Ulrich Beck, *Risk Society* (Newbury Park, Cal.: Sage) 1992.
103 Ulrich Preuss, *Constitutional Revolution* (New Jersey: Humanities Press) 1995, p. 109.
104 Dan Ortiz, 'Creating Controversy: Essentialism and Constructivism and the Politics of Gay Identity', 79 *Virginia Law Review* 1833, 1842 (1993). Dan Ortiz distinguishes between two concerns in the battle over homosexual identity: the first has to do with how a person comes to fall into a particular identity category, the second, with how the identity category is formed and its status determined: 'How one becomes a member of a group is separate from how that group's identity is given meaning.' These should not be conflated.
105 Motherhood supposedly has a high social status but it should nonetheless not be imposed.

8   Justice, causation and private law

N.E. Simmonds

The distinction between public and private law

Some legal distinctions are drawn with great clarity and precision. Thus, contract lawyers would distinguish between reliance loss and expectation loss, common mistake and mutual mistake, void and voidable contracts, or discharge by frustration and discharge by breach. Laymen need not concern themselves with the significance of these concepts; but lawyers, if called upon, could offer impressively precise and convincing accounts of such distinctions, even if in a minority of cases the application of the distinction may give rise to problems at the borderline.

Other legal distinctions are less clear, and this is sometimes true of distinctions that are, in a sense, fundamental to the legal system as a whole. Thus lawyers take for granted the fact that developed Western systems of law are divided into the two sectors of 'public' and 'private' law. The distinction forms a general background for lawyerly understandings, but not one that lawyers could articulate with great confidence. They could readily assign various departments of law to the one sector or the other: there would, for example, be universal agreement that administrative law, tax law, planning law, welfare law and constitutional law are all varieties of public law; similarly that contract, tort, property, and restitution are instances of private law. Yet what precisely is the criterion that underpins the classification? What indeed is the *significance* of the distinction?

Unlike the distinctions of contract doctrine mentioned above, the distinction between public and private law will only rarely play a dispositive role in the decision of litigated disputes (it may play a part, for example, in questions relating to the jurisdiction of particular tribunals, or the appropriateness of particular procedural rules) and then it is likely to be addressed in terms of that particular context, rather than as a highly general distinction requiring general definition. Legal practitioners and judges are concerned with the immediate business of representing clients or deciding particular cases. It is therefore left to the legal theorists to speculate about the public/private distinction.

Attempts to elucidate the distinction generally form part of a broader theoretical exercise, seeking to ascribe to the distinction a significance that would not be universally recognised. Thus it is not easy for us to say what the 'ordinary lawyer' takes the distinction between public and private law to signify. As F.H. Bradley observed in a different context:

> It is not so easy to say what the people mean by their ordinary words, for this reason, that the question is not answered until it is asked; that asking is reflection, and that we reflect in general not to find the facts, but to prove our theories at the expense of them. The ready-made doctrines we bring to the work colour whatever we touch with them; and the apprehension of the vulgar mind, at first sight so easy, now seems, because *we* are not vulgar, to present a difficulty.[1]

Unable to proceed from the common understanding of this distinction, therefore, we can only proceed from theoretical articulations that are inherently contentious. Fortunately, our task is made somewhat easier by the fact that legal theorists can be divided into two broad schools of thought on this issue.

On the one hand are those who treat the distinction as a thing of little genuine significance: simply a traditional classification that may serve a certain limited purpose (or perhaps a pernicious, mystificatory purpose) but that conceals an underlying unity. On this view, the law as a whole serves a diversity of social policy goals, and they can be pursued by techniques and mechanisms traditionally associated with private law, or by those associated with public law. The differing techniques are to be judged solely by their efficacy, and they possess no deeper significance.

This sceptical position on the public/private distinction can actually be arrived at by either one of two quite different routes. Exemplifying the first route we have severe legal positivists such as Hans Kelsen, who seek to avoid any dependence upon moral ideas in the working out of legal concepts and definitions. For such theorists, a genuine cognition of law must confine itself to the contents of posited rules, and cannot include a speculative reconstruction of the moral conceptions that might be thought to underpin the rules, or the broad social purposes served by the rules. If such theorists offer us definitions of the distinction between public and private law, we are likely to find that their definitions do little to clarify our understanding, for they will proceed in entirely formal terms. Thus, we might be told that public law involves remedies of this or that sort, or decisions by this or that sort of tribunal; while private law involves remedies of this or that other sort, or decisions by this or that other sort of tribunal. These 'explanations' are unlikely to explain anything that might have puzzled us: their whole object is to show that legal distinctions can be defined in terms which are entirely internal to the system of legal rules and principles, while avoiding questions concerning the deeper significance of the distinctions.

Legal theorists who are committed to this type of self-contained and value-free explication of legal concepts have sometimes concluded that the distinction between public and private law is unreal or mystificatory in character. Thus, Hans Kelsen commences his discussion of the issue by observing that 'no one has yet succeeded in arriving at a fully satisfactory statement of the difference between private and public law'; he is led to conclude that 'critical investigation reveals no foundation in the positive law for this entire distinction'.[2]

Although rejecting the distinction himself, Kelsen does endeavour to describe the conventional understanding, in the following terms:

> The most widely disseminated view turns on a classification of legal relations, with private law representing a relation between coordinate subjects of equal standing legally, and public law representing a relation between a superordinate and a subordinate subject – between two subjects, then, one of which is of higher standing than the other. The typical public law relation is that between state and citizen.[3]

The distinction is, in Kelsen's view, one which 'dominates our whole juridico-scientific systematic'; yet it is simply 'a mask worn by certain political or natural law elements as they creep into the characterization of the positive law'.[4] It is, he tells us, one of a number of dualisms in legal thought that serve a basically ideological function, in this case by creating 'the illusion that the field of public law alone . . . is the domain of political power, which is totally excluded from the field of private law'.[5]

Although Kelsen's focus is a very narrow one, being concerned with the purity and objectivity of legal knowledge, one might feel that a range of inferences could reasonably be drawn from his position. Thus Kelsen's analysis might lead one to the conclusion that it is a mistake to view the market as a sphere of natural liberty that is wholly independent of the state's intervention: market transactions operate against a background of entitlements that are established and enforced by law and sustained by the state's coercive power.[6] Whatever distributive or aggregative consequences flow from the exercise and existence of such entitlements are the indirect products of the state's decision to confer and protect rights with that content.

In fact it is far from clear that such inferences would be justifiable. For legal positivists such as Kelsen base their rejection of the public/private distinction upon a general self-denying ordinance: they refuse to incorporate within the conceptual structure of 'legal science' (the systematic study of legal doctrine) moral or political conceptions that go beyond the contents of the posited rules. They take no view upon the soundness or otherwise of those moral or political conceptions when they are proffered upon normative grounds, rather than as representations of the existing law.

There is, however, an alternative route to scepticism concerning the public/private divide in law. Theorists in this second group of sceptics are perfectly willing to analyse law in terms of sweeping political conceptions that go beyond the material to be found in posited rules; but they favour a political theory that attaches no intrinsic importance to the divide between public and private law. An example would be those enthusiasts for the 'economic analysis of law' who explain the law's content in terms of the value of 'wealth maximisation'.[7] The monistic character of this theory, combined with its instrumental view of law, ensures that the theory will tend to downplay the significance of those legal doctrinal distinctions that play little part in the actual disposition of cases. Playing little or no such dispositive part, they can be of no great instrumental significance; and in so far as they purport to reveal something of the moral values or relations embodied in law, they are misguided rivals to the theory of wealth maximisation itself. Thus, for the economic theorist, the terms 'public law' and 'private law' describe different legal techniques or institutions that can be called upon in the service of economic efficiency. The terms are, at best, a useful shorthand; and, at worst, an unhelpful obfuscation of the law's unity of aim and underlying policy.

Sceptics do not occupy the field of legal thought alone, however. To many ordinary lawyers, private law seems essentially different in character from public law, and distinctly less political. Their view is partly borne out by the surprising historical continuity of ideas within private law, for it is true to say that the doctrines of private law governing transactions in the 'global' economy of instantaneous communication have a history that can be traced to the late scholastics and beyond, to the lawyers of ancient Rome.[8] In consequence, and in spite of numerous differences of detail, there are culturally diverse societies all over the world that employ broadly the same categories and conceptions in their systems of private law.[9] The continuity of this history is made obvious by the traditional preference of lawyers for the adoption of the views of others: as the legal historian A.W.B. Simpson observes, 'At least in the Western European legal tradition of private law successful creative work consists in a combination between intelligent plagiarism and systematisation of what is lifted from others.' Simpson explains this tendency partly by reference to 'the close connection between private law and certain moral ideas which have remained relatively static over long periods, thus constantly generating similar principles and problems'.[10] Nothing comparable can be said of public law.

Of course, most lawyers would recognise that, even in the context of private law disputes, judges regularly invoke considerations of general social policy: they are not exclusively concerned with conceptions of individual moral responsibility of the kind that might plausibly be said to remain 'relatively static over long periods'. Such social policy questions, however, crop up within a context of ideas about entitlement and responsibility that are specific to private law and that cannot easily be dissolved into the general considerations of some aggregative theory such as utilitarianism or wealth-maximisation.[11] Moreover, the very general conceptions of individual responsibility that are implemented in private law leave open a host of detailed questions that can properly be resolved with an eye to their impact upon more general policy considerations. The integrity of private law is preserved to the extent that such issues are dealt with in a manner *consistent with* the principles of individual responsibility; the particular solution adopted need not be *entailed by* those principles.[12]

Supporting many of these unstructured intuitions of ordinary lawyers, the distinction between public and private law has its enthusiasts amongst legal theoreticians, who consider it to be the focus for a whole range of moral ideas. One such theorist is Ernest Weinrib, whose book *The Idea of Private Law*[13] is a remarkable confection of arguments built up around the distinction between private and public law. While assembling an ambitiously eclectic collection of philosophical ideas, Weinrib manages to articulate and systematise a number of very traditional attitudes towards private law, such as the belief that private law is centrally concerned with justice between individual parties, rather than with wider social goals; and the belief that private law is somehow more truly 'legal' and less political than public law. We will examine Weinrib's position before speculating about some more plausible ways of explaining those traditional beliefs.

Weinrib on legal formalism

Weinrib defends a position that he describes as 'formalism'. Formalism maintains that legal doctrinal argument is wholly distinct from political argument; in Weinrib's account, it is private law that is truly formalistic in this sense, while arguments within public law are more political in character. It is important to make clear at the outset, however, that Weinrib's conception of 'formalism' differs from some more familiar jurisprudential ways of employing that word.

Take, for example, Hart's discussion of 'formalism' in Chapter 7 of *The Concept of Law*.[14] By 'formalism', Hart seems to mean the conjunction of two claims: (i) that law consists entirely of posited rules, identifiable by their source of enactment, and (ii) that every dispute can be decided by the application of such posited rules, without any need to enter into more open-ended questions of justice, or social policy. Weinrib, by contrast, endorses the more expansive conception of formalism put forward by Roberto Unger.[15] According to Unger, any legal theory that claims the existence of a distinction between legal doctrinal argument and open-ended political argument is an instance of 'formalism': in Unger's view the formalism described[16] by Hart is merely an extreme end-point of a much broader position.

Weinrib also agrees with another aspect of Unger's account of formalism. Unger argues that any attempt to defend formalism will have to fall back upon the claim that law is the expression of a coherent and integrated moral vision. This is because the distinction between law and politics cannot be sustained simply by appeal to a set of posited rules, such as statutes or rules established in precedents: the minute one comes to apply such rules, one will be forced into deeper questions about the values served by the rules. If one hopes to defend the distinction between law and politics, therefore, one must argue that the rules implicitly embody a coherent set of principles that can inform interpretation of the rules. The principles will constitute, not moral or political values at large, but those values that can be derived or interpreted from the set of legal materials as a whole; at the same time they will serve to guide and inform the construction of individual provisions to be found in those same materials. It is in this way that the distinction between law and politics is to be sustained. This is the strategy of argument pursued by Ronald Dworkin.[17]

Weinrib agrees with Unger that, if law is to be distinguished from politics, law must contain (as Weinrib puts it) an 'immanent moral rationality'. Beyond this point, the two part company. The conservative Weinrib believes that such an immanent moral rationality is discoverable in law; while the radical Unger denies this.

The forms of justice

Formalism in Unger's sense gives us only one of the many resonances that Weinrib seeks to assemble around the idea of 'form'. For example, Weinrib claims that the formalism of private law (for it is private law that truly exhibits the requisite independence of politics) hinges upon the distinctive form of private law, which is a bipolar relationship between plaintiff and defendant. This bipolar form is central to private law both doctrinally and procedurally. Procedurally, private law is centrally concerned with claims made by one party against another; typically, the remedy sought is an order to the defendant to compensate the plaintiff. Substantively, private law doctrines require a causal relationship of 'doing and suffering' to have obtained between plaintiff and defendant. According to Weinrib, the autonomy of private law from politics consists in the fact that individual rules are assessed, not by their political desirability, but by their 'coherence' with the form of private law.

Weinrib suggests that the distinct form of private law was first identified and analysed by Aristotle, in his discussion of 'corrective justice' in the *Nicomachean Ethics*.[18] The form of relationship expressed in the idea of corrective justice is the locus of a special morality with its own repertoire of arguments. Distributive justice, by contrast, is the central concern of public law, and it depends upon a distributive principle that must be politically chosen. In distributive justice, the relationship between the parties is mediated by a distributive principle, whereas in corrective justice it is direct. Thus, it is one thing to complain that you stole my property (the relationship is direct) and another thing to complain that I have received less than my due, while you received more than yours: here, we may have no direct connection, but may be related only by a distributive principle that defines our 'due'.

Thus far we have the 'formalism' that consists in law's distinctness from politics, and the 'form' of private law (corrective justice) itself. Yet Weinrib has not yet finished with the fertile notion of 'form'. For he argues that corrective justice aims to restore the equality of the parties that preceded the particular transaction giving rise to the dispute. What exactly does this preceding baseline of equality amount to? One answer would be that it is provided by a conception of distributive justice. Such an answer would subordinate corrective to distributive justice, by presenting corrective justice as the procedure whereby an originally just distribution is rectified after being upset by some individual transaction of taking or harming or promise-breaking. Weinrib rejects this view for reasons that we will examine in due course. He is then faced once again with the problem of identifying the baseline of equality that is supposedly restored by corrective justice.

With a surprising willingness to draw upon diverse philosophical traditions, Weinrib invokes Kant's theory of justice at this point: the relevant equality is the equality of the parties as agents. This equality of agency, or equal freedom, is itself a 'formalism', in so far as it concerns itself with the 'form' of the will rather than with its content: that is, it is concerned with the impact that my actions have upon your freedom, rather than with the moral worthiness of my action, or its impact upon your desires.

Corrective and distributive justice

Weinrib is far from being alone in seeking to defend the integrity of private law from the distributive and aggregative considerations that apply within the realm of public law; nor is he alone in relying for this purpose upon the notion of corrective justice. In common with all such theorists,[19] however, he faces the difficult problem of giving sufficient content to the bare notion of corrective justice without falling back upon those very distributive and aggregative ideas.[20] Corrective justice requires, let us say, that wrongdoers should have to compensate those whom they have wronged. Yet how are we to determine what counts as a 'wrong'? Will the notion of corrective justice itself provide an answer to that question? Or will any such answer only serve to expose a deeper reliance upon distributive justice? Will a 'wrong' turn out to be the violation of a 'right', so that we need a distributive theory of what rights people possess before we can ascribe content to corrective justice? If the requirements of corrective justice are actually determined by considerations of distributive justice, corrective justice is not in reality a distinct form of justice at all, but simply a procedural and rectificatory aspect of distributive justice. Yet how can corrective justice be given a distinct content otherwise than by reliance upon a theory of distributive justice?

It is surprising that Weinrib chooses to address this problem by invoking a Kantian theory of equal freedom, for such a theory has itself frequently been accused of emptiness. These accusations were first formulated by Hegel and Schopenhauer,[21] but they have been repeated many times since. One might reasonably expect Weinrib to address these familiar criticisms, given that he is seeking to respond to a problem of alleged emptiness (the emptiness of corrective justice) by invoking an allegedly empty theory. He appears not to address the problem at all, however.[22]

Why should we not adopt the simple view that distributive justice is the logically prior notion, and that corrective justice deals with situations where a just distribution has been upset by some individual transaction (of theft, or fraud, or promise-breaking, or careless injury, etc.)? This would give content to the requirements of corrective justice. Admittedly it would, in a sense, collapse corrective into distributive justice, and would thereby present the distinction between public and private law as of relatively little significance; but so what?

Weinrib offers various arguments on this point.[23] In the first place, he argues that to treat corrective justice as dependent upon distributive justice would give the judge a reason for allowing the 'Robin Hood' defence. In other words, the judge would have reason in principle[24] to consider the justice or injustice of the underlying distribution of resources when considering an apparently wrongful taking, for such a wrongful taking might have produced a *more* just distribution than would have obtained in the absence of the taking. Judges in private law cases, however, treat the parties as equals: they do not investigate the background distribution of resources, but look solely at the particular transaction that is in dispute. One cannot, Weinrib tells us, rightly treat people as equals unless they are truly equal in some respect.[25] Hence, he concludes, the relevant equality must be equality as agents or choosers (the Kantian notion of equal freedom) and not equality as resource-holders.

Weinrib's argument lies open to an obvious objection at this point, for it is simply not true that one cannot rightly treat people as equals unless they are equal in some relevant respect. We might, for example, treat people as equal with regard to their holdings in distributive justice even though we know that they are almost certainly *not* equal in that respect. Thus, courts might well exclude the Robin Hood defence because consideration of the overall distributive situation would require the consideration of information not in the court's possession, and parties who are not in front of the court. The court would find it difficult to establish with any certainty what precisely the resources of the plaintiff and defendant really were; and still more difficult to establish how these resources related to the resources of all other citizens. Even if it is clear that the plaintiff (victim of theft) is rich and the defendant (thief) is poor, and equally clear that some re-distribution should take place, it might well be grossly unfair to place the whole burden of redistribution upon the plaintiff's shoulders. When his position is compared with that of other rich people, it might become clear that he should not bear much of the burden at all, but this type of comparison would be well-nigh impossible for a court to make. It is a far more suitable question for the (public) tax and welfare sector.[26]

On the other hand, individual transactions *can* upset just distributions, and they involve detailed questions of fact and circumstance that it would be difficult for the institutions of the tax and welfare sector to investigate and address. It therefore makes sense for the courts to investigate the upset to distributive justice that can be assumed to stem from the particular transaction, on the assumption that the pre-existing situation was just from a distributive point of view. In other words, the courts can be justified in treating as equals those who may well not be equals in reality.

Weinrib also argues that gifts and natural catastrophes may upset distributive justice as well as injuries or thefts or frauds; yet we do not think of corrective justice and private law as enforcing the restoration of gifts. Therefore, he concludes, corrective justice and private law cannot be thought of as simply rectifying upsets to distributive justice.[27]

So far as natural disasters go, some of the considerations that we have just been considering provide a relevant response to Weinrib's argument. The court's practical inability to consider the overall distributive situation and the impact of the disaster upon that situation combine with the desirability of placing the responsibility for insuring against many such losses upon the individual's shoulders.

Where gifts are concerned, we might well wish to dissent from the Rawlsian view that justice is an overriding virtue,[28] preferring to assign justice a high value, but one that must be balanced against competing considerations. One such competing consideration might be the importance of the family, and of friendship. Since most gifts are made between family and friends, this might give us good reason for not seeking to rectify the upsets that they cause to distributive justice.[29] Alternatively, it might simply be the case that, in not requiring any detailed investigation of fact and circumstance, the rectification of such upsets caused by gifts can be handled very conveniently by the tax and welfare sectors.

Thus it seems that Weinrib's arguments fail to demonstrate the distinctive nature of private law, since most of the differences that he points to can be explained very well in terms of a varied set of considerations, including considerations of administrative convenience. Weinrib regards such explanations as unsatisfactory, because they fail to reveal the distinct 'immanent moral rationality' of private law. To one who doubts the existence of such a distinct morality, however, this will hardly be viewed as a serious deficiency.

Competing values

Weinrib's theory is a version of legal formalism in so far as it claims to separate juridical questions concerning the legality of this or that doctrinal principle from political questions concerning the need to protect certain interests or to advance desirable goals. Proposed doctrinal principles are to be judged, not by their tendency to advance some schedule of interests or goals or values, but by their 'coherence' with the 'form' of corrective justice. He objects to conventional justifications of tort law (for example) because they invoke a plurality of values that are only contingently and loosely related to the form of private law adjudication. Thus, tort law is conventionally justified by reference to the goals of 'deterrence' and 'compensation'. By making tortfeasors pay damages, one deters people from engaging in the careless or injurious conduct that can lead to such liability; by paying the damages to the injured plaintiff, one helps to spread losses and make them easier to bear. The connection between deterrence and compensation is purely contingent, and the goals could be achieved by a system that did not embody the bipolar form of private law at all.

Thus, in relation to traffic accidents, one might make all careless drivers (regardless of whether their careless driving caused an injury) pay a fine into a general fund; while all persons injured in traffic accidents (whether or not their injury was caused by anyone's carelessness) could be compensated from the resulting fund. The 'bipolar' relationship of private law, wherein the defendant must have injured the plaintiff, would be abandoned by such a system of pooling, but the goods of deterrence and compensation would be achieved more fully. The goals of deterrence and compensation are independent goals that are only artificially related within the context of private law, but do not find their natural expression in the form of private law; in relation to those goals, private law appears only as a rather imperfect instrument for their advancement.

Weinrib objects to such conventional understandings of the basis of private law, because the justifications invoked are 'truncated': that is to say, they are not applied consistently across the whole range of potential applications that would seem to be dictated by their content. If our object is to deter carelessness, for example, we should penalise careless actors who, by pure chance, have not actually injured anyone; and if our object is the spreading of losses, we should compensate all those who suffer injury whether or not the injury was caused by carelessness. Thus, a consistent adherence to the postulated values would lead us to abandon the forms of private law in favour of a more distributive approach: the said values must, therefore, provide a poor theoretical justification for private law. Weinrib tells us that, where a theory incorporates a plurality of 'elements' in this way, 'Each element is inherently expansionary, since its claim is no weaker with respect to one section of the legal universe than it is to another. Since all elements have a similarly autonomous status, the result of their confluence is a scramble for empire among competing forces.'[30]

This rejection of plurality and 'truncated justification' within a juridical theory is fundamental to Weinrib's theory. It is this that underpins his insistence upon the need for 'coherence' in theories of private law, and in legal doctrine. He defines 'coherence' as ruling out plurality, since 'Coherence signifies a unified conceptual structure, the constituents of which express a single idea.'[31] Unfortunately for him, his own theory is grounded upon a plurality of precisely the type to which he objects.

One problem with a theory that separates corrective justice from distributive justice, treating the two as autonomous conceptions possessing their own integrity, is (as we have seen) the problem of how to ascribe a detailed content to corrective justice without reliance upon a distributive theory. Another problem concerns the relationship between the two conceptions. It is here that we discover Weinrib's own pluralism.

It is perhaps possible to imagine a theory that would give each form of justice a restricted scope, treating it as relevant only to a quite specific type of situation. Distributive justice might, for example, be thought to concern the distribution of those resources which I am justly entitled to control. Suppose, for example, that the owner of some divisible resource contemplates making a gift of that resource to a group of others, and thereby faces the question of how the resource should be divided amongst them. Thus, their parents may wonder how they should distribute their property amongst their children. Corrective justice might be thought to govern individual transactions of wrongdoing or injury.

This is not the approach adopted by Weinrib, who claims that the two conceptions of justice do not lay 'exclusive claim to a certain slice of the empirical world. . . . either of the forms of justice can apply to any external incident.'[32] His theory dictates the need for 'coherence'; but what this means is that we should not mix justifications that rely upon the form of distributive justice and justifications that rely upon the form of corrective justice. When deciding whether any particular type of 'external incident' is to be regulated by the one form or the other, we are faced with a radical and (seemingly) rationally ungrounded choice.

Weinrib's inability to clarify the relationship between the two forms of justice, and the resulting dependence of his theory upon such a radical moment of choice, is clearly a serious deficiency in his argument. In fact it reproduces the very type of pluralism that he is otherwise so concerned to resist and reject. For, according to Weinrib, distributive justice and corrective justice each offer a model of justice that could appropriately regulate any type of incident. Each form of justice is the embodiment of a type of claim that is perfectly general in scope. Do we not have here 'a scramble for empire among competing forces' consequent upon the fact that the plural elements 'have a similarly autonomous status'? The exclusion of plurality is basic to Weinrib's entire conception of 'coherence' and, therefore, to his 'formalism'. The reproduction of precisely such an instance of pluralism at the very heart of his own theory therefore seems to be a fatal flaw. With the presence of such a plurality of values, his theory succumbs to his own critique; but were he to drop his objection to pluralism, his entire case for formalism would dissolve.

In actual fact, there is no real problem with a situation of competition between values. Weinrib's conflation of 'coherence' as entailing monism with coherence as meaning 'intelligibility' helps to conceal the otherwise obvious fact that mutually competing values do not lead to a situation of unintelligibility.[33] Nor are 'truncated justifications' problematic as Weinrib imagines them to be. 'Deterrence' may provide a reason for wrongdoers to be required to pay penalties; and the desirability of spreading losses ('compensation') may provide a reason for victims to receive compensation. Judged in isolation, therefore, these two values might be more fully realised by a 'pooling' system of the type described earlier (careless actors pay money in, regardless of harm caused; injured victims draw money out, regardless of the level of care shown by the person who caused their injury). Each of these values, however, must compete with the value of liberty, which might be construed as giving us a reason to let losses lie where they fall, without the coercive intervention of the state;[34] they also compete with the need to avoid incurring extensive costs in the administration of justice. Perhaps the balancing considerations of liberty and low administration costs are outweighed only in those cases where deterrence and compensation combine to support a single institutional response: that of a private law remedy.[35] Once we appreciate the fact that other values (such as liberty, or administrative efficiency) may have a bearing upon our pursuit of the goals of deterrence and compensation, we will appreciate that Weinrib's instances of 'truncated justification' are in fact instances of the competition between values.

Perhaps Weinrib is here misled by his own adoption of Unger's notion of formalism. Like Unger, Weinrib seems to assume that there is something deeply troubling about the need to balance competing values, since there is no reason in principle for striking the balance in one place rather than another.[36] In fact all that this demonstrates is that there could be other, equally reasonable, ways of striking the balance; it does not demonstrate that this particular way of striking the balance is itself unreasonable, or that all such balances are ungrounded in considerations of reason.

Justice divided

Weinrib's problems with the radical choice between the forms of distributive and corrective justice might well encourage us to reject the idea of any such plurality within the notion of justice. Surely, we might say, justice of all values must be single, unified and univocal in its requirements. Adopting such a view, we might then have good reason to interpret corrective justice as but the procedural mode whereby distributive justice is restored when once upset by some transaction of wrongdoing or injury. Alternatively, we might construe the scope of distributive justice as confined to special contexts where the owner of a divisible resource contemplates its distribution amongst a class of persons. Either view would restore unity to our conception of justice. With the consequent disappearance of any truly fundamental distinction between corrective and distributive justice, the significance of the distinction between public and private law would once again be called into question.

Despite the failure of Weinrib's own arguments, however, there are some good reasons for suspecting that there *is* a fundamentally important distinction that might be described as that between corrective and distributive justice.[37] Consider, for example, the parable of the labourers in the vineyard:

> The Kingdom of Heaven is like this. There was once a landowner who went out early one morning to hire labourers for his vineyard; and after agreeing to pay them the usual day's wage he sent them off to work. Going out three hours later he saw some more men standing idle in the market-place. 'Go and join the others in the vineyard,' he said, 'and I will pay you a fair wage'; so off they went. At noon he went out again, and at three in the afternoon, and made the same arrangement as before. An hour before sunset he went out and found another group standing there; so he said to them, 'Why are you standing about like this all day with nothing to do?' 'Because no one has hired us,' they replied; so he told them, 'Go and join the others in the vineyard.' When evening fell, the owner of the vineyard said to his steward, 'Call the labourers and give them their pay, beginning with those who came last and ending with the first.' Those who had started work an hour before sunset came forward, and were paid the full day's wage. When it was the turn of the men who had come first, they expected something extra, but were paid the same amount as the others. As they took it, they grumbled at their employer: 'These late-comers have done only one hour's work, yet you have put them on a level with us, who have sweated the whole day long in the blazing sun!' The owner turned to one of them and said, 'My friend, I am not being unfair to you. You agreed on the usual wage for the day, did you not? Take your pay and go home. I choose to pay the last man the same as you. Surely I am free to do what I like with my own money. Why be jealous because I am kind?'
>
> (Matthew 20: 1–16)

Let us set on one side the theological significance of the parable, which is presumably concerned with God's generosity to those Gentiles who come late to the Judaic Christian faith.[38] The majority of modern readers will, I think, react to the story with conflicting moral intuitions. We tend to feel that valid claims of justice are to be found on both sides of the argument.[39] Situations where claims of justice appear to conflict are, of course, not at all unusual. Notice, however, that the conflicting claims in this parable are connected with quite different perspectives that we can adopt upon the situation as a whole. On the one hand, we may think of the narrative as describing a series of discrete transactions involving the exchange of promises (to work, and to pay wages). From this perspective, the owner of the vineyard is quite correct. Yet, on the other hand, we may think of the vineyard as a deliberately organised set of arrangements which distributes benefits and burdens in a certain way. From this perspective, we may well conclude that the vineyard is organised in an unjust way.

Much of the debate within political philosophy and jurisprudence concerns the choice between these two perspectives. On the one hand is the view that a market economy is appropriately viewed only as a series of discrete transactions, the ultimate outcomes of which were neither planned nor intended by any individual or body: on this view the civil justice that regulates individual transactions is genuine, whereas 'social justice' is a spurious concept.[40] On the other hand is the view that market transactions occur within, and are structured by, a framework of institutions (property rights, enforceable contracts, etc.) that are maintained by the authority and coercive power of the political collectivity, and that are (at least within limits) alterable; the consequence, it is argued, is that we bear collective responsibility for the outcomes of the market, and cannot deny that those outcomes raise legitimate questions of 'social justice'.[41]

We have here an interesting example of how the development of political institutions, in particular the institution of the state, transforms our moral situation. The state itself[42] may be the unintended result of a multiplicity of actions directed to other goals; but once it is in existence, it provides us with the ability to deliberately alter the rules governing social life.[43] Rules which may have resulted from the convergence of uncoordinated actions therefore become alterable. The systemic effects of uncoordinated actions may well be unintended, but they are not always unforeseeable. To the extent that those effects can be foreseen as the likely result of channelling conduct through a specific set of legal institutions (rules of property and contract, for example), and to the extent that those institutions are alterable by the organs of the political community, we bear a collective responsibility for them. Attempts to alter such rules will themselves have a host of consequences, many of which may be unforeseeable, and it may be suggested that the risk that such consequences may be damaging to individual or collective interests will frequently justify a refusal to attempt such deliberate alterations. This familiar conservative argument, however, should not be understood as denying the existence of the collective responsibility; rather, it is a specific argument concerning the weighing of risk that should be integral to the exercise of that responsibility.

The emergence of the centralised organs of the state, therefore, creates a collective responsibility that would not otherwise exist. This new form of collective responsibility, however, must not be allowed to erode the notion of *individual* responsibility. This could happen all too easily if all of the consequences of my actions were to be ascribed to the framework of rules and institutions within which those actions occurred, and without which my actions would not have had precisely these effects. If the political community is to maintain conceptions of individual responsibility side by side with conceptions of collective responsibility, it must espouse principles that have the effect of attributing causal responsibilities to individuals as well as to the collectivity. The duality of perspective that explains our reaction to the parable of the labourers in the vineyard must somehow be incorporated within the conceptions of justice that are endorsed and pursued by the state.

The attempt to maintain a coherent juridical theory that gives proper recognition to both collective and individual responsibility, and does not allow the one to eclipse the other, plays a central part in the philosophy of law. For example, the long-running debate between the 'interest' and 'will' theories of rights can be reconstructed in terms of this issue;[44] and the entire debate about the determinacy and objectivity of legal doctrine can be seen as arising from a concern to separate the adjudicative determination of the precise ambit of legal rights (on the one hand) from questions of distributive justice concerning the rights that should be conferred by law (on the other). More recently, efforts have been made to discover a theory of distributive justice that is 'compatible' rather than 'competitive' with the individual's pursuit of private projects;[45] and these efforts have linked up with a more general endeavour to explain the relationship between the private law and the state's public policy objectives.

The distinction between private and public law is, no doubt, multi-faceted and not reducible to any single watershed issue; but there can be little doubt that the division between collective and individual responsibilities, currently under consideration, plays a major part in explaining the division of legal systems into public and private realms. Nor can there be much doubt that many of the current debates surrounding the relationship between distributive and corrective justice are really attempts to address this general issue. If the biblical vineyard were itself a political state, it would be viewed as a single organisational structure for the purposes of public law, and as a series of discrete transactions for the purposes of private law; attaining a just 'basic structure'[46] would be seen as a matter of distributive justice, whereas the procedural propriety of transactions within that structure would be regarded as a matter of 'commutative' or 'corrective' justice.

The rough intuitive distinction between the distributive or 'social' justice of the basic structure, and the more procedural (or 'civil') justice of transactions within that structure cannot be expected precisely to map the conventional distinction between public and private law. Legal categories of this kind are drawn in a way that is responsive to a great diversity of different considerations and shaped by various historical contingencies: they are unlikely to be the direct embodiment of any very elevated philosophical view. Nevertheless, there are good grounds for suspecting that we have here at least one part of the key to the distinction's moral significance. For, when Weinrib's basic starting point is excavated from the implausible philosophical claims in which he chooses to bury it, it remains a valid insight: private law is centrally concerned with the bipolar relationship of causal connection between plaintiff and defendant, while public law is centrally concerned with the implementation of certain distributive principles (or aggregative projects) that are independent of any such bipolar causal relationship.

Causation

That the direct causal connection obtaining between plaintiff and defendant might be central to the distinct character of private law is, in some respects, a familiar idea; for theoretical assaults upon the integrity of private law doctrine have frequently focused upon the issue of causal connection. The object has generally been to suggest that the issue of causation is used in adjudication as a cover for the introduction of general social policy issues concerning distributive or aggregative objectives. This does not result from some intellectual unscrupulousness on the part of judges or lawyers, but simply derives from the fact that the issue of causal connection has (it is alleged) little genuine content: its content is derived from elsewhere, so that when we seek to address some question such as 'Was the defendant's act the cause of the plaintiff's injury?', the issue simply collapses back into a broader range of issues concerning desirable policy goals.

Legal theoretical discussions of causation have therefore formed one important part of a much broader attempt to subvert the categories and concepts of private law, by exhibiting private law's lack of even relative independence from the state's distributive or aggregative objectives. For example, take the area of contract law. One conventional view here maintains that the justice or injustice of contractual enforcement depends upon the procedure whereby the contract was formed, rather than upon its impact upon the overall distribution of wealth. If the consent of the parties was voluntary, and not based upon a mistake[47] or induced by fraud or duress, the contract is binding. Considerations of overall distributive or 'social' justice should be kept out of contract law itself, and should be addressed by the mechanisms of tax and welfare. Yet a rival view suggests that notions such as that of 'voluntary consent' and 'duress' actually derive their content from a set of assumptions about distributive justice, so that the option of keeping such issues out of contract law is simply not available: the issues can be openly recognised or actively concealed, but the law would lack content without their constant presence.[48]

Similar attacks directed at the legal concept of causation have been very widely influential. Let us suppose that a factory is destroyed by fire. The loss may have resulted from the conjunction of many different events and circumstances: the dropping of a match; the presence of combustible material; the presence of oxygen in the atmosphere; the springing up of a light breeze which fanned the flames; the night-watchman's lack of attention; the late arrival of the fire brigade. Not all of the essential preconditions for the occurrence of an event are regarded as 'causes' of the event. In attributing responsibility for harm, the courts must select from the range of preconditions those factors that can appropriately be regarded as having caused the harm. But how is that selection made? Is the inquiry a *factual* one? Or is it in essence a question of social policy?

In the first half of the twentieth century, jurists associated with the American 'legal realist' movement adopted a position which has come to be known as 'causal minimalism'. Causal minimalists argued that the distinction between the causes of an event and its essential (but non-causal) preconditions was simply a cover for policy judgments by the courts. According to such theorists, the only genuinely causal issues addressed by courts were issues of 'but for' causation: i.e. the identification of the factors but for which the event would not have occurred. So far as the factual questions go, they argued, all such preconditions were equally entitled to be treated as the 'cause' of the event: the presence of oxygen in the atmosphere has as good a claim to be the 'cause' of the fire as has the dropped match. In deciding that some preconditions are causes and others are not, the courts are making a policy judgment about where it is desirable to locate responsibility and impose liability. Consequently, legal principles proclaiming the existence of liability for the causation of harm are not (it was argued) the stable juridical principles that they appear superficially to be: they might better be regarded as empty frameworks offering ample scope for flexible policy judgment.

If soundly based, the claims of causal minimalism would have dramatic implications. Liability in private law is to a very large extent based on the causation of harm. Private law demarcates certain rights or protected interests, and imposes liability upon those who are (intentionally, negligently, or on the basis of strict liability) causally responsible for damage to the relevant interests. It is assumed that, while questions of general social policy may enter into the conferment of rights and the choice of general rules, adjudicative decisions about the infringement of those rights and the violation of those rules are manifestations of the intellectual integrity of private law doctrines, and are not simply matters of pliable social policy. If, however, issues of causal responsibility are in fact just policy issues in disguise, the integrity of private law is an illusion. Adjudication (on this view) loses its character as an application of coherent doctrines, and individual rights are revealed as having no genuine stability or tolerably clear parameters.

In their classic work *Causation in the Law*,[49] Hart and Honoré mounted a powerful attack upon this line of argument. The causal minimalists had moved too swiftly from the observation that there were no simple principles regulating the courts' causal judgments to the conclusion that there were no principles at all, but merely an open-ended contest of policies. In fact, as Hart and Honoré demonstrated, the causal principles employed by the courts are complex but orderly, subtle but intelligible. They reflect similar causal judgments made in the course of everyday life, embodying principles which are fundamental to our sense of possessing a distinct identity. In particular, the central model of causation which underpins many of our judgments is one of 'intervention on a stage already set'. Factors which are constant

and normal will not be treated as causes, even when they are essential preconditions for an occurrence. Only those factors which can be regarded as
interventions or departures from the normal course of events will be
judged to be causes.

Hart and Honoré fully accept that this model shows causal judgements to
be in a sense relative to perspective and focus of interest. Thus a man's
stomach pains may be attributed by his doctor to ulcers; but the man's
wife may attribute them to the eating of parsnips. The difference is that the
doctor treats the eating of parsnips as a part of the normal course of
events, and regards the ulcers as the abnormal feature that explains the
incidence of pain in this case. The wife regards her husband's ulcers as a
part of the normal background to life, and attributes his pain on this occa-
sion to the parsnips. The wife and the doctor are in effect asking different
questions. The doctor is asking 'Why does this man suffer pain (on eating
parsnips) when most men do not?'; the wife is asking 'Why (given the
existence of his ulcers) is my husband suffering pain *now* when usually he
does not?' This seeming relativity of causal judgments invites the conclusion
that only the question of 'but for' causation is a factual issue, with all other
supposedly 'causal' issues being in fact a matter of policy. But, Hart and
Honoré urge, such a conclusion would be overly simplistic and inherently
misleading. Our values and interests may shape the questions that we consider it relevant to ask; but they do not determine the answers that we give
to those questions. Moreover, even if our common-sense causal judgments
exhibit a degree of contextual relativity, they are not mere functions of
social policy judgments. Causal judgments in law reflect a background of
common-sense understandings: they are not a cover for decisions about
desirable social goals.

More recently the arguments of the causal minimalists have been recycled.
Ronald Coase's brilliant and hugely influential article 'The Problem of Social
Cost'[50] has been credited with a major insight into the nature of causal
relationships in law. Consider a recent statement of this view (this time
giving credit to Calabresi[51] as a well as to Coase):

> Ronald Coase and Guido Calabresi independently invented the
> economic analysis of law when they realized that every injury is a joint
> product. Both injurer and victim cause any injury. . . . In all but the
> most bizarre cases, the accident could have been prevented had the
> victim stayed home, taken a different route, or whatever. Thus, any
> injury is always a joint product, which must somehow be divided between
> the parties.[52]

It would be quite remarkable if, in the course of a brief but brilliant article on
economics, Coase had developed a general and innovative view of causation.
If that was his intention, he clearly failed, for the great insight which is
ascribed to him actually amounts to no more than the basic starting point

of causal minimalism generally (and therefore of Hart and Honoré's response to causal minimalism): namely, the great multiplicity of essential preconditions that constitute 'but for' causes of an event.

In fact, it should be perfectly obvious that Coase was not offering a general philosophical or jurisprudential thesis about causation, but developing a highly innovative contribution to economics. I have argued elsewhere[53] that Coase's remarks concerning causation must be read in the context of an overall concern with aggregative or allocative issues. From that perspective, it is indeed true that the common-sense distinctions we make between essential preconditions and 'causes' are quite irrelevant. It is, however, obviously fallacious to infer from that specific failure of relevance a general claim that such distinctions are lacking in significance or content. The intelligibility of the principles that discriminate between causes and conditions has been demonstrated by Hart and Honoré;[54] there remains an interesting question concerning their relevance (or lack of it) to questions of justice.

Hart and Honoré say little about the moral relevance of the principles that they unearth. In the Preface to their second edition, however, they offer a few tantalising reflections that address this issue. Thus, they argue that the causal principles are required by 'the distinctive form which the legal control of conduct takes'.[55] Rather than aiming at 'Brave New World conditioning', the law appeals to individuals 'as intelligent beings who are assumed to have the capacity to control their conduct'.[56] At the same time, they argue, it would be unreasonable for the law to demand that people should not be the condition *sine qua non* of harm. Thus 'the limits to responsibility set by common sense causal principles are appropriate to the law as a system designed to minimize harm by an appeal to individuals to control their conduct.'[57] In addition, they offer the observation that the common-sense causal principles sustain 'the individual's sense of himself as a separate person whose character is manifested' in his actions:

> This sense of respect for ourselves and others as distinct persons would be much weakened, if not dissolved, if we could not think of ourselves as separate authors of the changes we make in the world. If we had to share the authorship of such changes with numerous prior agents, of whom it could be said that, had they not acted as they did, we should not have been able to bring about the change, we could no longer think of ourselves as separate authors in the way we now do.[58]

Our suspicion should be that a diversity of considerations contribute to the moral underpinnings of the common-sense causal principles and their role in the law. One element in a complex picture can be developed from the remarks of Hart and Honoré just quoted. The law depends for its determinacy upon a background of shared understandings, for in the absence of such shared understandings the texts of the law could not yield convergent interpretations, and so shared rules. Yet the law may also lend determinacy to the very background understandings that help to sustain it.[59] The common-sense causal principles, as Hart and Honoré point out, make possible our sense of ourselves as individuals. Articulated and stabilised in law, they form a public expression of that mutual recognition that constitutes us as individual agents.[60]

There is, however, another aspect to the role of the common-sense causal principles, in addition to this expressive and constitutive one. When discussing the parable of the labourers in the vineyard, we saw how our moral intuitions seem to embody a duality of perspectives. On the one hand, we feel concern for the justice of individual transactions, where we are inclined to address the issue in terms of individual responsibilities: the workers had got what they had agreed to, so what just complaint could they have? On the other hand, we feel concern for the overall justice of the way things are organised. Sometimes, for example, we are inclined to think of this as a matter of the 'basic structure' within which individual transactions take place; or we might think of society as something that has been deliberately organised by a single central authority. These assumptions conceal from us the depth of the problem, however. For in a real sense, there *is* no 'basic structure' within which individual transactions 'take place': the basic structure is itself the result of a huge multiplicity of individual transactions. Those transactions would not have had precisely these effects (or even been possible) were it not for the framework of legal rules that govern them; but those legal rules are themselves expressive of judgement concerning the justice of the particular transactions. Our conflicting intuitions concerning justice (revealed by the parable of the labourers in the vineyard) do indeed conflict, and cannot be neatly reconciled by an intellectual division between containing structure and contained transactions.

If we are to acknowledge the reality of both collective and individual responsibilities, without allowing the one to eclipse the other, we must develop institutions that embody this duality. Given the absence of any natural boundary between the two forms of moral concern, we must employ artifice, and the distinction between public and private law is a part of that artifice. No one should expect a doctrinal distinction of this sort to precisely trace out some significant moral principle or distinction: here as elsewhere, doctrinal distinctions are the product of historical contingency combined with the residues of tradition, rather than a direct expression of philosophical insight. Where we are to employ artifice, however, we must make use of the materials available, and it is in this way that doctrinal distinctions can come to be filled with moral resonances that they only imperfectly capture.

Our moral concern to exercise collective responsibility (so far as we can) over the overall profile of our community conflicts with our desire to preserve the individual's responsibility for the consequences of his or her action. The conflict stems directly from the fact that the structure of society is not a box within which individual actions are located: it is the context that forms and gives consequence to individual actions while at the same time being itself the unintended consequence of individual actions. Within law, this tension between collective and individual responsibilities manifests itself in our concern for the integrity of private rights.

In exercising, through our political organs or representatives, our collective power to shape the overall character of the community, we do not seek to determine the legitimacy of every action by reference to the contribution it makes to the attainment or dissolution of our favoured collective goals. To do this would be to fail to attribute intrinsic moral significance to individual responsibility. The solution, embodied in that state of affairs that we call 'the rule of law', is to take collective decisions that accord to individuals various rights, and then to judge individual actions by reference to the rights so defined. If this way of balancing conflicting values is to be a reality, the rights must not be defined in terms that collapse their bounds back into questions of the favoured distributive or aggregative goals being pursued at the level of the collectivity. Hence, there are in general good reasons for not making the legitimacy of the exercise of a right dependent upon the consistency of the right-holder's motive with favoured collective goals,[61] or the contribution of the right-holder's action to the advancement of such goals.

When rights conflict, however, there may be little option but to resolve the dispute by reference to collective values. Thus, the impact of my actions upon collective goals may be disregarded if my actions encroach upon the rights of no one else;[62] but if actions of mine, performed within the apparent scope of some general entitlement that I possess, come into conflict with your rights, the precise demarcation of the bounds between our rights cannot be carried out without invoking the collective goals and social policies that led to their conferment in the first place.[63] If the adjudicative determination of the scope of existing legal rights is to be relatively independent of the state's distributive and aggregative goals, therefore, the number of apparent conflicts between rights must be reduced so far as possible.

This gives us an explanation of the role of common-sense causal principles in private law that is distinguishable from (although consistent with) Hart and Honoré's explanation in terms of the maintenance of a sense of individual identity.[64] If I could be held causally responsible for all of those events for which an action of mine was an essential precondition, my responsibilities would be infinite and endless. Many of these events would be instances of harm or injury or encroachment upon the general entitlements of others. Conflicts of rights would therefore be all-pervading. This is not, of course, to say that I would be legally liable for all of these events, for *causal* responsibility is not the whole of legal liability; but each of these instances would be a case of apparent conflict between rights, thereby requiring resolution by reference to collective goals. The legitimacy of practically all of my actions would then be judged by reference to their impact upon such collective goals.

Causation and alterability

We have identified a conflict between the value of individual responsibility and the collective determination of society's general character. We have related this conflict to the contrast between 'distributive' (or 'social') and 'corrective' (or 'civil') justice, and thus to the contrast between public and private law. Finally, we have seen how the common-sense causal principles identified by Hart and Honoré can be partly explained by reference to their capacity to limit the number of conflicts between individual rights, and so the number of occasions on which the precise determination of the scope of rights must turn upon considerations of the state's public policy (distributive or aggregative) objectives. In conclusion, however, we need to note one respect in which the emergence of institutions (including the state) that make it possible to deliberately alter the structures and conditions of social life, while making some such reconciliation of individual and collective values necessary (as we have seen), may also undermine the very basis for that reconciliation. These concluding remarks will do no more than gesture in the direction of some complex issues, but the chapter would be incomplete if those issues were not adverted to at all.

Hart and Honoré trace the scepticism that underpins causal minimalism to a failure to grasp the complex nature of the principles whereby our common-sense judgements distinguish between 'causes' and mere 'conditions'. Thus, they show that there is no unitary conception of causation that underpins our ordinary thinking, but rather three quite different models whereby the causally responsible factor may be selected from the huge multiplicity of conditions 'but for' which the event in question would not have occurred. Two of these models'[65] can be disregarded for present purposes, the better to concentrate upon what Hart and Honoré themselves regard as the central case. The central model of causality that underpins our common-sense judgments (Hart and Honoré suggest) is the notion of 'intervention on a stage already set': 'An act is the cause of harm if it is an intervention in the course of affairs which is sufficient to produce the harm without the co-operation of the voluntary actions of others or abnormal conjunctions of events.'[66] Since, according to Hart and Honoré, we commonly regard omissions as capable of being causes, the same model would apply to a failure to initiate or arrest some physical process, if that failure was a departure from the ordinary course of events, amounting to 'an intervention on a stage already set'.

The analysis offered by Hart and Honoré therefore suggests that causal judgments in law and common sense are relative to a taken-for-granted background that constitutes the 'stage already set', upon which a cause 'intervenes'. We may therefore conclude that such causal judgments will seem most secure and determinate in contexts where the background may indeed be taken for granted as an established background like a natural landscape. The more that we come to appreciate the alterability of human arrangements, the less secure such causal judgments will seem; and the more sophisticated our political and other institutions become, the more we will appreciate such alterability.

We are now in a position to see how the *concepts* of private law may have exhibited considerable continuity, while the law has nevertheless grown more pliable. Where once a famine might have been attributed to the unexpected absence of rain (for example), we now have public bodies that might be expected to anticipate such events and do something to avert their possible consequences. Their failure to act may then be viewed as the cause of the famine. When once the car crash might have been attributed to the icy road (or to the driver's negligence) it might now be attributed to the Highway Authority's failure to grit the road. When once the death of a child through starvation and neglect might have been attributed to the failures of the child's parents, it might now be attributed to the local authority's failure to identify the child as at risk, and remove it from the custody of its parents. In a traditional society where no organisation is equipped to address questions such as the maintenance and improvement of roads, or the supervision of parental care for children, responsibility for these events may seem straightforward: it rests with the driver of the car, and with the parents of the child. But once we have highway authorities, and public authorities empowered to remove children from the custody of their parents, the question becomes rather more complex. One might even argue that our awareness of the possibility of such interventions renders the distinction between injustice and misfortune entirely problematic.[67] The more extensive the protective scope of the state's authority, the less we will be inclined to regard tragedies as the result of ill-fortune, and the more we will seek to ascribe blame; the more extensive that authority, the less we will be willing to accept the idea of uncompensated loss.

The analysis of Hart and Honoré reveals the extent to which our assignments of causal responsibility possess a degree of certainty only when they are made against the background of contexts that can be taken as more or less settled and relatively unalterable. The deeper our appreciation of how the effects of an action may be shaped by the action's context, and the deeper our grasp of how open to alteration that context might be, the more problematic our ordinary causal judgments become. Yet the integrity of private law and of corrective justice appeared to depend upon the centrality of such causal judgments. If the plaintiff's complaint is that the defendant injured him, we need to decide whether the injury was indeed caused by the defendant's driving, or by the Highway Authority's failure to repair the road. Yet this judgment becomes harder to make in abstraction from a set of understandings about what highway authorities can be expected to do, and this from questions of distributive justice. Is it fair, we may find ourselves asking, that this or that motorist (even if somewhat careless) should have to bear the cost of damage that would not have occurred had the Highway Authority acted differently?

The principal institutions and ideas of private law developed within societies that did not possess a highly developed state apparatus capable of envisaging the extensive restructuring of social life, or the revision of established practices. At the same time, those institutions and ideas have provided a valuable resource for the maintenance of individual responsibilities, and the integrity of individual rights apart from the state's distributive agenda. Their long-term fate remains a matter for speculation.

Notes

1 F.H. Bradley, *Ethical Studies*, 2nd edn (Oxford: Clarendon Press 1927) p. 2.
2 Hans Kelsen, *Introduction to the Problems of Legal Theory*, translated by B.L. Paulson and S.L. Paulson (Oxford: Clarendon Press 1992) pp. 92, 94.
3 *Ibid.*, p. 92.
4 Hans Kelsen, '"Foreword" to Main Problems in the Theory of Public Law', in *Normativity and Norms*, edited by Stanley L. Paulson and Bonnie Litschewski Paulson (Oxford: Clarendon Press 1998) p. 7.
5 Kelsen, *Introduction to the Problems of Legal Theory, op. cit.*, p. 95.
6 Robert Hale is an important theorist who reaches related conclusions from the perspective of a very different tradition of legal thought. For excellent discussions of Hale's views, and references to his scattered writings, see Barbara H. Fried, *The Progressive Assault on Laissez Faire* (Cambridge, Mass.: Harvard University Press 1998); and Matthew Kramer, *In the Realm of Legal and Moral Philosophy* (London: Macmillan 1999) ch. 7.
7 Richard Posner, *Economic Analysis of Law*, 3rd edn (Boston, Mass. and Toronto: Little Brown 1986).
8 See, for a mass of relevant information, Reinhard Zimmerman, *The Law of Obligations: Roman Foundations of the Civilian Tradition*, translated by Tony Weir (Oxford: Clarendon Press 1996).
9 See James Gordley, *The Philosophical Origins of Modern Contract Doctrine* (Oxford: Clarendon Press 1991).
10 A.W.B. Simpson, 'Innovation in Nineteenth Century Contract Law', in Simpson, *Legal Theory and Legal History* (London: Hambledon Press 1987) p. 178.
11 See Charles Fried, 'Rights and the Common Law', in R.G. Frey (ed.), *Utility and Rights* (Oxford: Blackwell 1985).
12 For example, suppose that we take the view that the responsibility of promise-breakers to compensate their promisees clearly entails a duty to pay for *all* the losses flowing from the broken promise. We might then also hold that the promisees' right to full compensation should not be restricted by reference to considerations of collective welfare, and we might reject on that basis the rule (of English law) that the contract-breaker need only pay for losses that were reasonably foreseeable at the time of making the contract. In fact, however, the general moral responsibility of promise-breakers is not so clear: does it extend to *all* losses, or only those losses that were foreseeable at the time the contract was made? Given the compatibility of the general conception of responsibility with either view, there can be no objection to the adoption as law of one or other view on the basis of general social policy considerations.

    The position set out in the first paragraph of this note is sufficient to demonstrate that there is no necessary incompatibility between reliance upon social policy argument and private law's claim to embody principles of individual responsibility. We must also remember, however, that a variety of considerations (including administration costs, and the need to avoid the involvement of the courts in open-ended and non-resolvable controversies) ensure that private law can never be a perfect expression of moral conceptions of responsibility, even to the extent contemplated in the first paragraph. See Simmonds, 'Bluntness and Bricolage', in *Jurisprudence: Cambridge Essays*, edited by H. Gross and R. Harrison (Oxford: Clarendon Press 1992).

13 (Cambridge, Mass.: Harvard University Press 1995).
14 (Oxford: Clarendon Press 1961).
15 Roberto Unger, *The Critical Legal Studies Movement* (Cambridge, Mass.: Harvard University Press 1986).
16 And rejected: Hart criticises formalism on the grounds that it ignores 'the open-texture of language' which inevitably gives rise to 'penumbral uncertainty'.
17 Ronald Dworkin, *Law's Empire* (London: Fontana 1986).
18 Book V.
19 See, for example, Richard Epstein, *A Theory of Strict Liability* (San Francisco: Cato Institute 1980). See Simmonds, 'Epstein's Theory of Strict Tort Liability' (1992) *Cambridge Law Journal* 113.
20 Cf. Richard Posner's comment that 'when one turns to the detailed articulation of . . . doctrine, the theory of corrective justice quickly runs out of steam'; Richard Posner, 'Wealth Maximisation and Tort Law', in *Philosophical Foundations of Tort Law*, edited by David G. Owen (Oxford: Clarendon Press 1995) p. 108.
21 G.W.F. Hegel, *The Philosophy of Right*, s. 135, translated by T.M. Knox (Oxford: Oxford University Press 1952); Arthur Schopenhauer, *The World as Will and as Representation* (3rd edn, 1859), vol. 1, translated by E.F. Payne (New York: Dover 1966) p. 528.
22 At one point Weinrib says that his argument could be developed 'in Hegelian' terms as well as 'in Kantian terms'. This seems to involve reading Hegel's discussion of 'abstract right' in isolation from the rest of Hegel's theory. See Weinrib, *op. cit.*, p. 81n.
23 *Op. cit.*, p. 79.
24 Weinrib notes that the Robin Hood defence might be excluded for 'administrative reasons not relevant to the theoretical point in issue'; *op. cit.*, p. 79n. By so denying the theoretical relevance of such administrative reasons, however, Weinrib begs the entire question. For those who see little substantive significance as attaching to the distinction between public and private law, the best explanations of the particular *form* of private law are very likely to focus upon issues of administrative convenience rather than more substantive matters.

Similarly, Weinrib argues that, if corrective justice is conceived of as dependent upon distributive justice, 'transactional injustice would not be a wrong directly done to the sufferer': it would 'consist not in something that the defendant has done to the plaintiff, but in the defendant's having more and the plaintiff less than each's fair share of the distribution'. This too would be found untroubling by Weinrib's opponents, however. For those who see corrective justice as subordinate to distributive justice, the distinction between private law and public law is not very deeply significant. Private law focuses upon transactions in which the defendant has done something to the plaintiff; but this focus is explained (on this view) by pragmatic and administrative considerations, and not by fundamental matters of moral principle.
25 *Op. cit.*, p. 80.
26 See Charles Fried, *Contract as Promise* (Cambridge, Mass.: Harvard University Press 1981) pp. 105–6.

27 *Op. cit.*, p. 79.
28 John Rawls, *A Theory of Justice* (Oxford: Clarendon Press 1972) p. 3.
29 The family is a source of injustice in numerous respects, yet it is nevertheless of value. We tolerate some relatively small injustices for the sake of other values. When the injustices stemming from the family become too severe, we may seek to redress them, even at some cost to the value of the family itself: thus we do in fact tax testamentary and *inter vivos* gifts when they exceed certain amounts. On the general problem, see James Fishkin, *Justice, Equal Opportunity, and the Family* (New Haven, Conn.: Yale University Press 1983).
30 Ernest Weinrib, 'Law as a Kantian Idea of Reason' (1987) 87 *Columbia Law Review* 472 at p. 477.
31 Weinrib, *Idea of Private Law*, p. 72. In spite of defining 'coherence' in this way, Weinrib does not hesitate to equate 'coherence' with intelligibility: see e.g. *op. cit.*, p. 11 *et seq.* He is thus guilty of an equivocation between two different senses of 'coherence'. As Raz observes, 'coherent' can mean 'consisting of mutually supporting elements' or it can mean 'intelligible'. A system can include mutually competing (or non-supporting) elements while still being perfectly intelligible; Joseph Raz, *Ethics in the Public Domain* (Oxford: Clarendon Press 1994) p. 264.
32 *Op. cit.*, p. 70. Weinrib cannot really mean this literally, since he claims that corrective justice involves a relationship of 'doing and suffering' involving a causal connection between the two parties: it could not apply to an 'incident' where I won the national lottery while my brother fell ill.
33 See n. 31 above.
34 This interpretation of the implications of liberty as a value is, of course, highly contestable. The mere possibility of such a view, however, affects Weinrib's argument.
35 A similar point is made by John Gardner:

>   We need to marshal all the reasons in favour of something in order to defeat the whole army of objections which are lined up against it. The problem is not that of letting considerations do less than the justificatory work of which they are capable, but of wishing that they could do more, and having to call in reinforcements when one realizes they cannot.
>
>   John Gardner, 'The Purity and Priority of Private Law' (1996) 46
>   *University of Toronto Law Journal* 459 at p. 472.

36 See John Finnis, 'On "The Critical Legal Studies Movement"', in *Oxford Essays in Jurisprudence: Third Series*, edited by John Eekelaar and John Bell (Oxford: Clarendon Press 1987).
37 Whether these terms are ideal (e.g. should we speak of 'corrective' or of 'commutative' justice?) and whether the concepts are drawn from Aristotle or from his later commentators, are matters that do not concern me here. It is far from obvious that questions in the theoretical analysis of private law should be closely linked to questions concerning the proper interpretation of Aristotle, or the history of the Aristotelian tradition of scholarship. Nevertheless, the long continuity of the debate concerning the relationship between these two notions is some evidence that deep and genuine problems underlie the debate.
38 I am indebted to Matthew Kramer for elucidating the theological significance of the parable.
      I have discussed the parable in 'The Possibility of Private Law', in J. Tasioulas (ed.), *Law, Values and Social Practices* (Aldershot: Dartmouth 1997), at p. 156. Other jurisprudential discussions of the parable include Wojciech Sadurski,

Giving Desert its Due (Dordrecht: Kluwer 1985) pp. 33 *et seq.*; and Michael Detmold, *The Unity of Law and Morality* (London: Routledge and Kegan Paul 1984) pp. 105–7.

39 This reaction is, apparently, not universal: Wojciech Sadurski, *loc cit.*, sees no merit in the owner's position, and construes it simply as an assertion of power. It is perhaps significant, however, that Sadurski invites us to refer to the workers who worked all day as 'blacks', and those who worked only one hour as 'whites'. This is done, he tells us, purely for ease of reference(!) but one suspects that it is done in the hope of altering our ordinary reactions to the parable.

40 F.A. Hayek, *Law, Legislation and Liberty*, vol. 2 (London: Routledge 1976).

41 This would seem to be one of the implications of the work of Robert Hale, n. 6 above. It is presumably an unstated premise in innumerable contemporary discussions of social justice.

42 I do not propose to embark on an attempt to elucidate the concept of the state. In the present context I use the term to refer to centralised political institutions having the juridical authority to alter the legal frameworks within which individual transactions occur. I set on one side the question of how far that juridical authority is matched by factual power.

43 Subject to the qualification in the preceding note.

44 See my contribution to Matthew Kramer, N.E. Simmonds and Hillel Steiner, *A Debate Over Rights* (Oxford: Clarendon Press 1998).

45 R. Dworkin, *Law's Empire* (London: Fontana 1986) ch. 8.

46 John Rawls, *A Theory of Justice* (Oxford: Clarendon Press 1972).

47 Legal systems vary in the extent to which they recognise mistake as a defence.

48 A. Kronman, 'Contract Law and Distributive Justice' (1980) 89 *Yale Law Journal* 472. For criticism of Kronman, see Kramer and Simmonds, 'Getting the Rabbit Out of the Hat: A Critique of Anthony Kronman's Theory of Contracts' (1996) *Cambridge Law Journal* 358 [reprinted in Matthew Kramer, *In the Realm of Legal and Moral Philosophy* (London: Macmillan 1999) ch. 9].

49 H.L.A. Hart and T. Honoré, *Causation in the Law*, 2nd edn (Oxford University Press 1985).

50 Coase, 'The Problem of Social Cost' (1960) 3 *Journal of Law and Economics* 1.

51 Guido Calabresi, 'Some Thoughts on Risk Distribution in Torts' (1961) 70 *Yale Law Journal* 499.

52 Arthur Ripstein, *Equality, Responsibility and the Law* (Cambridge: Cambridge University Press 1999) pp. 35–6.

53 Simmonds, 'Epstein's Theory of Strict Liability' (1992) *Cambridge Law Journal* 113, at pp. 118–19.

54 Although their work receives little careful attention from the modern causal minimalists. Thus, Ripstein observes that 'Their analysis is of little help' to those who seek 'to explicate the notion of wrongdoing in terms of causation', since 'it focuses on tracing the causal consequences of independently identified wrongdoing' (Ripstein, *op. cit.*, p. 38). This is, however, quite misleading as a description of Hart and Honoré's work. Other such critics prefer not to mention Hart and Honoré at all, casually dismissing all such views as 'premodern' (whatever that means); see Mark Kelman, *A Guide to Critical Legal Studies* (Cambridge, Mass.: Harvard University Press 1987) p. 24.

I am, of course, not suggesting that the work of Hart and Honoré is beyond criticism, and it certainly raises a host of problems; but it needs to be addressed, rather than ignored or dismissed.

55 H.L.A. Hart and T. Honoré, *Causation in the Law*, 2nd edn (Oxford: Clarendon Press 1985) p. lxxix.

56 *Loc. cit.* Cf. Lon Fuller, *The Morality of Law*, rev. edn (New Haven, Conn.: Yale University Press 1969) pp. 162–7.
57 *Op. cit.*, p. lxxx.
58 *Op. cit.*, p. lxxxi. Further relevant reflections can be found in Tony Honoré, 'Responsibility and Luck' (1988) 104 *Law Quarterly Review*, 537; and Honoré, 'Being Responsible and Being a Victim of Circumstance', *Proceedings of the British Academy*, vol. 97, p. 169.
59 See Simmonds, 'Between Positivism and Idealism' (1991) *Cambridge Law Journal*, 308.
60 'Self-consciousness . . . exists only in being acknowledged'; G.W.F. Hegel, *Phenomenology of Spirit*, trans. A.V. Miller (Oxford: Oxford University Press 1977) p. 111.
61 Traditionally English law is contrasted with civilian systems such as French law by the absence in the former and the presence in the latter of a general doctrine of 'abuse of rights'. See F.H. Lawson, *Negligence in the Civil Law* (Oxford: Clarendon Press 1950) pp. 15–20; F.H. Lawson and B.S. Markesinis, *Tortious Liability for Unintentional Harm in the Common Law and the Civil Law* (Cambridge: Cambridge University Press 1982) vol. 1, pp. 52–7.
     In fact the position in English law is not straightforward. Compare *Bradford Corporation* v. *Pickles* [1895] AC 587, with *Hollywood Silver Fox Fur Farm.* v. *Emmett* [1936] 2 KB 468. David Howarth is probably correct when he suggests that the key issue is the type of loss suffered by the plaintiff; David Howarth, *Textbook on Tort* (London: Butterworth 1995) pp. 503–4.
62 See *Bradford Corporation* v. *Pickles*, n. 61 above.
63 See *Hollywood Silver Fox Fur Farm* v. *Emmett* [1936] 2 KB 468.
64 Hart and Honoré do not appear to regard the causal principles as having a role in private law that they do not possess within public law. This is probably connected to their belief that the principles could and perhaps should form a part of any moral theory, even one of an aggregative or distributive type. Thus, they suggest at p. 69 of *Causation in the Law* that a utilitarian theory might invoke the causal principles as a restriction upon the relevance of an act's consequences. In my view, this would make no sense for a theory constructed around an aggregative or patterned distributive goal. This is not to say, of course, that employment of the causal principles might not be justified within such a theory by instrumental considerations, such as the need for relatively simple and easily administrable rules.
65 One person by words or deeds providing another with reason for doing something; and the provision of an opportunity, commonly exploited for good or ill, which is so exploited. Like the central model discussed in the text, each of these models has negative variants: the failure to provide reasons, or opportunities.
66 Hart and Honoré, *op. cit.*, p. 5.
67 See Judith Shklar, *The Faces of Injustice* (New Haven, Conn.: Yale University Press 1990).

9 Private contract and public institution

The peculiar case of marriage

Ursula Vogel

Introduction: what is marriage?

In most Western societies today more than one in three marriages will end in divorce. The number of couples who live together without the formal credentials of a marriage certificate is rising; so is the number of children who – to use the telling phrase – are born 'out of wedlock'. Single parenthood, teenage pregnancy and the increasing public visibility of same-sex partnerships complement the picture of a traditional form of life that has lost its way. According to the most apprehensive critics we are witnessing a deep crisis which strikes at the roots of liberal society's moral cohesion and political stability.[1] Other observers will find in the same facts but confirmation of the inexorable demise of a legal fiction which is irretrievably unjust and has ceased to accord with people's experiences and expectations.[2] Both sides will, however, agree that what is in a state of crisis or decline is the 'institution of marriage'. No phrase is more frequently invoked in public debates about the future of marriage; none proves more elusive when we inquire into its exact meaning.

One might of course say that the term refers to no more than the simple fact that marriage is a legal institute. Unlike friendship or the informal domestic partnership, the conclusion of a valid marriage is bound to formal prerequisites and procedures and gives rise to a specific set of enforceable rights and obligations. But these criteria of a legally constituted relationship would seem to apply to many contractual transactions or associations – such as the acquisition of a house or an employment contract – which do not attract the same amount of public concern and disquiet.

What special claims, then, are made on behalf of marriage when it is prefaced by the word 'institution'? If we probe into the typically defensive or polemical connotations that are carried by the phrase in ordinary speech we get some indication of the distinctive features that set the 'institution of marriage' apart from other legal or contractual relationships. The first of these features entails a strong indictment of the corrosive tendencies of modern individualism. Marriage, it seems, must be understood as something more than what two individuals intend and are able to make of a shared life. The common reference to the marriage 'vows' implies that the nature of the commitment is qualitatively different from the obligations that individuals incur through voluntary entry into other kinds of contractual associations. The institution of marriage, in the words of a German court judgment from the 1950s, must be considered as 'an independent, objective order which is not based solely upon the principle of individual autonomy'.[3]

The second thread of meanings implied in the concept revolves around beliefs that attribute to marriage a timeless, immutable essence. Its present form is seen to embody the necessary structures which pertain to the human condition as such and which will thus be found in all societies as a response to the demands of biological and social reproduction and to the needs of human bonding within the boundaries of intimate, affective relationships.[4]

The third characteristic thrust in the defence of the institution of marriage refers to its special function in maintaining the order of society and the state. This is a puzzling and profoundly ambiguous claim. On the one hand, marriage provides the paradigm of relationships that demarcate a private, quintessentially non-political sphere. On the other hand, it is uniquely invested with political purposes and a status of public significance.

This chapter will trace the modern understanding of the 'institution of marriage' to a radical shift in the orientations of European legal thought in the first half of the nineteenth century. In this particular context, the institutional discourse both reflected and spearheaded a comprehensive reaction against the legacies of Enlightenment rationalism and its alleged complicity in the revolutionary onslaught upon the foundations of Europe's traditional social order. However, as the first section of the chapter will indicate, this reaction drew upon authoritative models and perceptions of marriage which the medieval canon law had fashioned from the inseparable unity of contract and sacrament. The second section will then discuss the move towards an understanding of marriage as a purely civil contract which occurred in the natural law schools of the seventeenth and eighteenth centuries. The explosive political consequences of this shift manifested themselves in the legislative programme of the French Revolution which forced the separation of church and state in the recognition of the civil marriage and of the divorce by mutual consent. It is against this background that we can best understand the institutionalist discourses of the nineteenth century. In order to strike at the freedom of divorce the reaction had to move marriage into a discursive terrain that would be inaccessible both to the language of individual rights and to the regulatory powers of the state.

We shall see that at all stages in this historical process the question 'what is marriage?' was enmeshed in larger questions about the foundations of a legitimate political order. The political core of the marriage debates can be explored from three interrelated perspectives. The first encapsulates centuries of political and ideological struggle between church and state over who was to regulate marriage. Whose law was to determine and enforce the criteria which would confer public recognition upon one particular form of sexual union whilst striking all others with the mark of invalidity or punishable deviance? Who as a consequence, decided upon the legitimacy of children, upon familial affiliation and rightful titles to property? In other words, who could lay claim to the credentials of sovereign power?

The second perspective highlights the extensive regulatory involvement and coercive presence of the public power in the terrain of marriage. According to the abstract scheme of systematic classifications that became dominant in modern jurisprudence since the end of the eighteenth century, marriage belonged in the domain of the private law. However, within that general framework of voluntary contractual arrangements it stood out as a contract *sui generis* which affirmed a public, coercive relationship. In the traditions of legal thought with which we are concerned here reference to the public interest and to the imperatives of public order constituted the dominant mode in which the arrangements of marriage were explicated and justified.

We can get a sense of what is involved in the peculiar normative structure of marriage if we imagine it in the form of a tripartite contract. On this reading, the promises or vows exchanged between husband and wife would be directed not only at the other partner. They addressed and were affirmed by a third party, be it the kinship community, God, or the state. Thus medieval Christendom conceived of marriage as an unbreakable bond between husband, wife and God.[5] Analogous formulations can be found also in historical contexts where the separation of state and church had deprived religion of any substantive part in the marriage ceremony. 'The public is always party in questions of marriage': this is how the framers of the Code Napoléon justified their aim to reinforce the permanence and dignity of the matrimonial bond which the divorce legislation of the Revolution had allegedly surrendered to the arbitrariness of private volitions. In concluding a marriage contract, so the argument ran, the individual does not act solely on behalf of personal interests, but on those of the community – '*on stipule pour l'état*'.[6]

The third political dimension of marriage manifests itself in the constitution of gender as a political relationship of rule and subordination. European marriage laws, from the early medieval period to the end of the nineteenth century, converged on one point. They defined the asymmetric rights and obligations of husband and wife in an unmistakably political language – as *imperium maritale, puissance maritale, Herrschaft, baron and feme*. What was encapsulated in these terms was a husband's power over the personal conduct of his wife as well as over her property. She was, to summarise briefly, incapable of performing legally valid actions in her own person. Without his authority she could neither conclude contracts nor engage in business or paid work outside the home. In her own right she could not dispose of the goods she had brought into marriage and she similarly lacked an independent standing in court. We shall see that in the discourses which undertook to vindicate this peculiar legal relationship by reference to a coherent system of normative principles the political ordering of gender was presented as instrumental or secondary to the preservation of the public order as a whole. A close reading of the texts, however, will reveal the mutual dependence of the two régimes of order. For, the very question of what constituted order and disorder already presupposed the supremacy of male over female as the defining characteristic of ordered human existence. To put it differently, the order of gender and the political order were so intertwined in the construction of marriage that it is impossible to determine which was prior or dominant. The assertion of one necessarily reinforced the other.

The sacramental contract: Christian marriage laws

The Christian understanding of marriage and its consolidation in the jurisdictional powers of the Catholic church meant a radical break with the tribal and familial customs of ancient Europe. With regard to the acts and actors that established a valid marriage, the centre of gravity shifted from the collective authority of families, dynasties and local communities to the two individual partners. *Solus consensus facit nuptias* (consent alone makes a marriage): in adopting the maxim of the Roman law, Christian doctrine made the voluntary agreement between a man and a woman the sole requirement of the matrimonial bond. Before, towards the end of the eleventh century, the rituals of solemnisation became more clearly defined with regard to specific procedures and the prescribed public space of the local church, a valid marriage required no other testimony than the simple verbal promise of two individuals to take each other as husband and wife.[7]

While the centrality of consent gave to the Christian marriage the formal structure of a contract, its simultaneous status as a sacrament anchored the agreement between two human beings in a sphere beyond their individual will and freedom. 'The consent of husband and wife signifies the union of Christ and his church which is effected through love.'[8] Among Christians, the marriage contract was *eo ipso* a sacrament – a sign and vehicle of divine grace, like baptism or the Eucharist. In the fusion of contract and sacrament marriage acquired the characteristic features of an 'institution': the contract expressed the consensual formation of the bond but also committed the individuals to obligations which did not originate in their own choice. Marriage was thus a creation of the human law and, at the same time, pre-ordained in a higher, divine order of things.

In important respects, Christian law placed personal freedom at the centre of marriage. According to the maxim of consent-alone, no external power was allowed to forcibly interfere with the mutual agreement between the two partners. Neither the will of parents nor the authority that kings, feudal lords and slavemasters held over their subordinates could break or prevent a bond for which there was sufficient evidence of consensual origin. The freedom granted by the consent principle should, on the other hand, not be understood as opening up a wide space of individual autonomy.

Its meaning was confined to the absence of coercion from the act of consent, i.e. to the guarantee of free will against force, error and duress. In most practical respects marriage confronted the individuals as an order whose imperatives preceded and transcended their personal will. Not only was the right to contract a marriage fenced in by an extensive catalogue of impediments, such as the known incapacity to beget offspring or the manifold instances of 'incest' entailed in relations of even remote consanguinity. Freedom of consent at the entry gate of marriage did not entitle the spouses to determine the purposes and practices of their union even in the most 'private' domain of personal life. The former were prescribed in the imperative of procreation, the latter in a detailed code of sexual conduct by which the law, in conjunction with the confessional and the rituals of penance, sought to enforce that end.[9]

Most importantly, the consent requirement did not entail freedom of exit. Invested with sacramental properties, and in this regard qualitatively different from any other contractual bond, the marriage contract committed individuals to an indissoluble union. Under church law divorce was, and still is for practising Catholics today, absolutely prohibited. The only remedy for a severely damaged relationship lay in the separation of bed and board which precluded remarriage for both partners. In the period of the French Revolution divorce was to become the pivotal issue that divided the institutional and the contractual conceptions of marriage. The safeguard against individual wilfulness which church law had derived from the sacred status of marriage would reappear in the emphasis upon the primarily public tasks of the 'institution of marriage'.

What was the place of women and men in this legal order? The answer is more complex than a superficial glance at the easily identifiable patriarchal features of the Christian marriage would suggest.[10] To begin with, Christian doctrine established a kind of equality between the sexes that was unknown in the ancient world. It assumed that in the realm of faith and salvation women and men were 'co-heirs of the gift of grace' (I Peter 3: 7) and that in this respect the distinctions of sex, like those of ethnicity, nationality and social rank, were to count for nothing (Galatians 3: 28). As for marriage, the principle as well as the procedures of consent affirmed women's personhood by asserting their equal participation in the act of promise-making; the sacrament instituted by this act was understood as given by each of the spouses to the other. Moreover, it is important to stress, if only because it is commonly overlooked, that in those domains of marriage over which the church exercised sole jurisdiction the canon law enshrined the equal treatment of the sexes. In contrast with the civil laws and with the dominant orientations of later secular discourses, that equality applied in particular to the sexual rights and duties of marriage. In relation to sexual fidelity, adultery, and the 'conjugal debt' (the debt of sexual intercourse) a husband owed as much as he was owed. Upon violation of these obligations, and in matters of separation and annulment, a woman had the same recourse to and the same standing in the ecclesiastical courts as a man. In a literal sense, 'equality between men and women in sexual behaviour was a Christian invention' and at variance with the perceptions and beliefs entrenched in local customs.[11]

However, 'outside the marriage bed, man was always the woman's master'.[12] As far as the domestic order of marriage was concerned, church doctrine lent authority to – and entrenched for a long time to come – the hierarchical status ascriptions that it found embodied in the secular law. The church never challenged the severe restrictions which the civil laws inflicted upon the personal and property rights of a wife. It recognised the husband as the head and ruler of his wife and emphasised her duties of obedience and submission. It even endorsed the marital right of chastisement and correction of misdemeanour (which might be of considerable import, for example, in cases where the courts had to decide whether instances of domestic violence justified a wife's petition for separation).[13]

A language of equal worth in one domain and, in another, a language of mastery and servility – what kind of explanation could bridge the divide? Of the many conceivable ways of approaching this question by means of doctrinal, sociological or institutional analysis, only one will be pursued here because it bears upon the general argument of this chapter. Given that a literal, non-contextualised understanding of the Scriptures remained the unquestionable source of authority for Catholic as well as Protestant legal thinkers until the end of the seventeenth century,[14] a prominent and much quoted passage from St. Paul's letter to the Ephesians would have been a central reference point (Ephesians 5: 22–33). The letter links the 'great mystery' of marriage, through which a man and a woman are joined together as one flesh, to the sacred bond that unites Christ, the head, with the body of his church. It is a bond of love on the part of the husband (Christ) and of reverence on the part of the wife (the Christian congregation). Portrayed in the asymmetrical, yet complementary relationship between head and body, on the one hand, and between love and obedience, on the other, gender difference seemed entailed in the very structures of the sacred order.[15] In the context of the biblical analogy the 'inequality' of husband and wife required no special justification. The very notion of formal equality would have seemed incommensurate to the imagery and symbolic meanings that set marriage in relation to the mystery of Christ's love for humanity. It is this incommensurability with the common norms of contractual relationships and the language of individual rights which we will find reiterated in the institutional marriage discourse of the nineteenth century and its attempt to weave the subordination of the wife into the texture of ethical love and equal dignity.

Once divine revelation ceased to be the exclusive source of true knowledge about the legal order and once conceptions of a hierarchically ordered universe gave way to the homogeneous universe of modern science, the marriage contract was reconstituted as a purely civil contract and assimilated to the uniform norms of a secular legal system. In this respect, the natural-law doctrines of the seventeenth and eighteenth centuries, to which we shall now turn, enacted an irreversible turn in the modes of legitimation. However, some important legacies of the canon law of marriage remained entrenched in its secular reconstruction. Links of continuity can be observed not only in the technical details of an extensive and sophisticated system of matrimonial causes. They are manifest above all in the architectonic structure that defined the place and function of marriage in relation to the legal order as a whole. These structural continuities, which operated independently of the substantive tenets of religious faith, can be summarised as follows. First, marriage performed a similar function for the secular state as it had done for the church: control over it constituted sovereign power. Second, the contract preserved the structure of a *pactus supra partes* (a pact above the parties). Its consensual components remained constrained by and subordinated to the ends of a transpersonal order. Third, although these purposes no longer represented the primacy of divine over human law, they established an analogous hierarchy in which considerations of public order ranked above the claims of private autonomy. Fourth, gender remained the privileged site in which the meanings of order and disorder were constructed and enforced.

A civil contract like any other: marriage in modern natural law

I shall examine the marriage doctrines of modern natural law by looking at its continental variation as represented by Samuel Pufendorf (1632–94), Christian Thomasius (1655–1728) and Christian Wolff (1679–1754). These thinkers and the extensive networks established by their schools had a direct and lasting influence upon future developments of the law, both in theory and practice.[16] Due to its hegemonic status at the Protestant universities of eighteenth-century Europe, natural law evolved as the master language spoken by the jurists, state officials and reformers of the absolutist state. It was in this context, and in this language, that at the end of the century the political battles over marriage were fought.

Following the lead of the Reformation, on the one hand, and of the exemplary methods of scientific reasoning, on the other, natural law doctrines severed the marriage contract from its foundation in the sacramental order. Like all other legal associations in civil society, marriage had to be considered as a 'worldly business', a *causa mere civilis*, i.e. a purely legal relationship.[17]

What distinguished 'modern', secular natural law from its medieval predecessor was the claim that valid knowledge about human nature and the right ordering of civil society was to be derived from the self-sufficient capacities of human reason alone. This domain of reason had to be sharply demarcated against the province of the divine law, on the one hand, and against the mere facticity and historicity of the civil laws, on the other.

On the basis of these demarcations, modern natural law constructed the foundations of the legal and political order from two sources: from the rational and social nature of man, and from the uniform attributes of voluntary contractual agreements by which alone human beings could be assumed to exchange their natural freedom and equality for the constraints of the civil law.

What did the shift from sacrament to contract imply for the law's power to regulate marriage, for the freedom of the individuals, and the construction of gender in the relation of husband and wife? Most importantly, in the period of enlightened absolutism natural-law arguments about marriage came to be harnessed to the claims of state sovereignty. For if marriage was a civil contract like any other, it followed that it belonged under the exclusive jurisdiction of the civil magistrate. With its polemical thrust against any rivalling power, the civil-contract marriage provided the most powerful weapon to vindicate the secular state's bid for supreme and undivided control over its terrain. 'Le loi ne considère le marriage que comme un contrat civil': the introduction of the civil marriage in revolutionary France and its guarantee in the separation of state and church gave practical legal force to the philosophical idea that it was the contract alone, unemcumbered by the prescriptions of religious faith, which conferred public recognition upon the matrimonial union.[18] As a consequence, the religious consecration of marriage lost its public dimensions. The commitment to a sacred institution became what it is today – a matter of private belief and personal choice.

Another, if much more contested, change sanctioned by the natural-law contract lay in the recognition of divorce. The early formulations of the issue, such as those of Pufendorf and his school, made no concessions to the freedom of individuals to end their marriage at will. Following in the steps of strict Protestant doctrine, they allowed for termination solely on grounds of adultery and wilful desertion.[19] But even when set out in these narrow confines, the argument still underlined the crucial point that an indissoluble marriage, like an interminable contract, could not be vindicated within the system of natural law without undermining its foundations. Its logic demanded that in cases where one party had violated the central clauses of the agreement the other be released from its obligations. Moreover, as the development of natural law doctrines in the eighteenth century shows, the contractual paradigm contained an internal dynamic towards further contractualisation which would press against the restriction of divorce to severe cases of fault. Thomasius and Wolff conceded the legitimacy of dissolving a marriage by mutual consent of the two partners once they had fulfilled their procreative obligations. The Prussian Civil Code extended this provision to all childless couples, on the grounds that the very nature of a contract implied its terminability upon free agreement by the contracting parties.[20] In the language of the revolutionary legislation, finally, the contract became so closely associated with the postulate of individual freedom that the resistance to divorce could be portrayed as implying nothing less than the loss of the most sacred rights of liberty.[21] In this respect the institutional reaction of the nineteenth century would have a point: a purely contractual understanding of marriage was unable to defend the imperative of a life-long bond.

While the natural-law contract thus opened up some spaces of private freedom, it left the internal order of the conjugal society firmly embedded in the hierarchical structure of marital *Herrschaft* and wifely subordination. True, considered by its hypothetical origins, marriage derived from a contract between two equal agents. However, the 'regular and complete agreement' which spelt out the concrete rights and obligations of husband and wife will, if we follow Pufendorf, display a pattern that Pateman has identified as a contract to establish male sex right over women's bodies: since marriages are initiated by men and for the one and only reason to acquire children of their own flesh and blood, it is incumbent upon a wife to promise 'that she will nobody but him grant access to her body'. Although husbands will 'usually' make a similar commitment, it is not absolutely required in the form of an explicit promise. Second, the imperative of orderly procreation requires husband and wife to unite for the purpose of a stable shared life, with fixed abode, settled property and orderly household arrangements. This demand, too, is specified as a woman's obligation to live with her husband without interruption, not to leave his house without his permission, not to sleep separately and not to refuse him, without good reasons, the use of her body. Third, a woman must recognise her husband as 'head and director' of the marriage association and submit to his commands in all matters that pertain to the tasks of domestic life.[22]

Pateman's account of the sexual contract rightly emphasises the distinctly modern constitution of the patriarchal marriage in the natural-law doctrines of the seventeenth and eighteenth centuries.[23] At issue is not an unreflected continuation of assumptions that pertained to the medieval status contract, but an explicit act of individual consent by which a woman submits to her husband's rule. Pufendorf, for example, went to considerable lengths to refute the common run of traditional arguments that served to entrench women's subordination: neither divine punishment for Eve's transgression, nor the testimony contained in the positive laws of most nations nor even the clear evidence of men's physical and mental superiority would satisfy the justificatory demands of the natural law: 'There can be no obligation demanding obedience from a wife before she has by her own consent submitted herself to the will of her husband.'[24] Moreover, and that marked the decisive difference from the status contract, this consent had to take the form of a special 'pact of subordination' which was added on to the marriage contract proper.

However, and here I take issue with Pateman's interpretation, it is not the contract on its own which accounts for women's subordination. The construction of marriage in natural law does not vindicate the claim that female subjection is essentially, or invariably entailed in the individualist premises of the modern contract and that the latter must therefore be deemed in principle incapable of affirming women's independent agency. The following brief summary of a complex set of arguments is meant only to highlight the point that it is not the contract itself which establishes patriarchal rule. Rather, the patriarchal marriage owes its specific features to particular legal traditions which supply the abstract principles of natural law with the required substance of definite rights and obligations.

First, the marriage contract in natural law remained embedded in the teleological framework of Christian provenance which tied the rights and duties of the spouses to the predestined task of procreation. The propagation and rearing of offspring was conceived not, as it would be today, as a matter of private choice. It was a strict duty that all individuals owed to the public good of species preservation. Second, the imperative of procreation did not in the main instance aim at the reproduction of optimal numbers of human beings. Even less did it refer to the sentimental values and the emotive inclinations which predominantly motivate the desire for children in our society. Marriage was necessary in order 'to constrain procreation by laws'.[25] That is, marriage had to contain the limitless sexual appetites and promiscuous inclinations of human nature within the strict boundaries of an exclusive and permanent legal union. Third, the particular conception of order with which marriage was aligned centred in the imperative of certain paternity, i.e. in the maxim derived from the Roman law: 'the father is he to whom marriage points' (*pater is est quem nuptiae demonstrant*). What distinguished order from disorder and civil peace from the confusions of a lawless state of nature was the enforcement of the presumption 'that any child born to a woman is the offspring of the mother's husband'.[26] Fourth, Pufendorf derived the model of a conjugal order that would guarantee the natural, biological ties of fatherhood not from the Roman law but from Germanic customary law, which invested a husband with stringent possessory claims upon his wife's body and a strict control over her movements and actions.[27]

However, this particular construction of the patriarchal order of marriage, cogent though it may seem on its own terms, needed to pass the test of contractual legitimation. And this is the crucial point that sets the natural law marriage apart from the essentialist anchoring of women's subjection in the 'institution of marriage'. Pufendorf assumed that all 'regular marriages' would entail a woman's consent to place herself under marital *Herrschaft*. But he had to concede that the irregular marriage, such as that of the Amazon – who reserved her independence as well as her power over her children – was legitimate if it had been properly contracted.[28] Natural law, in other words, was incapable of ruling out exceptions to the conventional patriarchal norm. Convention could not override or obliterate the contractual test of justice which demanded recourse to the original equality of individuals and their voluntary agreements. This meant that the epistemological premises of natural law left the order of marriage in a state of indeterminacy and variability. Thomasius's radical epistemological move, which disconnected the pure commands of the law of nature from any admixture of customary beliefs and practices, concluded that women's subjection to marital rule was not strictly necessary in order to fulfil the demands of natural justice. The latitude of the natural law was still more provocatively asserted in his claim that even polyandry – the marriage between one woman and several men – could not in principle be excluded from the range of legitimate options (since it met the requirements of orderly procreation and contractability and since natural fatherhood could, without damage to the social order, be replaced by social fatherhood).[29] Christian Wolff, whose interpretation of natural-law norms reflects the influence of the canon law and the Roman law, conceived of marriage as an equal society. Although he left the juridical form of the husband's prerogatives in place, he circumvented them in the emphasis upon the equal obligations and the cooperative partnership of both spouses in relation to the tasks of parenthood.[30]

The debates about the implications of the marriage contract in natural law never reached the point of asserting the equality of women as a matter of right. But the need to secure the legitimacy of patriarchal rule in the forum of contractual reasoning left an important critical legacy. The debates showed that the contract could not absolutely guarantee a relationship of *Herrschaft* and subjection against other conceivable and legitimate forms. It was this ambivalence or unreliability of the contract as regards the essential constitution of gender which the institutional discourse sought to remedy.

From contract to institution: marriage as a 'sacrement civil'

In the long nineteenth-century reaction to the crisis of order sparked by the French Revolution and the ensuing European wars, marriage and the family emerged as favourite targets of public debate and reactive politics.[31] In a mode of response that is not unfamiliar today politicians, legislators and opinion-makers turned upon the family to portray the effective cause of an all-pervasive disintegration of authority. Efforts to curb the liberal divorce laws of the revolutionary period became a predominant feature of legislative politics in both Germany and France.[32] In the domain of jurisprudence the consensual divorce similarly served as a potent symbol to expose the complicity of Enlightenment rationalism, and its individualist and contractualist principles, in the destructive tendencies of the modern age. Condensing complex developments into a simple formula we might say that the move from 'contract' to 'institution' in legal discourse aimed to reconstitute marriage in a metajuridical sphere of secular sacredness.

We shall consider the formation of the institutionalist discourse in two exemplary contexts. The first will refer to the making of the French *Code civil* of 1804 and in particular to the arguments by which Etienne Portalis, its leading draftsman, combated the legacies of the revolutionary divorce legislation. Throughout the nineteenth century the Napoleonic code enjoyed canonical status as Europe's unrivalled example of a modern system of private law which guaranteed to all citizens the rights of private property, formal equality of legal status and security of contractual exchanges. Within this system, marriage had the function of securing society against the threat of instability and further disruption by radical politics and of reinstating the principle of authority against the subversive dynamic of natural rights. For the second example we shall turn to Karl Friedrich von Savigny and his contribution to the Prussian reforms of the 1840s and 1850s which similarly sought to reverse the liberal divorce law of the Prussian civil code. As minister of the Prussian government, Savigny was closely aligned with a powerful coterie of ultra-conservative junkers who aimed at the restoration of a rigidly authoritarian order under the rule of king, aristocracy and church. However, as the most eminent academic jurist of his generation and the leading representative of the emerging science of private law (*Privatrechtswissenschaft*) he stood at some distance from those ideological orientations. In this latter capacity he was concerned with the elaboration of a modern legal system in which the guarantee of private autonomy and contractual freedom would be held in balance by the altogether different norms that were appropriate to the unique character of conjugal and familial relations.

Despite the manifold differences that separated the social and constitutional structures of post-revolutionary France from the autocratic political regime and hierarchical status society of mid-century Prussia, and despite the specificity of philosophical and jurisprudential traditions which shaped the French and the German debates, the institutional marriage discourse betrays remarkable similarities in both contexts. This applies not only to the practical intention of banning all but the most narrowly circumscribed causes of divorce. The affinities manifest themselves even more clearly in the search for new normative foundations that would sustain this political aim.[33]

It would be a serious misunderstanding to confine the institutional reaction to the terrain of a narrowly 'reactionary', backward-looking creed. In the post-revolutionary bourgeois society of the nineteenth century the promise encoded in the 'institution of marriage' – the guarantee of both privacy and public order – commanded a broad consensus that reached across otherwise entrenched political and ideological divides.[34] Simple attributions of ideological partisanship would similarly detract from the fact that the intellectual and political challenges to which the institutional discourse responded were complex and ambiguously poised between modern and anti-modern tendencies. As we have seen, the legal definition of marriage by the attributes and procedures of a purely civil contract had become the indispensable condition of the modern state's exclusive claim to sovereign power. To deny these contractual foundations would have implied a replication of the dual sovereignty of state and church. The contractual paradigm played a similarly constitutive role in providing jurisprudence with the credentials of a modern scientific discipline. The postulated cohesion and homogeneity of a system of private law depended upon the abstract uniformity of contractual norms in all legal transactions, including marriage. For political and scientific reasons alike, certain components in the contractual legacies of the Enlightenment and the revolution had to remain intact.

Given these constraints upon the re-definition of marriage, the task was to forge a 'new coherence' of contractual and non-contractual principles.'[35] Required was a discourse which would not jeopardise the state's claim on the civil marriage and which could, yet, vindicate the political goals of the reaction, namely to uproot the legitimacy of the consensual divorce and to reinforce the patriarchal order of the conjugal relationship. In response to this double challenge the institutional discourse affirmed the competence of contractual norms for a closely delimited sphere which included the formal conditions of concluding and dissolving a marriage and, on the margins, some optional arrangements with regard to matrimonial property.[36] The essence of marriage, on the other hand, i.e. the nature of the conjugal bond, was to be severed from any assumptions that would have implied the predominance of individual rights and private autonomy. In this respect, the union of husband and wife was to be endowed with qualities that were fundamentally different from and, indeed, incommensurable with those that pertained to other contractual associations under the private law. Napoleon demanded of his code that it enshrine marriage as a 'sacrement civil'. It was a fitting analogy. For it captured the aspiration of the institutional discourse to fashion a modern, secular equivalent for the sacred, immutable and unassailable status of the Christian marriage bond.

The 'institution of marriage' owed its distinctive features (and its enduring popularity) to the fusion of two discursive strategies. The first, or essentialist, discourse removed the essence of marriage from the domain of the law and equally from the subjective will of the marriage partners. Instead, the meaning of the conjugal bond was entrusted to the higher authority of Nature (Portalis), or *Sittlichkeit* (Savigny). The second strategy supplied the normative language of the law which the first was altogether lacking – authoritative definitions of right and wrong, coercive power and categories of punishment. Importantly, the enforcement of the essence of marriage fell to the imperatives of the public law and the sanctions of criminal justice. The following argument will emphasise the mutual dependence and complicity of the sentimental and the coercive discourse. They might seem to establish separate spheres of private and public orientations. In fact, they complemented each other in a highly effective manner. For the essence of marriage – the seemingly private realm of sentiment and ethical love – stood in need of coercive enforcement. The public interest in marriage, on the other hand, could hide its punitive implications behind the veil of an essentially private, non-political association.

'What is marriage in itself'?[37] This question took centre stage in the speech in which Portalis submitted the drafted sections of the *Code civil* to the

Council of the 500 (convened by Napoleon for the deliberation and enactment of the new law). The emphasis upon marriage 'in itself' was meant to
transcend the narrow confines of traditional formulations, be they those of
theology (sacrament), jurisprudence (contract) or philosophy (procreation
and sexual order). Following Rousseau, Portalis drew upon the resources
of a romantic, sentimental understanding of Nature as a dynamic, creative
and benevolent force in order to invoke the essence of marriage in the timeless 'romance of the human couple': man and woman equipped by the
wisdom of nature with the impulse of mutual sexual attraction as well as
with tender feelings and the capacity for reason; sexual desire maturing
into mutual concern and the recognition of the duties owed to a non-
ephemeral union; the birth of children and their need for parental care and
devotion completing the thrust towards a life-long bond. Nature herself,
Portalis could conclude, had stamped upon the conjugal union the essential
mark of a 'contrat perpétuel par sa destination'.[38]

Without any reference to the imposing authority of religion, state or law,
the speech implanted the political goals of the reaction in the seemingly non-
political essence of marriage. The rhetorical invocation of a 'perpetual
contract' had the effect of burdening the divorce by individual consent
with a violation of a fundamental condition of human existence and thus
with the stigma of arbitrary subjectivity. If we remember that the Revolution
had abolished all contracts in perpetuity (such as those that pertained to the
institution of feudal land tenure) and that the new code itself would affirm
this prohibition in the law of property and obligation, we get a first indication
of the extra-territorial status assigned to marriage in modern private law.
Moreover, the essentialist argument made gender difference part of the
original and immutable design of Nature. The essence of masculinity and
femininity was conveyed in alluring images of natural complementarity in
which strength and the capacity for reason and freedom stood in perfect
harmony with the attributes of physical weakness, empathy and gentle sub-
missiveness. Within this discursive frame there was no space for contractual
arrangements and no need for a woman's consent to her own subordination.
Indeed, the very language of formal legal transactions would have seemed
singularly inappropriate to convey the meanings of a relationship that was
inscribed in the essential structures of human existence.

Savigny's project to return the 'frivolous' divorce laws of the Prussian civil
code to the minimal provisions of individual moral fault (i.e. adultery and
wilful desertion) were more closely aligned with a Christian belief in the
divine consecration of marriage. However, both the imperatives of a secular
legal science and the need to influence a wider public required that the case be
conveyed without direct reference to the tenets of religious faith. Following a
common pattern of German thought in this period, Savigny expressed the
metajuridical and non-contractual essence of marriage in the language of
Sittlichkeit (i.e. of the demands of ethical life). Unlike the imperatives of
Kantian morality (*Moralität*) and its emphasis upon individual autonomy,

Sittlichkeit assumed that the individual's life would acquire meaning and substance only as an integral part of communal life and within the bounds of institutions that embodied the collective spirit of a particular community or culture. Understood as one of those institutions, marriage was to be defined by three distinct attributes.[39] For the individual it was a necessary form of human existence, and for the state an essential component of the foundations of political life. A third attribute singled out an additional specific meaning for women: they owed to the Christian marriage the elevation of the female sex (above, that is, the state of slave-like subjugation suffered by women in primitive nations). Outside marriage, that was the implication, women would lack even the basic prerequisites of an ethical life. These three features conferred upon marriage an ethical dignity which set it apart from other legal associations and from the world of ordinary contracts.

If we consider the practical implications of this essentialist definition of marriage, we will find that they point in the same direction as Portalis's construction from Nature. Marriage binds individuals into an objective order which is not of their own making and stands independent of their particular subjective will. *Sittlichkeit* thus rules out that the marriage bond be relinquished to the bidding of transient, self-seeking inclinations and, equally, that it be placed at the mercy of ruthless legislators. Set out in this way, the consensual divorce stood condemned as a manifestation of individual licentiousness and general moral corruption. The return to a strictly ethical code should, Savigny argued, also be applied to most other instances for which the shallow humanitarianism of the Enlightenment had opened an all too easy route to divorce, such as the affliction of one marriage partner with dementia, disfiguring physical illness or chronic alcoholism. Adverse conditions of this kind were not by themselves to count as sufficient cause for divorce unless they had the same irremediably destructive effects as adultery and wilful desertion.[40]

Savigny's strictures on divorce in the case of alcoholic addiction can also throw light upon the assumption that women are differently constituted by marriage in the sense of being uniquely indebted to it.[41] Although the case is presented in seemingly gender-neutral terms as regards the duties that fall to the non-afflicted 'partner', the reference to the character traits of patient solicitude and loving devotion will leave little doubt as to who had to uphold the dignity of marriage.

The profile of the institution of marriage that emerged from the essentialist discourse can be attributed to the skilful combination of several rhetorical strategies. The first suffused the specific, clearly delineated connotations of legal concepts (such as *marriage, contract, conjugal rights*) with elusive meanings. Reformulated in the language of a *veritable* or *perpetual* contract or the *true* nature of the conjugal bond, marriage took its place in a sphere of essences and unquestionable truths that was not accessible to the common juridical understanding of a contractual association and not open to contestations of the kind that we have observed in the field of natural law theories. A second and more radical move removed the characteristic attributes of marriage from any affiliation with the law and reconstituted them in a vocabulary of personal intimacy, love and ethical aspirations. It was this strategy in particular that proved able to accommodate the liberal emphasis on a private sphere which needed to be protected against the invasion by the law. However, it needs to be stressed that in this context privacy did not connect with individual liberty. Both Portalis and Savigny understood the formal guarantee of personal liberty as the defining feature of a modern system of private law and its dominant concern with the security of private property.[42] With regard to marriage, by contrast, and with a special focus upon the undesirability of the divorce by mutual consent, liberty stood for licence and undisciplined subjectivity. Instead of liberty, the institutional discourse placed an altogether different concept at the normative centre of marriage – dignity. No term was more frequently and ubiquitously invoked in nineteenth-century debates on the marriage law. Importantly, 'dignity' was not attributed to individuals in their capacity as autonomous agents. It pertained to the institution and its claim to transcend and erase that autonomy.

Taken by its distinctive claims, the essentialist marriage discourse seemed to lack any reference to the constitutive power of the law. For the purpose of discrediting the legacies of the Revolution, it had to assert that 'The legislator has nothing to do in this respect; Nature has done everything.'[43] Savigny similarly affirmed that the law was incapable of creating *Sittlichkeit*. However – and this is the salient point towards which the whole argument drives – the law could and should uphold marriage against the deviant impulses of individuals through educative and disciplinary measures.[44] At this point we can observe the sentimental discourse joining forces with a coercive discourse which asserted the primacy of public over private interests and subordinated the remedies of the civil law to the retributions of the criminal law. The following section will examine the shift from private to public in three examples. The first considers the definition of matrimonial property in the *Code Napoléon*; the second draws attention to Savigny's project of a change in divorce procedures; while the third focuses on the two dimensions attributed to adultery – a breach of the marriage contract, on the one hand, and an offence against the public order, on the other.

The *Code Napoléon* prefaced the section on matrimonial property with the categorical assurance that the law was not to impose authoritative regulations upon the material goods that the spouses brought into marriage (*Code civil*, Art. 1387). With regard to property, it seemed, marriage was to follow the pattern of voluntary contractual arrangements which applied to private property in general. Heated debates in the codifying commission turned upon the specific question whether this rule would allow a wife to alienate even her substantive property, i.e. land, without her husband's consent and whether, by yet further extension, this freedom of contract could be taken to the point where mutual agreement would result in the woman's management of the joint goods – an option which was bound to undermine marital power in all other respects. The *Code Napoléon* closed down this option. It ruled out any settlements about property that would impair the husband's legal powers as master and head of the marriage relation: 'The spouses cannot derogate either the rights that result from the power of the husband over the person of wife and children nor those that pertain to him as *chef*' (i.e. as master over matrimonial property) (*Code civil*, Art. 1388). Property in marriage thus moved into a normative domain of its own. For the uniform principles that pertained to property relations and transactions in modern private law contained no space to justify one individual's rights over another's property on grounds of a pre-ordained, non-contractual status of personal power. As the debates show, these anachronistic rights could only be vindicated by invoking the prior claims of a public interest.[45] A similar controversy was to occur nearly a hundred years later in the preparatory stages of the German civil code (enacted in 1900), when representatives of the German women's movement and the leaders of the SPD pleaded for the marriage law to adopt a system of separate property akin to the provisions of the Roman dotal law. While conceding the general merits of the case in terms of modern women's undeniable claim to personal independence, the main redactor – a jurist of proven liberal leanings – emphasised the law's prior interest in the unifying effects of the husband's control over matrimonial property. That is, from the higher viewpoint of the public interest, the institution of marriage had to rank above the independence of the wife.[46]

In both cases the institutional marriage discourse allowed a higher, or public interest to trump the formal guarantees of equal agency which modern codifications of private law accorded to all legal subjects. Both cases also show that this public good was inseparably intertwined with the re-affirmation of the husband's rights over the person and property of his wife.

Savigny's proposal to change the procedure by which courts were to deal with divorce cases offers a still more pertinent example of the endeavour to fortify the institution of marriage in the interest of the public order. In contrast with normal law suits, where a judge adjudicated between the claims brought by the two parties, divorce proceedings would in addition require the presence of a defender of matrimony (*defensor matrimonii*). It was to be the specific task of this third party to represent and defend the public interest in marriage. That meant that the case would be not be decided on the evidence submitted by husband and wife and not in prior consideration of their interests. Rather, the outcome would be determined by an objective judgement formed with regard to the interests of the state. From this perspective the only criteria for terminating a marriage would be derived from an impartial assessment of guilt in which the parties' own account of the crisis or breakdown of their marriage would carry little weight. Moreover, the pronouncement of divorce, especially on grounds of adultery, would automatically be followed by punishment of the guilty party in the form of a prison sentence. (The eighteenth-century Prussian code, against which the argument was directed, had imposed this punishment only upon demand by the innocent partner.) Only a *poena publica* (public penalty), Savigny claimed, would match the nature of an offence which was not merely a breach of contract, but a 'sacrilege against the institution of marriage'.[47]

The reinstatement of adultery as a criminal offence both in the *Code Napoléon* and in Savigny's proposed reforms shows to what extent the public order, which is at stake in the coercive defence of the institution of marriage, was affiliated with the patriarchal order of gender. The divorce law of the Revolution and of the Prussian code had defined the adulterous acts of husband and wife by the same criteria and penal consequences. The *Code Napoléon* returned to the customary law's double standard of sexual morality which exempted the husband from the charge and the consequences of adultery unless he went so far as to live with his mistress in the matrimonial home (*Code civil*, Arts. 227 and 228). Only in this latter, aggravated case of marital infidelity was a wife entitled to sue for divorce, while she herself was held liable for any adulterous act or extra-marital affair. If convicted, she faced imprisonment (i.e. the *poena publica*). The husband who found himself in court was guilty only to the extent of having to pay a fine (and the same applied to the partner of the adulterous woman). Superficially, a case for the special culpability of the adulterous wife could be made out by emphasising the need to protect a husband's name, honour and property against usurpation by a 'stranger'.[48] A wife, that is, had nothing to lose if her husband fathered a child outside marriage. However, that other side of the coin is precisely what invalidates such arguments. For with regard to illegitimacy the institutionalist reaction in both Germany and France successfully re-entrenched the disadvantages of the illegitimate child and the stigmatisation of the unwed mother, which the Enlightenment codes had remedied by providing both the child and its mother with legal claims against the father. Savigny's notoriously biased argument identified the corruption of *Sittlichkeit* and the threat that illegitimacy posed to the institution of marriage exclusively with the immorality of the deviant members of the female sex.[49] In a similar move, the French code had made it an offence to search for, and publicly identify, the father of an illegitimate child. The vindictiveness of the law turned exclusively upon the mother and her child.[50]

If we consider the public interest in marriage from the criminal law's treatment of adultery and illegitimacy we get a clearer sense of the gendered assumptions that sustained the institution of marriage. Unlike a husband's deviance, a wife's infidelity violated 'the most vital interests of state, family and public morality'.[51] The public order was more vulnerable to a woman's adulterous acts because the latter undermined not only the marriage bond but the patriarchal order as a whole, which was cemented by a husband's rights over the person and body of his wife. The inseparable link between

the public interest and the husband's interest manifests itself in the differential punishment that the law appended to female and male adultery –
imprisonment, on one side, compensation in the mode of the private law,
on the other. The corollary to this instance of the law's special vindictiveness
towards women and leniency towards men appeared in the definition and
penalisation of illegitimacy. The law protected the name and honour of the
'father' against the stigma of an extra-marital affair, while placing the full
costs of public shame and of material disadvantage upon the unmarried
mother and the child.

Considered by its enduring hegemony in modern legal and political argument, the institutionalist marriage discourse was immensely successful. The
elusiveness of its non-juridical language established a coherence that
wedded the progressive aspirations of nineteenth-century liberal bourgeois
society to the security and discipline afforded by a traditional patriarchal
order. Max Weber attributed the peculiar anachronistic status of marriage
in modern law to the residual quest for community in an increasingly con-
tractualised society.[52] Recent theories of modernisation have emphasised
the crucial interdependence between the fixation of gender in a hierarchical
status relationship, on the one hand, and the dynamic of individualisation
processes, on the other.[53] The history of legal discourses in the nineteenth
and twentieth centuries reveals a similar pattern of gendered modernisation.
The recognition of the civil marriage salvaged the cohesion that modern
secular law owed to the norms of the contract, while the incommensurable
status of the 'institution' closed the door to any furthergoing challenges to
which the universal principles of contractual freedom and equality would
have given rise. The civil sacredness of marriage created a terrain where
modern society was protected against the disruptive forces of modernity.

Conclusion: from public institution to private partnership

In the history of modern liberal societies marriage has been a 'latecomer to
contractualisation'.[54] From the limited concessions to the married woman's
independent property rights in the second half of the nineteenth century it
took more than a hundred years of incremental, small-scale and often
arrested reforms to dismantle the protected status of the institution of
marriage in private law. Since the introduction of the no-fault principle in
the divorce laws of the 1970s, on the one hand, and the recognition of the
independent and equal legal agency of the wife, on the other, marriage has
gradually adapted to the same norms that govern other contractual associations. As far as the law is concerned, the opposition between contract and
institution has been resolved in favour of the former. This does not mean
that the marriage contract is as open to individual choices and preferences
as a commercial contract. The law still imposes constraints upon contractual
autonomy that we do not find elsewhere. It upholds prohibitions of incest
and bigamy; it presumes and enforces special obligations of mutual financial

support that are not negotiable by the parties; it denies same-sex couples and cohabiting partnerships the status of a valid marriage. In most other respects, however, the lawgiver refrains from answering the question 'what is marriage?', leaving that answer to be determined by the individuals themselves. We have seen that nineteenth-century jurisprudence rejected the contractual paradigm because it undermined the imperative of a life-long union, made the public interest in marriage prey of the arbitrary will of individuals and destabilised the necessary authority of the husband and father. In all three respects, the marriage law has undergone a remarkable shift from an ascriptive order with pre-established purposes towards a partnership governed by the assumption of personal autonomy. The legally enforced essence of marriage has given way to a plurality of private meanings that individuals are willing and able to realise.

Especially with regard to the relationship between husband and wife, we seem to have reached that state of affairs which legal and political thinkers of the past sought to forestall by enforcing an order of rule and subordination. Marriage now is an association with 'two sovereigns' (Portalis)[55] and thus vulnerable to conflicting interests and in need of continuous negotiation and mutual agreement. Consent of both partners is required not only at the entry-gate but for all subsequent decisions.

In formal juridical terms at least, marriage is no longer ordered by gender. Indeed, it can be argued that the very terms 'husband' and 'wife' have become obsolete insofar as they have lost any connotations of differential legal status (although they still function to rule out the homosexual marriage). This means that we can no longer rely on marriage to provide society and the state with that guarantee of order and stability which, in the past, was cemented in the order of gender. Marriage can no longer be insulated against the recognition of individual rights and against the principle of equality that pertains to the status of democratic citizenship.

Notes

1 See the contributions to R. Whelan, ed., *Just a Piece of Paper? Divorce Reform and the Undermining of Marriage* (London, 1995).
2 See I.M. Young, 'The Family in the Age of Murphy Brown', in N. Hirschman and C. Di Stefano, eds, *Revisioning the Political. Feminist Revisions of Traditional Concepts in Western Political Theory* (Westview, 1996), pp. 251–70.
3 Quoted in B. Harms-Ziegler, *Illegitimität und Ehe: Illegitimität als Reflex des Ehediskurses in Preussen im 18. und 19. Jahrhundert* (Berlin, 1991), p. 268.
4 For a critique of this position as represented by Malinowski, see J. Collier, M.Z. Rosaldo and S. Yanagisako, 'Is There a Family? New Anthropological Views', in R.N. Lancaster and M. di Leonardo, eds, *The Gender/Sexuality Reader* (London, 1997), pp. 71–81.
5 P. L'Hermite-Leclercq, 'The Feudal Order', in C. Klapisch-Zuber, ed., *A History of Women*, vol. II (Cambridge, Mass., 1994), pp. 226–7; B.M. Hoggett and D.S. Pearl, *The Family, Law and Society. Cases and Materials* (London, 2nd edn 1987), p. 171.

6 J.E.M. Portalis, 'Discours préliminaire sur le projet du Code civil', in *Portalis, Ecrits et Discours Juridiques et Politiques* (Aix/Marseille, 1988), p. 44.
7 For a general overview of the theological, legal and cultural aspects of the medieval marriage, see H.J. Berman, *Law and Revolution. The Formation of the Western Legal Tradition* (Cambridge, Mass., 1983), pp. 225–30; C.N.L. Brooke, *The Medieval Idea of Marriage* (Oxford, 1991), chs 2 and 6; G. Duby, *The Knight, the Lady, and the Priest. The Making of Modern Marriage in Medieval France*, transl. by B. Bray (Harmondsworth, 1985), chs 2, 3, and 9; M. Ingram, *Church Courts, Sex and Marriage in England, 1570–1640* (Cambridge, 1987), pp. 125–67; D. Schwab, *Grundlagen und Gestalt der staatlichen Ehegesetzgebung in der Neuzeit bis zum Beginn des 19. Jahrhunderts* (Bielefeld, 1967).
8 Statement from Gratian's *Decretum*: quoted in Schwab, *Grundlagen*, p. 20, n. 28.
9 See Duby, *The Knight, the Lady, and the Priest*, pp. 25–9, 116–20.
10 See R. Metz, 'Le Statut de la Femme en Droit Canonique Médiévale', in *Recueils de la Société Jean Bodin*, vol. 12 (Brussels, 1962), pp. 59–113.
11 J.L. Flandrin, 'Sex in married life in the early Middle Ages: the Church's teaching and behavioural reality', in P. Ariès and A. Béjin, eds, *Western Sexuality. Practice and Precept in Past and Present Times*, transl. by A. Forster (Oxford, 1985), pp. 114–29.
12 Flandrin, 'Sex in married life', p. 118.
13 See Ingram, *Church Courts*, pp. 143, 183.
14 See Schwab, *Grundlagen*, p.171.
15 Duby, *The Knight, the Lady, and the Priest*, pp. 177f.
16 F. Wieacker, *Privatrechtsgeschichte der Neuzeit*, 2nd edn (Göttingen, 1967), pp. 249–322; K-H. Ilting, 'Naturrecht', in O. Brunner, W. Conze and R. Koselleck, eds, *Geschichtliche Grundbegriffe. Historisches Lexikon zur politisch-sozialen Sprache in Deutschland*, vol. 4 (Stuttgart, 1978), pp. 245–313; H. Möller, *Vernunft und Kritik. Deutsche Aufklärung im 17. und 18. Jahrhundert* (Frankfurt a. M., 1986), pp. 189–211.
17 Of particular relevance for this subsection are the following texts: Samuel Pufendorf, *Herrn Samuels Freiherrn von Pufendorff Acht Bücher vom Natur- und Völkerrechte* (Frankfurt, 1711 = German translation of the original Latin text of 1672), book VI, I; Pufendorf, *On the Duty of Man and Citizen according to Natural Law* (1673), ed. J. Tully (Cambridge, 1991), book II, 2; Christian Thomasius, *Institutiones Jurisprudentiae Divinae* (1688) (7th edn, Halle, 1730), book III, II; *Rechtmässige Erörterung der Ehe und Gewissensfrage* (Halle, 1698); *De Crimine Bigamiae* (Halle, 1721); Christian Wolff, *Grundsätze des Natur- und Völkerrechtes, worinnen alle Verbindlichkeiten und alle Rechte aus der Natur des Menschen in einem beständigen Zusammenhange hergeleitet werden* (Halle, 1754), III, I, 2; *Vernünftige Gedanken von dem gesellschaftlichen Leben der Menschen und insbesonderheit dem gemeinen Wesen* (4th edn, Frankfurt/Leipzig, 1736).
18 For developments in France and in other European countries, see H. Conrad, 'Die Grundlegung der modernen Zivilehe durch die französische Revolution', *Zeitschrift der Savigny Stiftung für Rechtsgeschichte (Germanische Abteilung)*, 67 (1950), pp. 336–72; quotation at p. 355.
19 Pufendorf, *Natur- und Völkerrecht*, VI, I. For extensive references to the treatment of divorce by the various authors and schools in the tradition of natural law, see M. Erle, *Die Ehe im Naturrecht des 17. Jahrhunderts* (Göttingen, 1952); P. Mikat, 'Rechtspolitische Erwägungen zum Zerrüttungsprinzip', *Zeitschrift für das gesamte Familienrecht*, 1962, pp. 81–8, 273–81, 497–504; 1963, pp. 65–76; A. Dufour, *Le Mariage dans L'Ecole Allemande du Droit Naturel*

(Paris, 1971), pt II; H. Rinckens, *Die Ehe und die Auffassung von der Natur des Menschen bei Hugo Grotius, Samuel Pufendorf und Christian Thomasius* (Frankfurt, 1971).

20 See U. Gerhard, *Verhältnisse und Verhinderungen. Frauenarbeit, Familie und Rechte der Frauen im 19. Jahrhundert. Mit Dokumenten* (Frankfurt a. M., 1978), pp. 423–9.
21 Conrad, 'Grundlegung der modernen Zivilehe', p. 355.
22 Pufendorf, *Duty of Man and Citizen*, book II, ch. 2; *Natur- und Völkerrecht*, book VI, I, 10. For Pateman's critique, see C. Pateman, *The Sexual Contract* (Cambridge, 1988), pp. 167–8, 184–5.
23 Pateman, *Sexual Contract*, chs 1 and 2.
24 Pufendorf, *Natur- und Völkerrecht*, VI, I, 12.
25 Pufendorf, *Natur- und Völkerrecht*, VI, I, 4.
26 Pufendorf, *Natur- und Völkerrecht*, VI, I, 10.
27 Reliance upon the Germanic legal heritage also explains why Pufendorf considered the requirement of consent by itself as insufficient to establish a valid marriage. A woman had to enter the house of her husband 'so that he can use her as a wife', *Natur- und Völkerrecht*, VI, I, 14; for the relationship of husband and wife as defined by the Roman law (in the classical period), see Y. Thomas, 'The Division of the Sexes in Roman Law', in P. Schmitt Pantel, ed., *A History of Women in the West*, vol. I (Cambridge, Mass., 1994), pp. 83–138.
28 Pufendorf, *Natur- und Völkerrecht*, VI, I, 9; VI, II, 5.
29 Thomasius, *De Crimine Bigamiae*, pp. 23–32, quote at p. 29; for the debate on polygamy in modern natural law, see U. Vogel, 'Political Philosophers and the Trouble with Polygamy: Patriarchal Reasoning in Modern Natural Law', *History of Political Thought*, XII, 2, pp. 229–51.
30 See Wolff, *Grundsätze des Natur- und Völkerrechts*, III, I, 2, 855–88 (see note 17); for the capacity of the contractual paradigm to affirm the equality of husband and wife, see D. Schwab, 'Die Familie als Vertragsgesellschaft im Naturrecht der Aufklärung', *Quaderni Fiorentini per la Storia del Pensiero Juridico Moderno*, 1 (1972), 357–76, esp. pp. 366–8.
31 See D. Schwab, 'Familie', in O. Brunner, W. Conze and R. Koselleck, eds, *Geschichtliche Grundbegriffe*, vol. 2 (Stuttgart, 1979), pp. 253–301.
32 For a comparative account of the legislation on divorce in nineteenth-century Germany and France, see D. Blasius, 'Bürgerliche Rechtsgleichheit und die Ungleichheit der Geschlechter. Das Scheidungsrecht im historischen Vergleich', in U. Frevert, ed., *Bürgerinnen und Bürger: Geschlechterverhältnisse im 19. Jahrhundert* (Göttingen, 1988), pp. 67–84.
33 For the texts relevant to this section, see Portalis, 'Discours préliminaire sur le projet du Code civil', in Portalis, *Ecrits et Discours Juridiques et Politiques*, pp. 21–63; 'Exposé des motifs du projet du loi sur le mariage', *ibid.*, pp. 79–110; K.F. von Savigny, 'Revision des Strafgesetzbuches von 1843' (1845), in Gerhard, *Verhältnisse und Verhinderungen*, pp. 451f.; Savigny, 'Darstellung der in den Preussischen Gesetzen über die Ehescheidung unternommenen Reformen' (1850), in Savigny, *Vermischte Schriften*, vol. 5 (Aalen, 1968), pp. 222–343.
34 On the consensus of liberal and conservative views with regard to the need to stabilise marriage and family against modern individualism, see S. Buchholz, 'Eherecht zwischen Staat und Kirche', *Preussiche Reformversuche in den Jahren 1854 bis 1861* (Frankfurt am Main, 1981); B. Schnapper, 'L'Autorité domestique et les hommes politiques de la Révolution', in I. Théry and C. Biet, eds, *La Famille*, pp. 221–36; Schnapper, 'Autorité politique et partis politiques de Napoléon à de Gaulle, in H. Mohnhaupt, ed., *Zur Geschichte des Familien- und Erbrechts* (Frankfurt, 1987), pp. 177–219.

35 I. Théry and C. Biet, 'Portalis ou l'esprit des siècles: la rhétorique du mariage dans le Discours préliminaire au projet du Code civil', in Théry and Biet, eds, *La Famille*, pp. 104–21.
36 Portalis, 'Discours préliminaire', pp. 44f.; for Savigny, see S. Buchholz, 'Savigny's Stellungnahme zum Ehe und Familienrecht', *Ius Commune*, 8 (1979), pp. 148–91, esp. 152–5.
37 Portalis, 'Discours préliminaire', p. 36.
38 *Ibid.*, pp. 36–8.
39 See Savigny, 'Darstellung', pp. 288f.
40 See Savigny, 'Darstellung', pp. 298–308.
41 *Ibid.*, pp. 298f.
42 For Portalis, see 'Exposé des motifs du projet de loi sur la propriété', in *Ecrits et Discours*, p. 127; for Savigny, see Buchholz, 'Savigny', pp. 152–6 (see note 36).
43 Portalis, 'Mariage', p. 110.
44 Savigny, 'Darstellung', pp. 242–51.
45 See *Conférence du Code civil, avec la discussion particulière du Conseil d'Etat et du Tribunal, avant la rédaction définitive de chaque projet de loi*, par un jurisconsulte, vol. 5 (Paris, 1805), pp. 211–24.
46 See J.P. Schäfer, *Die Entstehung der Vorschriften des BGB über das persönliche Eherecht* (Frankfurt, 1983), p. 221; S. Buchholz, 'Das Bürgerliche Gesetzbuch und die Frauen: zur Kritik des Ehegüterrechts', in U. Gerhard, ed., *Frauen in der Geschichte des Rechts* (Munich, 1997), pp. 670–82.
47 See S. Buchholz, 'Eherecht zwichen Staat und Kirche', pp. 1–36; quotation at p. 31.
48 See *Conférence du Code civil*, vol. 2, pp. 180, 222.
49 See Buchholz, 'Savigny', pp. 186–91.
50 See *Code civil*, Art. 340: 'La recherche de la paternité est interdit'; for a comparative account of nineteenth-century legislation on adultery and illegitimacy in France, Prussia and England, see U. Vogel, 'Whose property? The double standard of adultery in nineteenth-century law', in C. Smart, ed., *Regulating Womanhood: Historical essays on marriage, motherhood and sexuality* (London, 1991), pp. 147–65.
51 Savigny, 'Revision des Strafgesetzbuchs', in Gerhard, *Verhältnisse und Verhinderungen*, p. 451.
52 See Max Weber, *Wirtschaft und Gesellschaft* (Tübingen, 1972), p. 414.
53 See U. Beck and E. Beck-Gernsheim, *Das ganz normale Chaos der Liebe* (Frankfurt am Main, 1990), pp. 38–43.
54 R. Cotterell, *The Sociology of Law: An Introduction* (London, 1984), pp. 129f.
55 Portalis, 'Mariage', p. 102.

Index